Blowing Away

THE **STATE WRITING**
ASSESSMENT TEST

Blowing Away
THE STATE WRITING ASSESSMENT TEST

Four steps to better writing scores for students of all levels

Third Edition

Jane Bell Kiester

Maupin House

Blowing Away the State Writing Assessment Test
Four Steps to Better Writing Scores for Students of All Levels

By Jane Bell Kiester

Cover and book design: Mickey Cuthbertson

Kiester, Jane Bell, 1945-
  Blowing away the state writing assessment test : four steps to better
writing scores for students of all levels / Jane Bell Kiester.-- 3rd ed.
     p. cm.
  Includes bibliographical references.
  ISBN-13: 978-0-929895-93-2 (pbk.)
  ISBN-10: 0-929895-93-2 (pbk.)
  1. English language--Composition and exercises--Evaluation. 2. English
language--Examinations. I. Title.
  LB1576.K473 2006
  808'.042076--dc22

                              2006008050

Also by Jane Bell Kiester
> *Caught'ya! Grammar with a Giggle*
> *Caught'ya Again! More Grammar with a Giggle*
> *The Chortling Bard: Caught'ya! Grammar with a Giggle for High School*
> *Eggbert, the Ball, Bounces by Himself: Caught'ya! Grammar with a Giggle for First Grade*
> *Putrescent Petra Finds Friends: Caught'ya! Grammar with a Giggle for Second Grade*
> *Juan and Marie Join the Class: Caught'ya! Grammar with a Giggle for Third Grade*
> *Giggles in the Middle: Caught'ya! Grammar with a Giggle for Middle School*
> *Teach Spelling So It Sticks! Quick and Clever Ways That Work for Grades 4-8*

Maupin House publishes professional resources for K-12 educators. Contact us for tailored, in-school training or to schedule an author for a workshop or conference. Visit www.maupinhouse.com for free lesson plan downloads.

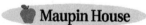 **Maupin House**

Maupin House Publishing, Inc.
2416 NW 71st Place
Gainesville, FL 32653

800-524-0634
352-373-5588
352-373-5546 (fax)
www.maupinhouse.com
info@maupinhouse.com

10 9 8 7 6 5 4

Dedication

This book is dedicated to the memory of my father, James Frederick Bell (1914–1995), esteemed professor, experimentist, physicist, Renaissance man, historian, writer, musician, encourager of and inspiration for daughter, and Daddy Extraordinaire.

I miss you.

Table of Contents

Acknowledgments

There are two people in my life who are extremely important to my writing—my husband, Charles L. Kiester, and my mother, Perra S. Bell. These two tireless, mostly uncomplaining editors read every edition of this book again and again, made invaluable (and sometimes sweeping) suggestions, corrected my errors, encouraged me when I was tired of working, put up with visiting with the back of my head, loved me even when I was grumpy from hours at the computer, and kept me honest. I love you both.

I would also like to thank some of my colleagues for their help in producing this book. We are all in this teaching business together, and I, for one, couldn't survive without their encouragement, suggestions, and support. Catherine Berg, a now retired ninth-grade teacher and friend who encouraged me to write the first Caught'ya book, also read this one. Without her input on the needs of high-school students, this book would not have been as accurate.

Mary Ann Coxe, a now retired colleague and friend (and head of English for Alachua County, Florida), who also encouraged me to write my first book many years ago, read the first edition of this book from the point of view of a supervisor, a former high-school teacher, and an official scorer of the Florida State Writing Assessment.

Renée Trufant has been a dear friend for more than thirty years, beginning when my six-year-old son won her heart at the check-out line at Publix supermarket where she was working. Her students' state writing assessment scores are very high. Renée has dynamite (and often wonderfully bizarre) ideas. Her contribution to this book is no exception. Thank you, Renée, for letting me pick your brain. Thank you also for all the long-distance brainstorming.

Tim McShane, eighth-grade English teacher at Westwood Middle School (where I taught) and author of *Boston Baked Bean* and *The Votive Pit*, among other plays, also read the original manuscript, made valuable suggestions, and encouraged me to finish this book despite my desire to write fiction.

Vanessa Alvarez, Nancy Embree, Dottie Hendershot, Jim Owens, Amy Rollo, and Renée Trufant kindly let me borrow samples of their students' writing so that I could provide examples for this book.

I also wish to thank all the students (who shall remain anonymous) who provided all the sample paragraphs and essays for this book. It is for you that I wrote this book. I wish you much success in your future writing endeavors.

And, finally, I wish again to thank Emily Gorovsky for her usual superb editing. What would I do without your fine hand?

Introduction

As of this edition, almost all fifty states have instituted a writing assessment test. It does not matter whether these tests are graded on a one-to-four scale, a one-to-five scale, a one-to-six scale, or by domains; they are all scored using essentially the same criteria. A top paper is a top paper, no matter what scale is used. All states require the same basic types of prose—expository, clarifying, descriptive, persuasive, or explanatory essays and/or personal, experiential, imaginative, or fictional narratives. Different states use different verbiage to identify the writing genres required on their tests, but an essay of any type still is an essay and a narrative, no matter how it is approached, still is a narrative.

Recently more states are requiring response to literature as a part of the high-school writing test, but a response to literature still is an expository essay that explains a premise. No matter what genre of prose writing is required on a state's writing test, no matter what grade level is being tested, no matter what state is doing the testing, the basic criteria for scoring each type of essay or narrative is essentially the same.

Most states test students in the fourth, seventh or eighth, and tenth grades, but a few vary by a grade level or so. The grade level tested does not affect the scoring process. A great essay at the elementary level is as good as (albeit less sophisticated than) a great essay at the high-school level. A poor example of an essay is incomplete and badly written no matter the grade level. (See the examples at the end of the book.)

That is why this book, although written by a Florida teacher (now retired) whose students faced and aced the Florida Writes! Test, is generic enough to be effective in any state at any level. The ninety examples of student writing (located at the end of the book) can be used with students at all grade levels.

Combined with completing a daily Caught'ya (see the **Bibliography** for a list of my Caught'ya books), the techniques and strategies suggested in this book are designed to help you get your students to write well both for the writing assessment test and everyday classroom assignments. By following the four steps in this book (and completing a daily Caught'ya), teachers have enabled students all over the country to achieve higher writing-test scores. The techniques within this book with a little added sophistication, also will help high-school students do well on the new writing component of the SAT.

The four steps to better writing are simple, easily implemented, and make sense to most of us who are under our state's "gun" to make our students write better (and therefore achieve higher scores on their tests). My successful experiences for more than a decade with this approach—as well as the testimony I've received from hundreds of teachers who have tried the four steps—convince me of their value with all types of students, from compensatory to gifted.

Until I retired in June of 2002, I continued to implement the four-step program in my classroom, and the writing scores of my students remained high. What is this successful system that evokes average scores from students with below-average skills in English and the highest scores from many of the others?

Read on. Whether you teach elementary, middle, or high school—and no matter in which state or province you teach—you can follow these four steps to higher scores.

What's Included in This Book

Step One gives you a play-by-play for teaching your students to write strong, vivid-verb paragraphs by replacing "dead" verbs with "juicy" ones and using graphic organizers to plan their writing.

Step Two shows you how to score the state writing assessment test, both holistically and by using domains, so that you can teach your students the basic criteria of scoring well enough for them to analyze and grade their own writing.

Step Three includes all the tools, tricks, and activities you need to teach your students to plan and write good essays and/or narratives with the required elements and avoid common writing pitfalls.

Step Four helps you teach your students to write with voice, great vocabulary, passion, flair, pizzazz, and from another's point of view so that your students' good writing becomes even better.

The CD contains the 90 student writing samples, scoring rubrics, graphic organizers, and other teaching tools, all found within the book, as well as 220 practice prompts, for easy access and duplication.

Step One

Teach Students to Write Strong, Vivid-Verb Paragraphs (SVVPs)

Strong, vivid-verb paragraphs are four to eight sentences long and address the characteristics of excellent writing.

All of these characteristics are required on state writing tests:

➜ "Verbal sophistication" and avoidance of using only passive voice

➜ Absence of verb-tense switching problems

➜ Variation of sentence structure

➜ Topic statement and concluding sentence

➜ Nitty-gritty detail (elaboration)

➜ Use of superlative vocabulary

➜ Use of similes and other figurative language

➜ Writing with voice, flair, and pizzazz

Strong verbs are action verbs which show what is going on. "Students **shouted** insults at the top of their lungs" is a good example of strong verb usage. Most students would have written "Students **were shouting** insults," a much weaker sentence.

Students usually write what author Rebekah Caplan calls "telling" sentences, such as the following: "The puppy *is* cute," or "I *am* bored." They do not naturally write sentences that "show" what they are trying to say and provide support for the topic sentence. For example: "The cute puppy **wriggles** in excitement whenever someone **comes** in the door." "I **twiddle** my thumbs out of boredom." These good "showing" sentences illustrate just how cute the puppy is and how bored the writer is. Much more powerful writing results from the use of strong verbs.

Children enter kindergarten speaking with strong verbs. Their dog **barked** at a neighbor. They **played** with their friend. Their mother **cooked** dinner. Their brother **hit** the ball and **won** the game. Somehow by third grade, probably because of the books they read, children unlearn the use of strong, vivid verbs. Unless we teach kindergarten, our students' writing skills depend to a large extent on how and how much the teachers before us taught writing.

To obtain the highest scores (and therefore the best writing) possible from your students, you need to convince your colleagues of all disciplines in at least one but preferably two grade levels below yours to start teaching their students to write strong, vivid-verb paragraphs. Even first- and second-grade students can be taught to write these paragraphs (see the examples on page 37 in this step)! High-school students may groan and protest, but they, too, need the practice. (Try a practice one, and watch them struggle.)

Even if you cannot convince your colleagues to give their students frequent practice writing strong, vivid-verb paragraphs, you can begin teaching your students how to write these paragraphs as early as the second week of school. This will ensure that they will be well prepared in time for the writing test.

The use of strong, vivid verbs = better writing = higher scores. If your state is one that doesn't overtly include "too much use of 'being' verbs" as part of the rubric, the people who score the writing test probably don't consciously notice the use of active verbs as they read the papers. But, I know that my students who were able to use these verbs consistently were the ones who earned the highest scores. The use of strong, active verbs really does make a difference!

Learning to write strong, vivid-verb paragraphs also is crucial because these paragraphs are a microcosm of the essays required on the writing test. They have a beginning, a middle that is the elaboration, and an end. In the strong, vivid-verb paragraphs, of course, each of the three parts is a sentence or two rather than a paragraph. Your students will get the hang of the general format that they will follow when writing an essay or a description in a narrative. (See **Step Three** for an explanation of a basic essay and narrative.) By means of the strong, vivid-verb paragraphs, you also can introduce the idea of including similes and vivacious vocabulary in writing, sure-fire score raisers.

The key is that in good literature and well-liked books, "dead" verbs are used fairly sparingly. Instead, strong, vivid, active "showing" verbs abound in descriptions, action, and dialogue. One of the reasons that the *Harry Potter* series is so vivid and popular with young and old readers alike is Ms. Rowling's use of strong, active verbs wherever possible (especially in the descriptions and dialogue).

For example, Fred and George, the Weasley twins, weren't "looking" at Harry and his scar, they "**gawked**" at him. They weren't "walking" into the room, they "**bounded**" in (which certainly fits the personality of the exuberant twins).

Maya Angelou, a wordsmith *par excellence*, didn't say that she "told a lie," she said that the "lie **lumped**" in her throat." How vivid an image! In a description of the church ladies making sausage, she painted a word picture so clearly that we can picture the ladies and smell the herbs.

> The missionary ladies of the Christian Methodist Episcopal Church **helped** Momma **prepare** the pork for sausage. They **squeezed** their fat arms elbow deep in the ground meat, **mixed** it with gray nose-opening sage, pepper and salt, and **made** tasty little samples for all obedient children...

Dickens, a past master of vocabulary, wrote that Rosie Dartle, as she was about to attack Emily, wasn't just getting up from her seat or starting a fight, she "**sprang** up from her seat, **recoiled**; and in recoiling **struck** at her, with a face of such malignity, so darkened and disfigured by passion..." Whew!

What vibrant word pictures strong, vivid verbs paint! I assure you that your students, no matter what age, can write similarly. Learning how to write these paragraphs, however, is not easy, but even your weakest student can master them as long as you keep the requirements to their level (more on this later).

So, how do we get our students to write strong, vivid-verb paragraphs? Read the rest of this step. It's not as hard as it looks at first glance.

Students Study Their Own Writing to Find the Verb They Use the Most

I cannot stress how much difference the use of strong action verbs makes in anyone's writing. And, it is important for students to know how much they rely on the "dead" verbs when they write. In order to take seriously learning any skill, students need to buy into the fact that they have a problem. To make the point that my students were using only one or two verbs in their writing (usually "is" and "was") and to have a "reality check," my students and I analyzed a piece of their writing. It doesn't have to be long. Any sample will do. And, what I did will work with third-grade through twelfth-grade students, especially the latter.

The first week of school, assign an essay. (It could be any type of prose including a short paragraph.) Then put up a bulletin board with the "dead" and "dying" verbs on it, and make a list on the board as well. Since bulletin boards are not my forte, I was delighted to leave mine up all year. My rationale was that it served as a reference for students for the rest of the year.

My bulletin board in all its simple glory

Once the bulletin board is up and the "dead" verbs are posted on the blackboard, divide your students into pairs. Returning the graded (or not) essays to the students and passing out one large marker to each pair, instruct them first to copy the "dead" and "dying" verbs on the top of their papers. Next tell them to read each person's paper out loud and put a big **X** over all the "dead" verbs. You will find that as your students do this, murmurs of surprise will arise from those shocked to find that they used mainly one or two verbs. While students put the **X**s over the helping verbs, it is a good idea to walk around the room, finding ones that they missed.

TEACHING NOTE: Please note that you do not have to use a big marker. Little stickers work just as well, especially at the elementary level. I know one high-school teacher who dramatically took a pair of scissors and cut out all the helping verbs, leaving gaping holes in his students' papers!

This lesson grabs students' attention, especially that of the more advanced students who "know everything." As the year progresses, you will want to repeat this eye-opening exercise about once every six weeks so that your students can monitor their own progress in the increased use of strong, vivid verbs. In this way, you can be aware of the decreased use of helping verbs and keep tabs on your students' progress. You may find that the resultant increase of active verb use is quite startling.

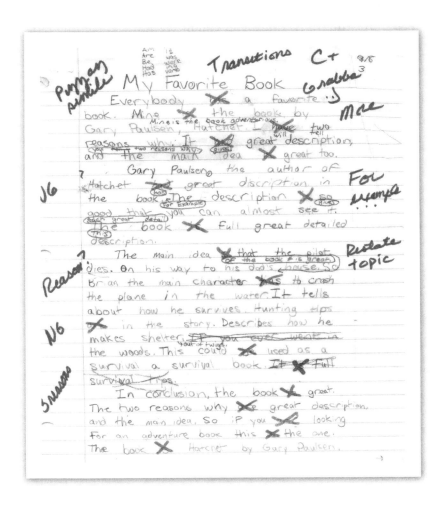

Sample paper written by an "average" student with "dead" verbs marked with Xs. Please note the following: "Dead" verbs written at top; "NG" = nitty-gritty detail is lacking; the nose tells the student that his "grabber" is boring and needs re-writing; the word "transitions" means that the student needed to work on writing more interesting transitions; and "pizzazz" and "simile" written at the top mean these are lacking in the essay. This student was about to rewrite his essay.

"Dead" Verbs to Avoid

What I call strong, vivid-verb paragraphs actually are artificially-constructed paragraphs based on Rebekah Caplan's idea of "showing-writing" from her book, *Showing-Writing: A Training Program to Help Students Be Specific* (University of California Press, 1980). Before your students can begin to use strong, vivid, active verbs, they must first learn which verbs to avoid. Why not include some fun in the process?

To introduce the concept of strong (action) verb usage in this manner, it is helpful to have a sense of drama. (Aren't most of us frustrated actors anyway?) The more drama used, the better the retention of the lesson. Students remember the unusual. With these maxims in mind, I used to introduce the use of vivid, active verbs over "dead," boring, helping verbs by burying them with great pomp, tongue-in-cheek eulogies, lugubrious music, and a lot of giggles.

Please note that only one grade level per school should do this to avoid redundancy (although students do not mind burying the "dead" verbs a second time), so you and your colleagues need to decide who gets the honor. I recommend third, sixth, and ninth grades. At first, I was the only teacher at my school who buried the verbs, so my students and I enjoyed the drama for some years. When sixth-grade teachers joined in the fun, those of us who taught seventh and eighth grade had to defer to them.

On the following page, you will find an illustration with a list of the "dead" and "dying" verbs. Primary grades need not worry about the "dying" verbs or the sense verbs as simply avoiding the helping verbs will be enough. The "dying" verbs are the ones students most often use as substitutions for the "dead" ones. These, of course, really are "dead" verbs themselves and not very illustrative.

First, using this list of "dead" verbs and the piece of writing that had the "dead" verbs marked with **X**s, ask your students to analyze their writing to find the "dead" verb they use the most. Usually it proves to be "is" or "was." Then, after hearing and viewing some samples (I saved ones from previous years), students write a brief eulogy. Some will be serious, but I think you will find (as I did) that most will be tongue-in-cheek or downright funny. My students and I always had a lot of fun sharing these.

As for grading them, completion was all that was necessary for an "A" since some students had access to computers, fancy equipment, and parents to help, and others had none of these things. There are a few examples on the next page to get you started.

"DEAD" AND "DYING" VERBS TO AVOID

(Sing to the tune of the "Volga Boatman's Song")

"DEAD" VERBS

am	is
are	was
be	were
had	any verb ending in "ing"
has	sense verbs ("looks,"
have	"smells," "sounds," "feels")

"DYING" VERBS (act as helping verbs)

become/became	make/made
act/acted	exist/existed
seem/seemed	resemble/resembled

MY POOR LITTLE "HAVE"

I used you too much
In this I mean such
Mrs. Keister took you away.

I guess it is good-bye
Oh why, oh why
I cannot believe it to this very day

Knowing I'll miss you a lot
But if I write you, I'll get caught.

That would not be good.
So, I leave you now,
To rest for a while,
Since I know I should

I realize now that you are deceased
As I leave my poor little "Have" to rest in Peace.

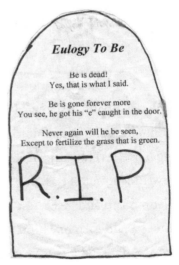

HERE LIES THE VERB IS.
DURING ITS LIFE IT GOT
PLENTY OF BIZ.
NOW IT'S TIME TO PUT
IS TO REST.
FINDING OTHER VERBS
BECOMES THE TEST.

Eulogy To Be

Be is dead!
Yes, that is what I said.

Be is gone forever more
You see, he got his "e" caught in the door.

Never again will he be seen,
Except to fertilize the grass that is green.

R.I.P

Three examples of eulogies. The second one is from a student in special education. The last one (so I was told by the author) is to be "rapped" with much enthusiasm.

Then, as a homework assignment or an in-class activity, students make a paper or cardboard representation/cutout of their favorite "dead" verb. They then construct a coffin (biodegradable only) to house that verb. The results can be hilarious and very inventive. I have included pictures of one coffin and one "dead" verb as examples. I had to beg my students to borrow them as they wanted to bury them.

I must warn you, though, that some students go overboard and even make tiny pillows and blankets for their deceased verb. Some of these coffins can be very elaborate, and some simply will be two sheets of paper taped together with a human-shaped paper doll inside labeled with the deceased verb. But, as long as a student makes *something*, I recommend that you give full credit for the exercise. This activity, after all, is supposed to be enjoyable.

**A coffin and "dead" verb from
another student's coffin.**

To facilitate memorization, I also taught my students to sing the "dead" verbs. I liked to use the "Volga Boatman's Song" (with the "dead" verbs as the words) since we could row between lines, but any familiar song in a minor key will do. Many teachers (who can't find a copy of the "Volga Boatman's Song") use "A Thousand Years from Now." Every day, we sang and sang (and rowed and rowed) until every student in the class had learned the "dead" and "dying" verbs. Only then did I cover up the bulletin board and give a test to write all the "dead" and "dying" verbs on a sheet of paper. As students wrote, I heard each one hum the "Volga Boatman's Song." The average grade was 100%.

After students have coffins in hand and can sing the verbs to avoid, you are ready for the burial. Choose a day for you and your students to dress in lugubrious clothes, take your eulogies and tiny coffins out to the "back forty" (or whatever bare space you can find on the edge of your school), and hold a mock funeral.

I always asked some students who were eager for extra credit to make a headstone out of cardboard. As we all solemnly walked to the edge of the campus, we sang the sad tune with the "dead" verbs. My "drama kings and queens" sobbed and carried on as we proceeded. I'm sure yours will do the same if you "ham" it up.

Once at the designated site, dig a hole with a shovel from home and bury the coffins containing the "dead" verbs. As each student lays his or her coffin in the hole, he or she should read the eulogy. After covering the "grave" and placing the biodegradable headstone on top, we walked back to the classroom, singing the "dead" verbs all the way.

After that day, students should be able to avoid the "dead" verbs in their writing as much as possible. When the sixth-grade teachers in my school took up my shovel, and I no longer went through the drama of burying the "dead" verbs, I still put up that bulletin board as a reminder, and we sang the "Volga Boatman's Song" on a daily basis for at least the first few weeks of school. It always started the year off right with a song and a laugh.

Replacing the Passive Voice with the Active Voice

After teaching the verbs to avoid, introduce students to strong, vivid verbs, and demonstrate how to substitute them for the "dead" verbs that they ordinarily use when they write. I did this with sentence writing. Those of you who teach Honors or AP English at the high-school level and whose students already may have mastered the art of using active verbs in their writing may still want to spend a day or two practicing with the sentences. Most advanced students need the review. To this end, I have included a more sophisticated practice sheet just for high-school students. It contains more serious and thought-provoking sentences than those on the worksheets for elementary- and middle-school students. My eighth-graders, however, loved the elementary sentences anyway because they needed to "crawl" with the primary sentences before they could "walk" with the more complicated ones.

TEACHING NOTE: *Teachers of lower grades or of classes with large numbers of students whose vocabulary skills are not up to par will want to keep a list of strong action verbs prominently posted in the classroom. Much of this list could come from the students themselves. The rest can be from Caught'yas (see the **Bibliography**) or from vocabulary found in reading selections and vocabulary books.*

First, with your students dictating and you writing, you should rewrite some of the following sentences so that they are "showing" sentences instead of "telling" ones. Sometimes the sentences will need to be inverted in order to change the "dead," passive verb into a strong, active one. It is a good idea to do a few of these a day for at least two weeks, eliciting the changes from your students. I suggest at least two weeks because you want to keep doing this with your students dictating and you writing until they completely understand how to change the passive voice to the active voice. No matter what grade you teach, I recommend beginning with the "primary" sentences that have the blanks.

We must learn addition before we can subtract and addition and subtraction before we can multiply, and all three before we can learn division. Similarly, your students need to take those baby steps in writing sentences that use strong, vivid verbs. Practice filling in the blanks before inverting the sentences or doing the ones that require a complete rewrite. Since most students at first try simply to substitute any other verb for a passive one, they make many mistakes until they get the idea that the sentence needs to be rewritten.

After writing a few strong-verb sentences each day with you at the helm, divide your students into groups, giving them a few sentences (no more than three) with "dead" verbs to rewrite as strong-verb sentences. I always asked each group to read over their three changed sentences and choose the best one to read to the class. After at least three days of changing the sentences in small groups and sharing the results (using the sample sentences in this book), you can make the students take more of an active part in their learning.

Give each group a number, and ask each one to write a "telling" sentence that uses a "dead" verb. They can make up one on the spur of the moment or use one from their own writing. Each group writes the "dead-verb" sentence on a piece of paper and passes it to another group. (That's why I numbered the groups.) Each group now has a sentence to rewrite. They rewrite that sentence, expanding it to become even more vivid and to contain even more details. Then, someone in each group reads the original sentence and the strong-verb rewrite. This always is fun.

After working with you and in groups, students should be comfortable changing "telling" sentences with "dead" verbs into "showing" sentences with strong, vivid verbs on their own. As a brief starter exercise, it is a good idea to give your students one or two dead-verb sentences a day to change into strong-verb sentences.

You also can put *one* "telling" sentence on the board for students to take home and turn into a dynamite "showing" sentence with strong, vivid verbs. Students love to share these. And, having only one sentence to write for homework helps ensure it actually gets done. I often found that whole families (usually at dinner) worked on coming up with a great "showing" sentence. Sometimes, after we shared, I gave a small prize for the best one.

Rewriting "telling" sentences into "showing" ones with detail—first with the whole class, then in small groups, and finally, individually—makes students accustomed to writing with the active rather than the passive voice. You can use the **Strong-Verb Practice Sentences** sheets (see pages 28-36 at the end of this step) or sentences culled from your students' papers.

Remember, rewriting "telling" sentences into "showing" ones with more detail is very difficult. At first it is awkward for your students, but they soon catch on to the idea. As you and your students practice, feel free to copy the following sheets for use in your classroom. But, I implore you to take it slowly and *not* assign an entire sheet at once. The sentences provided here are only suggestions, and most are very general. To help you, I have included *possible* rewrites for the sentences. These are *not* the definitive answers.

> **TEACHING NOTE:** One caveat—make sure that your students keep the same verb tense as the original sentence in their rewrite. This is good practice for maintaining verb-tense consistency so they don't ping-pong back and forth between present and past tenses.

Strong, Vivid-Verb Paragraphs

Once students can successfully write strong-verb sentences on their own and comfortably change any sentence on the worksheet(s) to the active voice, they are ready to write the strong, vivid-verb paragraphs. First they need to know what a strong, vivid-verb paragraph, or SVVP, is.

It is a paragraph that is composed of as many sentences as you feel your students can write, from four at primary levels to seven at the high-school level. It is not good to go below four (no room for details in the middle) nor above nine (too long a paragraph). 6-Honors

The **first sentence** is a "telling" one, a topic sentence that may contain a "dead" verb. The teacher or the students supply this sentence. (Please note that after students are comfortable with writing the paragraphs, you may wish to ask them to change this topic sentence to a "grabber"—see **Step Three**.) The **middle sentences** (two to seven of them) must all support the topic sentence and must use only strong verbs, none of which may appear more than once. The **last sentence** of this artificially constructed paragraph is a conclusion. It cannot be a repeat of the first sentence but can be similar to it. It also may contain a "dead" verb since it wraps things up.

Within the structure of the paragraph, depending on the skill level of your students, you can require that certain things must be included. Of course, as the age of the students increases, so can the number of such requirements. I suggest working from the list that you will find on page 20 of this step, where your students learn to plan the paragraphs. You also will want to require that your students write a paragraph in a particular type of prose—either expository, narrative, or persuasive. In this way, your students learn in the smaller structure of a paragraph what each genre is like.

Before beginning to plan or write any strong, vivid-verb paragraphs though, students need to read, or have read to them, some good examples. The grade level of the writers does not matter. If you never have had your students write strong, vivid-verb paragraphs, you won't have any great examples of theirs to read. Thus, I've included some at the end of this step. You also can write some of your own to use as examples the first year you teach SVVPs.

I offer a word of advice, however. As I said earlier, these paragraphs are *not* easy to write at first. I give workshops all over the country where I ask teachers (together in small groups) to write a strong, vivid-verb paragraph and then share it with the rest of the participants. In almost every workshop, teachers make mistakes and leave in a "dead" verb or two. It does not matter whether the workshop is for elementary, middle, or high-school teachers; at *least* one group leaves in a "dead" verb. I embarrassedly must tell you that I left in a "dead" verb in one of the examples in my second book.

Take heart, though. For us, learning to write SVVPs without mistakes takes only a little bit of practice before we teachers get the hang of it. When I do longer workshops where teachers successively write two SVVPs, all the second ones are error-free.

So, I suggest that you get together with a colleague or two, read the examples that follow, and practice writing a few of these SVVPs together, checking your work for any "dead" verbs. There are a bunch of possible topic sentences on page 43 at the end of this step, but you can begin your paragraphs with any "telling" sentence.

When you are comfortable with the structure and format of a strong, vivid-verb paragraph, you will be ready to share the following examples with your students and maybe include a few of your own!

The student examples of strong, vivid-verb paragraphs were written in various ways: as a whole class, in small groups, and as individuals. I have put them on separate pages so that you can make transparencies to show to your students or sample copies to be put into their notebooks.

Pre-Planning (Clustering) Strong, Vivid-Verb Paragraphs

Now that your students have seen some good examples of strong, vivid-verb paragraphs, it is time to teach them to plan (cluster) the subjects and verbs to use, especially for those middle sentences. Planning ahead using a graphic organizer helps avoid using "dead" verbs and makes it easier to write the actual paragraphs. This graphic organizer, by the way, is perfect for your right-brained students when they write essays and works extremely well for narratives, too.

You can begin this as a whole-class exercise. First, decide how many strong, vivid-verb sentences you wish to include in the middle of the paragraph. Then, put a blank cluster plan like the one on page 41 on the overhead. Please, feel free to make a transparency from that page. You can add or delete (white-out) an arm from the center oval as needed. Then, in the center oval, put a "telling" sentence, like "The room **was** a mess," Next, as a whole class, with you serving as the scribe, plan out a possible paragraph as you elicit suggestions from the class. You will find a sample of a completed cluster at the end of this step (see page 40).

The important thing to remember is to put only a subject and a verb on each of the "arms" of the cluster. For the compound and complex sentences (if you plan to require them), there should be two subjects and two verbs. In the case of the complex sentence, the subordinating conjunction (like "as" or "because") can be added later when you and your students compose the actual paragraph.) Of course, you always can include extra subjects and/or verbs for compound subjects and verbs.

When you and your students have a subject and verb for all the "arms" of the cluster, it is time to plan the last sentence and the title. The conclusion can be written out in full. When you have the completed cluster, the next step is to put the sentences into a logical sequence by numbering them in the order in which they would appear in a paragraph. Solicit suggestions from your students, siding with the general consensus, and put a number by each of the subject/verb combinations. You will want to do this three to six times with your class as a whole—they dictate; you write on the cluster; they decide the order. *Do not write the paragraph with these practice clusters.* That will come in the next activity.

See the cluster for the paragraph about the wild cafeteria that was used in the second middle-school example (page 38). As you look at that example, please note the way the students added information to the basic subject/verb of the cluster to make their sentences more interesting and changed the subject in order to vary it. They insisted on adding the sentence about the dean, but it was not required. (This SVVP was completed as a whole class.)

Remember, the plan/cluster should include only the subject and verb. Sometimes students prefer to list all the subjects first and then come up with the verbs. Of course, you write the original one on the overhead as your students dictate.

Writing Strong, Vivid-Verb Paragraphs Together

When your students understand how to pre-plan a strong, vivid-verb paragraph, they are ready to write some as a whole class with you as their scribe. To do this, cluster with your students as you did in the previous section, but this time, when you and your students are finished, hand the transparency with the completed plan to the student who is your worst behavior problem. I recommend this to keep him or her occupied and interested.

Put a blank transparency on the overhead for yourself. Then ask the student who has the transparency with the cluster (let's call him Herbert) to read the title you and the class had decided to use. Herbert reads from his transparency as you write on yours. Herbert then reads the topic sentence (the one in the oval provided by you). Again, you write it on the overhead for all to see. Now comes the fun part.

Herbert reads the subject and verb designated as #2. You write it on the board (not the overhead). Solicit from the class a possible strong, vivid-verb sentence using that subject and verb. Take several suggestions and put them to a vote if you wish. Write the chosen sentence on your transparency. Repeat this process with the rest of the subject/verb combinations, asking students to make one of them a compound or complex sentence (if you wish), to include a simile, or to use a "big, juicy" vocabulary word, etc. (See the list of possible requirements on page 20.) If a student makes a mistake and uses a "dead" verb, it is easy to gently help him or her come up with an alternative sentence that uses a strong, vivid one. *Do not let them repeat any verb.* ("Makes" is the most popular.)

When Herbert reads the concluding sentence, ask students if they wish to change it. Ask if they wish to change the first sentence (to make it a grabber) or the title. Remember, the actual sentences in the paragraph do not have to use the subject or verb in the plan; the only requirement is that the verbs be vivid, active ones.

When finished, you should have the entire paragraph written on the overhead. If you need a busy activity or think your students need an example in their notebooks (always a good idea), you can require that they copy the finished product. And, if you teach middle or high school, you'd better save the transparencies as subsequent classes always are curious about what previous classes have written.

I highly recommend that you repeat this process of planning (clustering) and writing three to five times or until your students get the hang of it. Whenever they suggest a sentence that contains a "dead" verb in it, stop and ask them to rethink it until they get it right. In this way, you are modeling the thinking process that they will use as they write their own paragraphs. You will be amazed, amused, and delighted at the paragraphs your students as a group dictate to you.

I also suggest something that really helped my students—a verb wall, ceiling, or bulletin board made from the really vivid verbs they come up with. As your students cluster these paragraphs orally, no matter what age they are, they will use some dynamite vivid verbs (especially if they do Caught'yas). Even if these verbs aren't difficult ones, any verb that paints a vivid picture (like "tiptoes" instead of "walks") is a great idea.

Doing this was easy and not any extra work at all. I kept a stack of 5" x 8" cards and a huge marker handy. The minute a student suggested a vivid, "showing" verb, I dramatically printed it as big as I could on the 5" x 8" card and either put it on the bulletin board or had a student get on a table and stick it under the acoustic tiles on the ceiling.

A plethora of "showing" verbs hung there until the day of the writing test when I had to remove or cover them all. At all other times, my students often gazed at the ceiling or the bulletin board for suggestions as they wrote. It was funny to watch a student crane his or her neck to search for a vivid verb on the ceiling!

On the bulletin board, by the way, I organized the great vivid verbs by meaning. For example, underneath "walked," I put (as students proffered them) "ambled," "trotted," "strolled," "tiptoed," etc. See the graphic of that bulletin board on the next page. This example is from a photo taken early in the year before too many verbs had been added. Random verbs that didn't fit into the "verb families" were stuck in between the acoustic ceiling tiles.

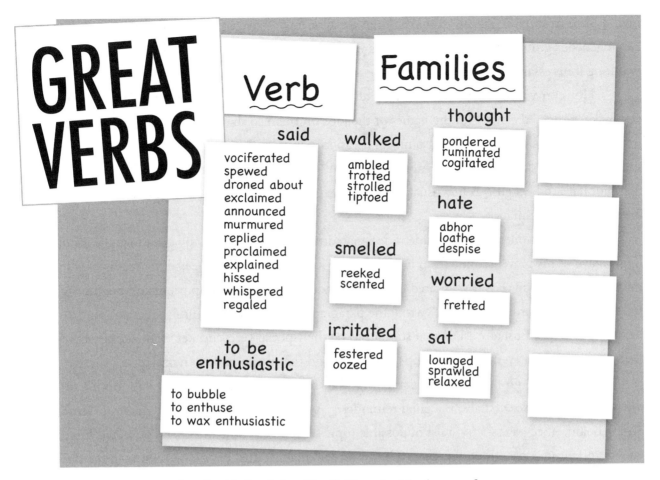

A word wall with "verb families." Note the blank space for more additions.

Writing Strong, Vivid-Verb Paragraphs in Groups and Individually

When your students feel comfortable clustering and planning the paragraphs as a whole class, the next step is to write a bunch of paragraphs in small groups. Teachers find that even if they teach eleventh grade, students need this group practice.

First, divide the class into groups of three or four. I liked to do this in a number of ways. You can use a "sorting hat" and put in the names of the four houses at Hogwarts (from *Harry Potter*), adding one or two (like Kiesterdon) for larger classes. Then stand at the door and, as students enter the room, let them reach into the hat and pick out a piece of paper with the name of their "house" on it.

You also can put colored strips of paper into a box, hold it high, and ask students to take one as they enter the classroom. Or, you can do the same with numbered strips. Sometimes I let my students group themselves (this can be dangerous), or I grouped them myself and handed them a seating chart as they entered the class. However you want to group your students will work just fine. I liked to vary the groups to shake things up a bit, but I have colleagues who always made heterogeneous groups at the beginning of the year and kept the same groups all year (with a little tweaking if necessary).

However you group your students, it always is a good idea to give each student a job. You can make laminated cards with the names of the jobs on them so that students can put the cards in front of them as they work. This also makes it easier to mix up the cards to assign new roles or have students take turns. I liked to use "mom" instead of "leader" to avoid arguments. The role of "mom" does not have to be a girl. A boy usually was assigned the "mom" role and had the responsibility of keeping the group on task.

The "questioner" was the student designated to come to me with any questions the group might have. This prevented me from having twenty kids in my face at once. The "reader" read the paragraphs to the class if we shared them and made sure that the group proofread the finished product. The "recorder" or "scribe" wrote the paragraph as the rest of the group dictated it. If I needed a fifth job, I usually asked that student to be the "special verb-checker" to make certain that there were no "dead" verbs in the group's paragraph and that no verbs were repeated.

Once in the groups, you can require that the "recorder" write the "dead" verbs on the top of the paper for all to see. (It also is a good reminder.) After that was done, I wrote the topic sentence on the board. (See page 43 for a list of possible topic sentences.) Students then combined forces and talents and wrote a paragraph together. The "recorder" made a final copy, and then each member of the group did the same. When I collected the paragraph from each group, I stapled the papers of all members together, graded the top one, and put the same grade on all of them so that each student could keep a copy in his or her notebook.

As your students work in their groups, it is a good idea to wander the room with a big marker in hand. When you reach a group, first check the cluster, putting a check on the subject/verb combinations that are correct. Make sure to check the clusters of *every* group.

Then, continue to roam the room as students write the actual paragraphs. This time put a big check over each strong verb and a big circle around any "dead" ones so that the group can correct their mistakes. In this way, students learn better and have a chance for success. As for we teachers, well, the papers are almost all graded by the time students hand them in!

The following day or after all the groups have completed the paragraph, the "reader" reads the paragraph out loud to the class. Often, if I was targeting only the verbs and a good vocabulary word, I could give the group a grade right then and there! If a mistake was made as the "reader" read, I asked the group to correct the mistake, and, if they could not, I elicited possible alternatives from the class. The bottom line was that *everyone* makes mistakes. We need each other's help to correct them.

A very effective alternative to sharing the paragraphs by reading them out loud is to have the "recorder" in each group write the final paragraph on a transparency to share with the class as the "reader" reads within the group. This adds an air of importance to the exercise. It also lets students participate more in their own learning process as they discover their own mistakes. And, you get to grade the paper without ever touching it!

Strong, vivid-verb paragraphs naturally lend themselves to learning some good active verbs as vocabulary words. As students share their paragraphs either by reading them aloud or putting them on the overhead, you might want to jot down and add those good, active verbs to the list on your wall or ceiling. This offers your students more choices as they compose future paragraphs. Invite them to add to the list as they find some "really good verbs" to use. This inevitably will drive students to the thesaurus.

Unless the teachers who preceded you taught strong, vivid-verb paragraphs, I strongly suggest that you make your students write the paragraphs in groups at least five to eight times before requiring them to write the SVVPs individually. When you do feel that the majority of your students are ready to write the strong, vivid-verb paragraphs on their own, write a topic sentence on the board and instruct them to write the "dead" verbs at the top of their papers and get to work. It also is a good idea to require that they read their paragraphs to a friend before turning them in. In that way, they can ferret out any "dead" verbs that still lurk in there.

Once students are comfortable with writing the strong, vivid-verb paragraphs on their own, they can write one or two a week, but I liked to vary the way we did it. Sometimes we wrote one as a whole class with me as the "scribe." (The students felt as if they were getting away with murder, but they were learning.) Other times, we wrote them in groups and shared either by reading aloud or writing on the overhead (always fun). And, of course, sometimes students wrote them by themselves, reading them to a friend for editing purposes. We never wrote the SVVPs the same way twice in a row. This kept the students hopping and prevented them from getting bored with writing the paragraphs.

Required Skills for Strong, Vivid-Verb Paragraphs

As you walk around the room checking your students' strong, vivid-verb paragraphs, encourage the use of good vocabulary and interesting transitions (more on this in **Step Three**). Make certain that students have access to dictionaries and thesauruses, and display (or hand out) a list of the things you require that they must put in the paragraph such as a good vocabulary word, transitions, literary devices, etc. In fact, if you hand your students a copy of the cluster (see page 41 at the end of this step) with your requirements written at the bottom, they can check off each item as they put it in their paragraphs. I have included the sample cluster sheet again on page 42 of this step, only this time there is a basic list of things that you may want to require students to include in their paragraphs. If you wish to use that sample cluster with your students before you make copies, you easily can "white-out" those you don't want to use or, conversely, add more. Of course, what you require will depend on the grade level you teach and the ability level of your students. Please note that you also will need to indicate the number of strong, vivid-verb sentences you require.

What you require your students to include in their SVVPs will depend on what grade you teach and the skill level of your children. Of course, older, more sophisticated students can make their own cluster and copy the requirements from the board.

I suggest using any or all from the following list:

➔ A particular genre of prose—expository, narrative, persuasive

➔ A title different from the topic sentence

➔ A topic sentence or a thesis statement (provided by you) that may contain a "dead" verb; you also can require that this sentence be turned into a good "grabber"

➔ Two to six sentences that use *only* strong, vivid verbs and that show detail and elaboration on the topic sentence—*no* verb may be repeated

➔ Great transitions (see **Step Three**)

➔ An example of a compound sentence and a complex sentence

➔ A simile, a metaphor, use of alliteration or other literary device

➔ The use of at least two big, "juicy" vocabulary words

➔ A quote (need not be long)

➔ Humor

➔ Use of direct address (great for persuasive paragraphs)

➔ A concluding sentence that is different from the topic sentence

All of the above (but not necessarily all at once) are important tools to establishing a writer's voice, and all are concomitants of good writing. Many states' writing tests overtly state that sentence structure must be varied, so it is a big help to practice using the different types of sentences in a short paragraph that can easily be checked. Almost all writing-test rubrics talk about "word choice" which translates to excellent command of good vocabulary and the use of words beyond the basic ones required for the grade level being tested. Using a quote and punctuating it correctly can establish a command of mechanics. The use of humor or literary devices demonstrates writing sophistication and adds to the voice that students will need to demonstrate if they are to have any chance of earning the highest score. (See **Step Four** for more elaboration on the above.)

If you frequently require the use of good vocabulary, transitions, literary devices like similes, quotes, varied sentence structure, etc. in a short paragraph, your students will find it easy to use them when they write a longer piece of prose. If you want your students to improve their writing, you will need to imbue these skills so well into their minds that using these tools becomes as natural as breathing. And, writing without them seems incomplete and odd.

Finding Possible Topic Sentences

Strong, vivid-verb paragraphs serve more than one purpose and require some real effort to write. But, you want your students to enjoy writing them. To this end, I suggest using weird topics that titillate the interest of students of any age. Years ago, I bought some shellacked moose poop jewelry in Alaska. My students wrote expository paragraphs explaining how disgusting my jewelry was, narrative paragraphs about how bizarre a person would have to be to buy such a thing, and persuasive paragraphs to convince me not to wear such revolting jewelry. (I needed no encouragement. I never could wear the earrings...)

Use anything you can find to spark good paragraphs that are written with humor and verve (and for which coming up with topic sentences is an easy task). I tried to compose a narrative topic, an expository topic, and a persuasive topic out of each object. Sometimes my students and I brainstormed for great topic sentences. If you can't get to Alaska, you easily and cheaply can buy disgusting and interesting things like plastic lizards, bugs, and other odd creatures on websites for novelty goods (www.rhodeislandnovelty.com, for example) and in catalogues such as *Oriental Trading Company.*

Some of these are cheap enough to give one to each of your students. Strange candy always elicits good topic sentences. I found huge gummy rats (black and red) in a local chocolate store.

Topic sentences:

➜ Explain why your teacher would want to keep a gummy rat on her desk.

➜ Persuade the cafeteria not to serve gummy rats as part of the lunch.

➜ Tell a story about what _____ would do if he/she found a gummy rat in his/her drawer.

➜ Explain what you would do with a gummy rat.

➜ Persuade your teacher to give you the gummy rat.

I'm sure you get the idea. You can give these disgusting-looking rats (or other equally repellent object or candy) as prizes to the students who write the best paragraphs. There are a lot of ways to make writing these paragraphs more than a chore. High-school students especially need to get away from the serious every once in a while in order to be reminded that humor is important and that learning can be a hoot. These paragraphs will give them a chance to be creative, to show their funny side, to put their passion into words, and to develop their voice.

The **Topic Sentence Suggestions** on page 43 provide some topic sentences that are a little less strange but have proven to spark some interesting paragraphs. You will want to instruct your students to write a narrative, expository, or persuasive paragraph. This will help prepare them for the genres on the writing test. Some topics lend themselves to more than one type of writing.

In addition, a great source of topic sentences (or ideas to generate topic sentences) is your students! You even could show a strange object (like that gummy rat) and ask students for topic sentences or titles for a strong, vivid-verb paragraph. They often come up with much more interesting ideas than we adults do.

As I mentioned in the beginning of this section, it is good to make writing the SVVP interesting, and to liven things up for a while. Besides the moose poop, etc., I liked to hold "Moldy Bread Contests" (recommended for grades five through ten). This yearly writing unit became so popular that the one year I skipped it, students got angry! It always was voted one of the best units on the evaluation sheet I asked students to fill out at the end of the year.

I got the idea from that good friend (and dynamite teacher) in North Carolina. *She* got the idea from a workshop (she doesn't remember which one) where the speaker had heard the idea from someone else, etc. You know how it goes, I'm sure. I give thanks to the original teacher who came up with the idea; it is a great one that sparked many a student to produce good strong, vivid-verb paragraphs. The whole thing takes about three weeks (since that is how long you need for the mold to grow), with one period a week to write and report and one period for the contest at the end. Any other writing (like essays) will, of course, extend the unit.

First, before you do anything else, check with your principal to see if holding a moldy bread contest is all right with the administration. While many people are allergic to mold in houses and pipes, few are allergic to bread mold, and the exposure in this activity is minimal. Your principal may object to your adding more mold spores to those which already lurk in your classroom walls, however. I did it safely for years with no one getting sick and only had a few parents object.

Next, with your principal's approval in hand, order some ribbons from a trophy shop with the phrases "Most Disgusting," "Most Colorful," and "Most Odoriferous" on them. You will need three per class if you can afford it.

Then write a letter to the parents of your students and require parent signatures on them. In it, explain what you are doing, ask them if their child is allergic to any kind of mold (most important), and obtain their cooperation with the project (and beg for brave souls to judge the contest). You *must* get these letters back to protect yourself. Any child who does not return the note or who has parents who object may not participate, and you will need to provide alternate topics for the journal, paragraphs, and essays.

Next, you will have to do a little research on mold. It needs three things to grow quickly: some warmth (although some certainly grows in *my* fridge), moisture, and food. Mold grows better in the dark than in the light. If you teach seventh grade or higher, you can require that your students do the research. Maybe you can persuade the science teacher to teach a brief unit on mold.

Once you get the letters back from the parents, you can begin. Instruct students to put a piece of bread into a see-through, airtight container (*not* Tupperware or parents will be angry since the container must be discarded). Tell them that bread without preservatives in it grows mold more quickly.

Teachers of younger students will want to keep the containers in a safe place in the classroom where no one will disturb or open them.

The same following rules must apply in all grades:

➔ You may put any food you wish on top of the bread **except** anything that has color to it or acid in it (like mayonnaise). Sugar (or nothing) works best.

➔ Moisten the bread slightly.

➔ You may brush the bread with any mold that you find in the fridge or cupboard to hasten the progress. Agar also is allowed.

➔ Shut the container and put it in a warm, dark place.

➔ Check the container daily (without opening it) and note any progress in a "Moldy Bread Journal." At the end of each week, draw a picture in your journal. If you choose to add something to the concoction, take the container outside. Record in the journal everything that was done to the bread, when, and why.

Next, students write a letter to a pet (dogs have been known to scarf up the bread) or human (visiting grandmothers tend to jettison the container) requesting that he or she leave their bread alone. Then, each week, you check the journals and come up with a topic for an SVVP that has to do with moldy bread. Of course, they can always describe the bread.

Topics for SVVPs could include:

➔ No mold grew on my bread this week.

➔ My dog was interested in the mold.

➔ Mold can be useful.

➔ My bizarre teacher made us grow mold on bread.

While all this is going on, find some willing parents, colleagues, or principals to act as judges in the "Moldy Bread Contest." In my school there was never a lack of volunteers. One of the science teachers donated lab coats, and I brought in masks, gloves, paper towels, plastic bags, tongs (one per judge), nose clips, etc. to make it funnier. One year my principal showed up in full academic regalia and kept saying "Here comes the judge." The more bizarre the costumes and getup (snorkel masks are always a hit), the more fun the contest.

Follow this procedure on the day of the contest:

➔ Give judges a paper with the three winning criteria on it—most disgusting, most colorful, and most odoriferous.

➔ Students put a card with their name on it and the unopened container of mold on the desk. Any student who opens the container is instantly disqualified.

➔ Judges walk around the room and write down the name of any student with a particularly interesting entry. Only one judge (usually the teacher) gingerly lifts the corner of the lid and sniffs. (The mold mostly smells musty, but there always is one that reeks to high heaven.) Finding the winner of the "Most Odoriferous" prize is never a problem!

➔ When notes are complete, judges confer, ribbons are given, and the containers are discarded into the trash bags and immediately taken to the dumpster.

The final writing assignment for this unit is not a strong, vivid-verb paragraph, but two essays. The first is a factual essay that explains in detail the student's participation in the unit, and the second essay lets the students critique the unit.

Scoring the Strong, Vivid-Verb Paragraphs

Once your students begin writing these paragraphs on their own, you are faced with grading them. Never fear! Whatever way you choose, it does not take long. And, if you walked around the room as your students wrote the paragraphs either in groups or individually, most of them already have been graded.

In **grades one and two**, I suggest you make only a positive comment or a check or whatever you use to denote a job well done.

For **grades three through five or compensatory classes at any grade level**, make it easy on yourself and simply encourage your students. While you can grade these any way you wish, I suggest that you give the student (or group) an "A" if the paragraph has been written correctly, a "B" if there is one mistake, and a "C" for more than one error. If some of the required elements have not been included, you could make these grades an "A-," "B-," and "C-." This encourages care on the part of the students, doesn't eat up too much of your time, and doesn't discourage your young students.

At the **sixth- and seventh-grade level**, how you grade probably will depend on the maturity of your students. If you have a batch of students who are below-level or whose writing egos would be threatened or discouraged by a tougher grading scale, use the one for grades three through five. If the students at your school need the challenge or you teach advanced classes, grade the paragraphs in the same manner as grades eight through twelve (below). As you decide which you will use, keep in mind that the grades on the paragraphs initially tend to be rather low until students learn the craft.

You will want to be more exacting in your grading for **eighth- through twelfth-graders**. A copy of the way I graded my eighth-graders' strong, vivid-verb paragraphs can be found on page 44 at the end of this step. At first, you will have to encourage your students not to give up as grades on the paragraphs initially tend to be rather low. Once students get the idea, you will find that most of them earn "As" and "Bs." I made copies of the grading sheet and gave it to my students so that they could refer to it as they composed their paragraphs.

Providing More Practice

Daily writing practice of some kind can be done in every subject. You can get ideas for great paragraphs from texts, thematic units, and the ideas below.

Art:

→ Write paragraphs about painters.

→ Critique a painting in a paragraph.

→ Explain why you painted (sculpted, etc.) your latest work.

Music:

→ Write a paragraph about a composer.

→ Critique a piece of music.

→ Explain why you like your favorite type of music.

P.E.:

→ Explain how to play soccer, baseball, football, etc.

→ Explain why _____ is your favorite sport.

→ Explain why _____ is a good athlete.

Social Studies:

Use the section headings in your book to generate topics for students.

→ Explain why you think our founding fathers wrote the Bill of Rights.

→ Explain why or why not you think the South should have seceded from the Union.

→ How is Canada different from the United States?

Science:

Use your unit headings to generate topics.

→ Explain how to make a magnet.

→ Explain how to make glue.

→ Explain why cockroaches are disgusting.

→ Explain how mold grows.

Math:

→ Explain how you figured out a word problem.

→ Write a paragraph about the process of division.

→ Explain how you got your answer.

Daily progress journals:

→ Students keep journals in a spiral notebook or composition book and take five minutes at the end of a period or the end of the day to write a short paragraph (daily is best, but who has that kind of time?) about what they did in class that day *or* what they learned in class that day.

Writing has become more and more a part of math, so math class presents the perfect opportunity for students to master SVVPs. Today, most states' math tests require students to explain in a short paragraph how they got an answer. In addition, in math, students, no matter what their age, struggle with word problems. Some students have trouble reading them. Others get so mixed up with the words that they can't see the math problem within. Teachers of any subject can help with this problem by having students actually write a word problem in the form of a strong, vivid-verb paragraph. Then, they can hand that problem to a partner to solve.

Or, better yet, if you don't teach math, you can meet with the math teacher beforehand and give the best paragraphs to him/her for practice during class. What better way to interest students in doing dreaded word problems than to have them figure out ones written by their peers?

To get students to compose the word problems, you can write a numeric problem on the board (the answer) and instruct students to make up a word problem that leads to that answer. Or, students can make up their own numeric problem and then write the paragraph. Encourage students to be funny.

I wrote the following paragraph to use in my workshops simply by rewriting a subtraction word problem that I found on the official practice test for Florida's FCAT. Needless to say, the original was very boring. Doesn't this paragraph appeal to you (and make more sense) more than a generic, dull, and sometimes confusing one on a subject in which you have no interest? I'm sure you will have no problem figuring out the answer.

Thirty teachers **endured** a long faculty meeting. Three **pleaded** desperation and **went** to the bathroom for the latest gossip. Seven **graded** papers under the table instead of giving the principal their full attention. One **filed** her nails (under the table, of course) and quietly **hummed** to herself to keep awake. Another teacher **fell** asleep and **drooled** on the agenda. Four more teachers **doodled** complex geometric designs on that same agenda. The rest were amazingly attentive. How many teachers **paid** attention at the faculty meeting?

Primary Strong-Verb Practice Sentences

1. The cat _____ in the chair.

2. A big brown dog _____ at the little cat.

3. The big dog then _____ the cat around the house.

4. My teacher _____ when the class talks too much.

5. Rabbits _____ when they smell danger.

6. The smelly, black and white skunk _____ the dog when the dog

   _____ it.

7. Our teacher _____ us how to write.

8. A yellow ball _____ down the stairs.

9. I _____ my best friend.

10. My friend _____ to school with me.

11. A big blue bird _____ the window.

12. When the teacher _____, I

    _____.

13. The school bell _____ when I _____ in the morning.

14. The wind _____ through the trees and _____ the leaves.

15. Cars _____ down the road and _____ their horns.

16. The flowers _____ the air with their smell. (Difficult)

17. In my messy room all my toys _____ the rug. (Difficult)

18. The bright yellow sun _____ on the kids on the playground.

Possible Answers for Primary
Strong-Verb Practice Sentences

1. The cat **curled up (sat, yawned, slept, etc.)** in the chair.

2. A big brown dog **barked (growled, whined, etc.)** at the little cat.

3. The big dog then **chased (pursued, followed, etc.)** the cat around the house.

4. My teacher **frowns (yells, sighs, shouts, etc.)** when the class **talks (chatters, prattles, etc.)** too much.

5. Rabbits **run (scamper off, quiver in fear, etc.)** when they **smell (sense, notice, etc.)** danger.

6. The smelly, black and white skunk **sprayed (peed on, bit, etc.)** the dog when the dog **attacked (growled at, chased, etc.)** it.

7. Our teacher **teaches (shows, demonstrates to, etc.)** us how to write.

8. A yellow ball **bounced (rolled, fell, etc.)** down the stairs.

9. I **hugged (called, played with, etc.)** my best friend.

10. My friend **walked (ambled, skipped, came, etc.)** to school with me.

11. A big blue bird **tapped (pecked at, hit, etc.)** the window.

12. When the teacher **talks (yells, teaches, etc.)**, I **listen (learn, cringe, pay attention, etc.)**.

13. The school bell **rings (peals, shrieks)** when I **arrive (come)** in the morning.

14. The wind **blows (rustles, moves)** through the trees and **rustles (shakes, moves)** the leaves.

15. Cars **drive (race, zoom)** down the road and **honk (toot)** their horns.

16. The flowers **perfumed (scented, filled up)** the air with their smell.

17. In my messy room all my toys **cover (mess up, litter)** the rug.

18. The bright yellow sun **shines on (warms, cheers up)** the kids on the playground.

Basic Dead-Verb Practice Sentences to Rewrite

The key is to show just how lonely, sad, happy, etc. the person is by telling something he or she would do. What do you do when you are sad? Mad? Happy? Lonely? It also helps to find the key words in each sentence.

1. The boy *was* lonely.

2. The little girl *was* sad.

3. The girl in the red dress *was* happy.

4. My teacher *is* slightly crazy and lots of fun.

5. My mom *is* mad at me.

6. My friend *is* mean to his sister.

7. These sentences *are* stupid.

8. The calico cat *was* a nice cat.

9. The little dog with the floppy ears *was* cute.

10. When I go to my grandparents' house, I *am* happy.

11. School sometimes *is* boring.

12. My room *is* a mess.

13. She *is* my best friend, and we *have* fun together.

14. The sky *is* blue with lots of fluffy clouds.

15. There *are* nasty brown roaches in my backpack.

16. The classroom *was* noisy.

17. The birthday party *was* awesome.

18. The skunk *is* smelly.

19. I *am* mad today.

20. It *was* fun.

Possible Answers for Basic Dead-Verb Practice Sentences to Rewrite

1. The lonely boy **sat** in the corner and cried.

   The lonely boy **played** all by himself.

2. The sad little girl **cried** piteously.

   The sad little girl **ran** to her mother and **sobbed** in her arms.

3. The girl in the red dress **danced** with joy.

   The girl in the red dress **twirled** around the room from happiness.

4. My crazy, fun teacher **plays** with us on the jungle gym.

   My crazy, fun teacher **likes** skunks and **collects** them.

5. My mom sometimes **yells** at me angrily.

   My angry mom **put** me in my room when I **broke** her favorite vase.

6. My mean friend **hits** and **teases** his sister.

   My mean friend **takes** his sister's dolls and **breaks** them.

7. These stupid sentences **take** a long time to rewrite.

   These stupid sentences **teach** me about strong verbs.

8. The nice calico cat **licked** my hand.

   The nice calico cat **curled up** in my lap and **purred**.

9. The cute little dog with the floppy ears **chased** its tail.

   The cute little dog with the floppy ears **rolled** on its back and **waved** its paws in the air.

10. When I **go** to my grandparents' house, I **get** anything I ask for.

    I **love** going to my grandparents' house because they **play** with me and **give** me lots of toys.

11. School **bores** me when I **must do** worksheets.

    Doing math problems or writing dumb sentences **puts** me to sleep.

12. My clothes **litter** the floor of my messy room.

    In my messy room, clothes **cover** the floor and math papers **spill** out of the trash can.

13. My best friend and I **play** games together all the time.

    My best friend and I **visit** each other's houses every day.

TEACHING NOTE: *Sometimes you need to reverse the order of the parts of the sentence as in the following examples.*

14. Lots of fluffy clouds **dot** the blue sky.

    Lots of fluffy clouds **float** in the beautiful blue sky overhead.

15. Nasty brown roaches **live** and **poop** in my backpack.

    Nasty brown roaches **eat** my lunch in my backpack.

16. The noisy classroom **hummed** with students at their learning centers.

    The students **talked**, **shouted** at each other, and **laughed** happily as they **played** in the noisy classroom.

17. We **stayed** up late at the awesome birthday party and **ate** cake.

    A clown and lots of animals **came** to the awesome birthday party.

18. The smelly skunk **sprays** the mean kid.

    The smelly skunk still **reeks** from spraying a dog.

TEACHING NOTE: *Sometimes you may want to take a totally different tack that doesn't even mention the adjective; it just demonstrates it with action.*

19. In my anger, I **want** to **lash out** and **hit** and **yell** at everyone today.

    My face **frowns** and **scrunches** up in anger.

20. My hair **stood** on end, and I **laughed** and **screamed** on the roller coaster ride.
    At Disney World, we **rode** on lots of rides, **ate** junk food, and **met** Mickey Mouse.

Intermediate Strong-Verb Practice
Sentences to Rewrite

Change the following "dead-verb" sentences into strong ones that create vivid images you can see. Paint word pictures with your sentences. You must include all the information in the original sentence. You may add more information if you wish. Note the verb tense of the "telling" sentence.

EXAMPLE:
"Dead-verb" sentence — She *was* angry.
Strong-verb sentence — The angry girl **flung** her arms about in frustration.

1. He *has* a long nose that *is* blue and ugly.

2. My friend *is* mean to me.

3. The girl *has* long, stringy hair that *is* past her shoulders.

4. The teacher *is* totally crazy.

5. There *are* nasty brown roaches in my backpack.

6. There *are* always lots of students in the hallways of school.

7. I know my teacher *is* happy because she *has* a big smile on her face.

8. The boy in the corner *is* lonely.

9. The music *was* wonderful and *had* a great melody.

10. The monster *has* bulb-like purple eyes popping out of its head.

11. The young lady *is* a real loud mouth.

12. We *were* the best in the class that day.

13. English teachers *are* always asking us to read something.

14. The adorable kitten *is* very playful.

15. The party *was* awesome.

16. The skunk *was* smelly. (Discourage the use of the verb "to smell.")

Possible Answers for Intermediate
Strong-Verb Practice Sentences to Rewrite

1. His blue, ugly nose **protrudes (hangs, sticks out)** from his face.

2. My mean friend **kicks** me under the cafeteria table.
   knocks my papers off my desk.
   steals my pen on a daily basis.

3. The girl's long, stringy hair **hangs** past her shoulders.

4. The totally crazy teacher **dances** on desks and **sings** the "dead" verbs.

5. Nasty brown roaches **inhabit (live in, eat everything in)** my backpack.

6. Lots of students always **crowd** the hallways.

7. I **know** that the big smile on my teacher's face **reflects** her delight.

8. The lonely boy in the corner **curls up** in the fetal position and **bemoans** his fate.

9. We **could not resist** listening to the wonderful, melodic music.

10. Bulb-like purple eyes **pop (bulge, stick)** out of the monster's head.

11. The loud-mouthed young lady **voices (shouts)** her disagreement.

12. That day we **dazzled** everyone else with our stellar behavior.

13. English teachers always **ask** us to **(demand that we)** read something.

14. The adorable, playful kitten **chases** the string and then **curls up** in my lap.

15. We **danced, ate, played games,** and **gossiped** at the awesome party.

16. The smelly skunk **sprayed** the vicious dog who **reeked** for days.

Advanced Strong-Verb
Practice Sentences to Rewrite

Change the following "dead-verb" sentences into strong ones that make vivid images you can see. Paint word pictures with your sentences. You must include all the information in the original sentence. You may add more information if you wish. Note the verb tense of the "telling" sentence. (Teachers, please note that the use of a gerund or a participle is acceptable.)

EXAMPLE:
"Dead-verb" sentence — The football coach *was* really pleased.
Strong-verb sentence — The football coach **praised** his players and **treated** them
      to pizza because they **won** the big game.

1. The halls *were* crowded with chattering students.

2. He *was* terribly lonely at home on a Saturday evening.

3. Shakespeare's play *Romeo and Juliet is* a tragedy.

4. After breaking up with her boyfriend, the girl *was* sad and depressed.

5. The high school's football team *was* great!

6. America *was* in a state of turmoil during the Civil War.

7. The Renaissance *was* a period of great creativity.

8. Shakespeare *has* a way with words.

9. The boy *was* guilty of a misdemeanor.

10. She *looked* guilty.

11. We *have* too much homework.

12. Drinking alcohol and then driving a car *is* dangerous.

13. He *was* depressed about his grades.

14. Love *is* a many-splendored thing.

15. He *was* green with envy.

16. Requiring two years of a foreign language for college *is* (beneficial/awful).

1. Chattering students **crowded** the halls.

2. Saturday evening **found** the terribly lonely boy at home with a book.

3. In Shakespeare's play *Romeo and Juliet*, the two lovers **die** at the end, making this play a sad tragedy.

4. After breaking up with her boyfriend, the girl **wailed** and **moaned** her distress to the winds and anyone who **would listen**.

5. The school's fabulous football team **won** the district championship last year and **completed** more touchdowns than any other school's team!

6. During the tragic turmoil of the Civil War, many soldiers **lost** their lives, and brother often **fought** brother, making it even more of a tragedy.

7. During the Renaissance, artists like Michelangelo and writers like Dante **created (crafted, composed)** major works that we **enjoy** and **celebrate** to this day.

8. Shakespeare's way with words and double entendres **delight** audiences even today, almost 400 years after his death.

9. The guilty boy **stole (lifted, pried, took)** hubcaps off cars, committing a misdemeanor.

10. Her face **mirrored (showed)** her guilt.

11. Our teachers **pile** too much homework on us. **or** Our books for homework **weigh** down our backpacks as our teachers **believe** in piling it on.

12. If you **drink** alcohol and then **drive** a car, you **risk** death or injury and **endanger** the lives of others as well.

13. His low grades **depressed** him.

14. Love, a many-splendored thing, **inspires** poets to write, painters to paint, and composers to compose.

15. The envious boy literally **writhed (stiffened, etc.)** with jealousy.

16. Requiring two years of a foreign language for college **prepares** us for higher learning. **or** Learning another language can **daunt (discourage)** even a good student.

Elementary Examples of Strong,
Vivid-Verb Paragraphs

"My Heart" (1st grade, expository)

A heart *is* in my body. It **pumps** my blood. It **runs** my blood around my body. It **makes** a noise thump thump when my doctor **listens** to it. I *have* a good heart.

"The Sad Boy" (first semester of 2nd grade, expository)

John *is* sad. He **cries** all the time like a baby. He **frowns**, and he never **smiles**. He **sits** by himself in the corner. John *is* very sad today.

"My Sister" (second semester of 2nd grade, expository)

My sister *is* a pain. She **takes** stuff out of my room. She **hurts** me by kicking me. She always **comes** in my room when I **don't ask** her. She **hogs** the t.v. too. That *is* why my big sister *is* a pain. (She really *is* not a pain.)

"The Funny Dog" (3rd grade/special education, narrative)

The dog *was* very funny. It **chased** its tail round and round, and it never **caught** it. When the funny dog **woofed**, its ears **flopped**. The dog **wagged** its tail so fast like a flag in a big wind. This dog *was* so funny I **bought** it.

"Mac's Adventures" (group of third-graders from Mississippi, narrative)

Please note that I left in a few "dead" verbs as this narrative was too good not to include. This is really a story, rather than an SVVP, but it shows how children can use strong, vivid verbs once they know how.

Do you **want** to hear a hilarious story? **Listen**. A long time ago, there *was* a dog named Mac. Poor Mac **lost** his checkbook and **couldn't pay** his debts.

While he **looked** for his checkbook, Mac **met** Dr. Hokey Pokey, the evil genius. Dr. Hokey Pokey **opened** his bag. He **put** his right arm in. He **took** his right arm out and **shook** drops of magic potion all over Mac. The potion **turned** Mac into a frog.

Mac **hopped** away to the riverside. His checkbook *was* on a lily pad! Mac **ripped** the Velcro open. He **clicked** his pen and **wrote** a check for $5,000.

Mac **said** to Dr. Hokey Pokey, "I'll **give** you this check if you **turn** me back into a dog."

Dr. Hokey Pokey **said**, "*It's* a deal."

And *that's* what *it's* all about.

Middle-School Examples of
Strong, Vivid-Verb Paragraphs
(Superlative vocabulary comes from Caught'yas)

"A Day in the CMS Cafeteria" (from Georgia, past-tense narrative)

Yesterday, the students in the cafeteria *were* wild. They **behaved** like kindergartners. Flying food **filled** the air and **covered** the floor. Principals **ran** from the chaotic scene as they **protected** their heads with trays. French dressing **saturated** Mrs. M's pulchritudinous hair. Mr. C **slipped** on the Jello that **carpeted** the floor, and he **landed** right on his behind. Milk **erupted** out of people's noses all over the tables. Yesterday *was* a wild and crazy day in the CMS cafeteria.

"The Wild Cafeteria" (my students dictated to me, past-tense narrative)

"**Prepare** yourself," **whispered** the dean to a teacher, "here **come** the wild bunch." *(Rewrite of boring topic sentence "The students in the cafeteria were wild.")* As students **got** their trays, they **threw** food from table to table. Some **shouted** invectives at the top of their lungs. Soiled trays **littered** the floor where students **flung** them. Students **stood** on the tables and **danced** to imaginary music. Others **burped** loudly to express their dislike of the school fare. One bold student even **yelled** at the dean, demanding that rock music play during lunch. The dean **croaked** over the loud speaker in a vain attempt to quiet down the students. Food **continued** to splatter on the walls. It *was* a typical lunch in the Westwood cafeteria.

"The Messy Room" (present-tense expository; rewrite of "My room is a mess")

"Crunch" **go** my CDs as I **walk** into my totally messy room! Clothes **litter** the floor. Sheets and blankets **hang** off the bed in great disarray. Half-empty Coke cans on their side **spill** their contents on the rug. Records **cover** my desk, burying last year's homework. A nasty smell of month-old pizza **wafts** from the overflowing trash can. Moldy school books **peek** out of my packed closet from underneath piles and piles of junk. Food stains from wild food fights **color** the walls. My room *is* a total disaster, and I **can't leave** it until I **clean** it up!

"Clinic Fun with Dr. S." (past-tense narrative)

The clinic lady's ice cold hands **shook** as she **signed** me in on her list of victims for the day. Then she **ushered** me in the freezing examining room, and she **turned** to leave. Next, the big metal door **slammed** behind me, causing me to leap in the air in surprise.

"**Come** on over, Sweetie," **rasped** Dr. S. in a gravelly voice as I **quivered** in fear.

Cold sweat **dripped** down my young visage as Dr. S **approached** with the rusty needle. (As mean as a salesman selling wrapping paper in July, Dr. S. **loves** giving shots.) Her aged hands **wound** around my upper arm just before the needle **stabbed** me. Ouch! I **hope** the common cold **doesn't** land YOU in her clinic!

High-School Examples of Strong, Vivid-Verb Paragraphs

(Please note that the topic and the verb tense are the same for both, but the genre is different)

"Boys Are Foolish" (persuasive)

Hanging out with my friends really *is* "sweet." We always **laugh** and **joke**, but we **enjoy** most poking fun at the boys who always **make** utter fools of themselves. Yes, boys, you **do** stupid things that we girls **would never think** of doing. In the first place, guys, you **find** all kinds of different ways to get your trucks filthy dirty when you **"Four Wheel"** in the mud. After you **mess up** your vehicles, you **wash**, **scrub**, **shine**, **wax**, **buff**, and **polish** them for hours. The next day, you **repeat** the process all over again. Why **waste** your time and energy this way? **Don't** you **know** that we girls **watch** you with disgust and **laugh** at your childish ways? Hey, guys, why not **act** like sensible young men instead of fools?

"Hanging Out with Friends" (expository)

Hanging out with my friends really *is* "sweet." When we **get** together to share the latest gossip, we **giggle** and **enjoy** each other's company, and all worries and parent hassles **disappear** as if they never **existed** at all. At the mall, as we **shop** for clothes together, thoughts of real life like school and homework **don't exist**. Our boy troubles **slip** out of our minds like soap as we **laugh** at each other when trying on different clothes. Stress **flies** out the window when my girlfriends and I **spend** the night together, laughing, eating pizza, sharing secrets, and talking about everyone else, especially boys. I **love** hanging out with my friends because it **makes** life "sweet."

"The Wild Cafeteria" Cluster

Title The Wild Cafeteria

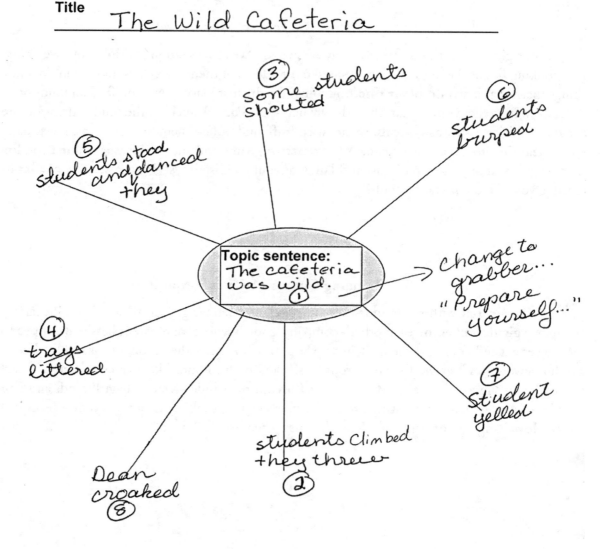

End sentence: It was a typical lunch in the Westwood Cafeteria.

Cluster/plan made as a whole class with me as scribe

Clustering the Strong, Vivid-Verb Paragraph

Title: _____

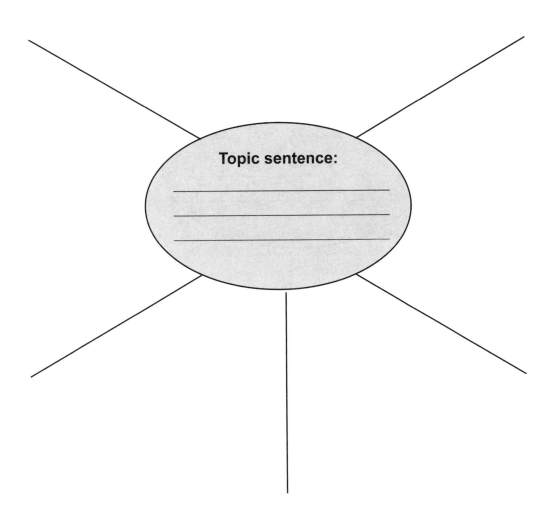

Topic sentence:

_____

_____

_____

End sentence: _____

_____.

Clustering the Strong, Vivid-Verb Paragraph

Title: _____

Topic sentence:

_____
_____
_____

End sentence: _____

_____.

INCLUDE (and check off as you put them in your paragraph):

___ 1. Title
___ 2. Topic sentence (Change it to a "grabber.")
___ 3. _____ strong, vivid-verb sentences—no repeated verbs
___ 4. At least two transitions
___ 5. Two vivacious vocabulary words
___ 6. Simile, metaphor, or other figurative language
___ 7. Compound sentence; complex sentence
___ 8. Concluding sentence (may have "dead" verb)

Topic Sentence Suggestions

(Ask your students for further suggestions, and/or
check their papers for "telling" sentences.)

Elementary School:

My little brother (sister, cousin, etc.) is a pain.

I was very happy (mad, sad, glad, etc.).

My teacher is strange (mean, nice, etc.).

My mom makes me angry.

School is boring (exciting).

The classroom was noisy.

The dog was cute (sad, mad, glad, etc).

_____ is my favorite toy.

The _____ is beautiful.

My best friend and I do lots of things together.

Gummy worms (accompanied by the real thing) look disgusting.

_____ was flatulent in class today. (disgusting but appealing to children)

Middle School:

The party was awesome!

The students in the cafeteria were wild.

He/She looks weird.

My room is a mess.

The old man was lonely.

My English teacher is strange.

Going to _____ is fun.

Going to see the dean is scary.

My backpack is filled with junk.

The students drove the substitute to insanity.

No one wants to eat in a school cafeteria.

Please, Mom and Dad, let me go on a date (stay out late, go somewhere, etc.)!

High School:

The party was awesome!

The last football (basketball, soccer, etc.) game was exciting.

The students were not on their best behavior.

The test was hard.

The world situation is depressing.

My room is a mess.

My parents are too strict.

School rules are too confining.

It was after midnight, and his parents were out of town.

The book _____ is _____.

Hanging with my friends is "sweet."

Do not go in my room, Mother!

FYI—How Your Teacher Scores the SVVP

Heading
Is the heading correct? You can lose the usual ten points out of 100 for the assignment if it is not. Do not be careless here.

Title
Is it different from the topic sentence? Are there capital letters in the right places? You can lose five points for this.

Plan and rough draft
Did you somehow plan the strong verbs and their subjects in a cluster, outline, or some other way? Have you included the corrected rough draft? Failure to include any part of this will cost you five points.

Topic sentence
Is it a complete sentence, and is it really a topic sentence? This is worth five points. Since the teacher usually gives you the topic sentence, this is a freebie grade. Be careful. Your teacher may ask you to turn the "boring" topic sentence into a "grabber."

Strong-verb sentences
In the six middle sentences, are only the main verbs highlighted? Are they all strong verbs? Are they all different? You will lose up to five points for incorrectly identifying the main verbs.

"Dead" verbs
Are there any in the middle six sentences? Except in the topic sentence and the concluding sentence, you will lose ten points for each "dead" verb used, for each strong verb that is repeated, and for each fragment (up to a total of 60 points)—one for each of the six sentences!

Sentence structure
Are the required types of sentences included? Do all the sentences make sense? Are all the sentences complete sentences (not fragments)? You can lose up to five points for this error.

Simile or other literary device
Is there an original simile? Has it been circled? This is worth five points.

Concluding sentence
Is it different from the first sentence? Does it wrap up the entire paragraph, or is it just another sentence? You can lose another five points here.

Spelling
Are there any misspelled words? You will lose five points for each, up to a possible 25 points, so be careful and check! Misspelling more than one word can earn you a negative grade! Be smart. Consult a dictionary, a spell-checker, or a parent.

Extra points
You can earn five extra points if your paragraph is typed, two extra points for each vocabulary word correctly used and circled (up to 10 points), and five extra points if the SVVP is really original, exceptionally well written, especially amusing, or otherwise distinguishes itself.

Step Two

Teach Students How to Score the State Writing Assessment Test

Just as in football where young players watch the great athletes and try to emulate those talented players, students who are to be good writers need examples to follow. No one walks cold onto a football field and knows instantly how to play the game and play it well. Similarly, no one walks into school knowing what comprises good writing and how to produce it.

And, just like the complicated rules of football, the scoring (even holistically) of an essay or narrative for the writing test is very complicated since there are many required elements. Students need to learn what constitutes good writing by reading both good *and* bad examples. That way, they can see for themselves what it is that makes one paper good and another incomplete and poorly written. The best way to do this is to make your students score papers using the same rubric that the official scorers utilize to grade the actual test.

The rubric is no secret. It is based on the five, six, or seven traits of writing (depending on which book you read). Sample student test papers from many states are available on the Internet and, in many cases, are provided in a booklet published by various states' departments of education to acquaint teachers with the specific requirements for a high score on the test. If students can understand the basic rubric, use it accurately to score papers (including their own), and point out what is missing in a poor paper and conversely what has been included in a superlative paper, their own writing will greatly improve.

Essentially, the traits of good writing are sticking to the topic at hand without inserting extraneous information; presenting good, original ideas; organizing thoughts well; providing support, detail, elaboration, etc.; achieving a "flow"; making few errors; creating a distinct voice; expressing passion and flair; using superlative vocabulary; and varying sentence structure. These are the elements that students will be looking for as they learn to score. I have condensed them (as have most of the states) into a simple, five-trait rubric that our students can understand.

As in teaching any new skill, you need to move in small steps to achieve your goal. The strategies explained in this step will enable you and your students to score essays and narratives with ease and also to recognize the specific elements that make one paper shine and another lackluster.

To aid you in this endeavor, at the end of this book, there are 90 examples of student writing (with scoring explanations) that you and your students can use for practice. No matter what grade level you teach, you can utilize all of these examples to teach scoring. Good writing is good writing. Mediocre writing is mediocre writing. And, poor writing is poor writing. High-school students can learn from elementary-school students' writing and vice-versa.

Scoring Holistically

Before you can teach your students how to score the essays and narratives required for the test, you yourself must be comfortable in your own ability to score. This is not easy to do by yourself without a lot of practice. Many school districts offer workshops in holistic scoring. If your district offers one, take it! Otherwise you can try my suggestions below. You will find the basic rubric for both essays and narratives at the end of this step. I also have included a more detailed six-point rubric that a few states still use. The six-point rubric breaks down the required elements into smaller increments for more clarity. The four-point, five-point, and domain-based rubrics are generally the same, only the elements are broken down differently. I have found that most rubrics are worded similarly. Each sample has been scored holistically as a whole and also by domains.

> **TEACHING NOTE:** *If you are a new teacher (or did not major in English in college) and are not already familiar with the format of a basic essay or a short narrative, this would be a good time to turn to **Step Three** and read the first section to give yourself an overview before you proceed.*

You can give yourself a one-teacher workshop on scoring the examples in the last section of this book, **90 Examples for Scoring Practice**. If you do this for at least 50 essays, you soon will feel quite comfortable scoring your students' writing. As you score (scoring explanations are after each group of papers for each topic), trust your instincts as a teacher who has graded many papers in the course of your career. Remember that when you score holistically, you only are looking for the basics, an overall impression. You are not reading carefully and analyzing.

As you use these papers for your own practice, however, try not to look at the scores before reading *all* of the papers for each topic. I suggest putting the number of each essay or narrative on a piece of paper and writing your score by that number (and maybe a brief explanation for that particular score as well). Then, when you reach the actual scores after each group of essays, you can compare them objectively with your scoring.

In the workshops that I give all around the country, the teachers work as a large group and then in small groups before they score the papers individually (at home). And, initially, while you probably will make more mistakes on your own than you would if you were working in a group, I predict that you will achieve the end result—feeling comfortable about scoring the essays and narratives. You then can use these same examples to train your students.

I offer you some hints on how to reduce the practice scoring time (and actual scoring time when you grade your students' papers) to the one to two minutes that the official scorers require. You can teach these hints to your students when they begin to practice scoring.

The following graphic contains the simple steps to follow to score a paper in a minute or less. Spending more than a minute or two will not help your students any more. Spending fewer than two minutes per paper will give you time to score more papers—lucky you! Each year, I scored about 1,500 to 2,000 essays depending on the number of students I taught. Using the method below, I rarely took home more than half an hour's worth of short essays and narratives. (More about this in the **Step Three**.) The longer essays, research papers, narratives, and plays that my students composed (which were *not* practice for the test) were an entirely different story.

TEACHING NOTE:

➔ *Learn the basic criteria for scoring (see page 56 at the end of this step).*

➔ *Glance at the first and last paragraphs to see if they are different, complete, and not formulaic.*

➔ *Briefly skim the middle for elaboration and details, vivacious vocabulary, and a clear voice. Glance at each paragraph to see if the elaboration is consistent.*

➔ *Use the score sheet to grade. H (High) = A, M (Medium) = B, and L (Low) = C.*

➔ *If you teach only English and/or reading, score the previous class's papers as the next class writes.*

➔ *Always use score sheets (page 59 in this step) to guide you and keep track of common errors.*

Practice Grading

Before you even begin to involve your students in scoring the essays and narratives, you will need a lot of sample papers to use. So where do you obtain these samples? There are many resources out there.

Use the samples in this book. First, you can use the anonymous samples written by fourth-, seventh-, eighth-, and tenth-graders that are included in the last section of this book, **90 Examples for Scoring Practice.** I used all of them with my students (except for the thirty-seven examples I added for this new edition). The papers come from seven different schools and the students of seven different teachers.

As I said in the last section, the analysis of the scores is on a separate page after each set of essays or narratives. Of course when you use these examples with your students, you will *not* include copies of the answers until after they finish scoring. Since these were not the actual papers on the test (even though the prompts may be the same as on the test since most states recycle them) and hence were not officially scored, they were graded by me and by the teachers who kindly let me use them in this book. I think, however, that the scores reflect fairly accurately what the papers would receive officially.

Obtain official state booklets. If you are lucky, the DOE in your state publishes a booklet each year with samples of the previous year's writing test. In my state of Florida, teachers in the targeted grades (fourth, eighth, and tenth) are given a yearly booklet, "Florida Writes!" In each of these booklets are twenty-eight examples of actual test essays and narratives scored on a six-point rubric (page 57 at the end of this step). For each of the two prompts that are given, there are two examples of each of the seven possible scores (including zero). My former colleagues and I copied the papers, took off the answers, mixed them up, and used them with our students. Of course, we made a key for ourselves.

Many other states publish yearly booklets. One state used to send back student papers that had been scored. With names removed, the good ones could be used as examples. Still other states post benchmark papers on the Internet. Use all the papers your state provides.

> **TEACHING NOTE:** *Remember that whether your state scores the test on a 1-6, 1-5, or 1-4 basis (or with individual domains), the basic criteria, required elements, and hence the rubric remain the same. The scores are either high, medium, or low no matter what number is assigned to it. Those states with rubrics of 5 or 6 have more wriggle room to recognize a really superlative paper, but that is the only difference that I can see.*

Take advantage of samples from other grade levels. After they initiated the writing test in my state, even though I taught seventh and eighth grade, I used examples from fourth-, eighth-, and tenth-grade tests to teach my students how to score. And, up until 2002 when I retired, I used examples from many years past. I repeat: Good writing is good writing no matter when it was written, why it was written, or by what grade level it was written.

Therefore, if you can get them or have saved them, copy the examples from your state's booklets for the past ten years, putting a piece of paper over the scores before you copy them so that students cannot see them when they score. Run off class sets, and number each paper for identification purposes.

Since you can use these year after year and can share with your colleagues, it is a good investment of time and paper. Be sure to make a key for the teachers. A fellow eighth-grade English teacher and I got together every year and ran off papers from the *Florida Writes!* book, reducing the work in half as we shared the class sets (and keys) to have the maximum number of examples.

Check different states' sites on the Internet. Many states post benchmark writing papers on their Department of Education website. You can search for the sites by using the name of the state and the words "writing assessment," "test samples," or "benchmark papers." Most of these are rather huge files since they are photocopied examples of actual student papers and not in jpeg format. Look for any state(s) you wish.

Make your own examples. Another way to obtain examples is to use ones that your previous years' students have written to practice for the test. You can remove the names and make copies of good, mediocre, and bad papers. The only disadvantage to using these examples is that they were not officially scored. It is a good idea to find a willing parent who can type the papers as they are, mistakes and all. You will want to do this so that no one can recognize the handwriting and so that your students can read them without difficulty. When typed, you then can make overhead transparencies or a class set of copies for your students to practice grading.

Basic Criteria of Scoring

Before students learn how to score the essays, they need to learn the basic criteria and then read (or have read to them) some examples of student writing with you referring to the basic criteria as you read. By becoming familiar with the basic criteria and seeing examples of good, mediocre, and poor essays *before* learning to score them, students become aware of what constitutes a good paper. Only *after* students have read, analyzed, and scored quite a few samples are they ready to learn and apply the elements of excellent writing to their own efforts.

I suggest that first you make an overhead of the **Basic Criteria for Scoring the State Writing Assessment Test** (page 56 at the end of this step) and go over it with your students. Then put a copy on the overhead of the **Focused Analytical Score Sheet** (page 59).

Now you are ready to read various examples of essays and narratives to your students. I suggest making a class set of each paper so that your students can follow along as you read and tell you what to mark on the **Focused Analytical Score Sheet**. If you don't have enough copy paper, or if your school counts how many copies you make, you simply can make an overhead of each sample, read it to your students as they follow along, put up the score sheet, and discuss the paper you just read.

As you read an example of an excellent paper, check off each required element as you come across it. As you read a mediocre or poor sample, circle what is missing. For example, if the writing sample lacks nitty-gritty detail, circle the words "nitty-gritty detail" and so on. After you read at least ten samples this way, your students are ready to begin scoring in earnest.

Scoring Essays and Narratives Together and Individually

Using the **Focused Analytical Score Sheet** (page 59 at the end of this step), begin teaching your students the high-medium-low method of scoring. You can use that page to make copies for your students to use as they practice scoring. You will notice that there are *two* scoring sheets on the page as I know copying is a pain and money is tight. (Sometimes during really lean years, I even reduced the score sheets to four on a page.) You need a lot of them because you or your students will staple one to every essay or narrative that they write or score. That is a lot of score sheets.

Once students understand the basic components of a good essay or narrative and have heard some excellent examples, they are ready to begin scoring. As with the strong-verb sentence and paragraph writing practice, scoring is best done by an entire class at first, then in small groups when students feel more confident, and finally, as individuals. You will want your students to become competent scorers for their own papers.

What you *really* want your students to do is to recognize what constitutes an excellent paper and what is lacking in a mediocre or poor piece of writing. Noting what elements made an essay or narrative earn a particular score is the way to achieve this goal.

First, either put an example of an essay or narrative on the overhead or pass out the example to your students (a packet of examples would be best). You can prepare a packet of mixed-up samples to score or run off some of the sets of examples that are in the last section of this book. If you make a packet, be sure to number each paper—Sample 1, Sample 2, etc.—for easy identification.

Next, pass out a copy of the **Focused Analytical Score Sheet** to your students. Read a sample (or the first example in a packet) to your students, and discuss its merits (or lack thereof) as a class. Ask students to look at the score sheet (but not to make any marks at this stage) as you debate the score and discuss what is good and/or lacking in the paper. It might be helpful to put a copy of the score sheet on the overhead so you can circle the missing elements, checking off the ones that are in the paper as you and your students discuss it orally. This models the process.

As you discuss each paper, use the list of helpful things to point out as your students score. You will find these on pages 52-53 in this step. You may want to keep a copy nearby for use in all the following scoring exercises. I suggest scoring and discussing the included or missing elements in at least ten papers before you turn your students loose to do this in small groups. Give each group a packet of papers to score (the number of which will depend on the grade level you teach) and one **Focused Analytical Score Sheet** for each example.

Once your students are in groups and they or you have decided who gets which job (and assuming that you use the same jobs as I suggested in **Step One**), you are ready to begin:

Procedure:

➔ The "reader" reads the papers, one at a time, to the group while each person follows along on his or her own copy. Or, the reader also can interpret words for the group as they all read silently.

➔ The "mom" keeps the others in the group on task, watches the time (two minutes to read and another three minutes to discuss), and leads (and ends) the discussion of the good and bad points of the essay or narrative they just read.

➔ The "recorder" writes the number of the paper onto a **Focused Analytical Score Sheet**, and then, with directions from his/her group, checks off things that were in the paper and circles the elements that were missing.

➔ The "questioner," card in hand, comes to you with any questions the group may have.

➔ As with the large group, I suggest scoring at least ten papers in groups in the above manner.

➔ Finally, pass out some papers (not many) to each student along with a **Focused Analytical Score Sheet** for each paper, and have students score them individually. After all are finished, hold a discussion on each one so that students can see if they scored accurately or not.

The next step is to have students attach a **Focused Analytical Score Sheet** to each essay or narrative *they* write and score it immediately after writing it. (This only works if you have at least an hour for the exercise.) When you score the papers *after* your students do, use a different colored pen, making clarifying notations on the score sheet.

If, however, your periods are shorter and your students do not have time to score their papers before handing them in, you can score each one on the score sheet and fold the sheet so that the student can't see what you wrote. The next day, on the backside of the score sheet, students put a score and explain why. Then, as a whole class, all your students open up the score sheet and check to see if they scored accurately.

As students get more and more proficient at scoring, you may want to ask them to score with the same scale and rubric that your state uses. My eighth-graders preferred having more options and actually got quite good at scoring accurately on a six-point rubric! They even become adept at spotting zero essays that were well-written but off the topic.

In fact, right after the actual test, I always asked each student to tell me what they thought they scored and why. Most gave me an approximate score as well as specifics they had included (like vocabulary words or using a quote or threading a theme). There were always a few who weren't sure and said that it was either a "5" or a "3" depending on how the scorer interpreted how much they got off topic. I wrote the predictions in my gradebook. When the scores came in, almost every student had predicted correctly. They knew what constituted good writing and were, for the most part, able to produce it on demand.

On page 58 at the end of this step, I have included lesson plans that reflect the detail explained above. I hope this will help you as you make your lesson plans. Of course, these exercises can apply to several of the standards for reading if you are required to teach those.

Helpful Things to Point Out

TEACHING NOTE: Elementary and middle-school teachers can do this for an exercise in reading. Or, if you are departmentalized and your school splits language arts and reading, ask the reading teacher to do it in order to give you more class time for students to write more paragraphs, essays, and narratives. Even first-graders can listen to a paper and analyze it orally.

As you read and discuss with your students the good examples of writing, there are some things you might want to point out. I always read at least one good example a day to subliminally drill into their heads what constituted a good essay or narrative.

It is a good idea to point out the following:

➔ Good grabbers that catch our attention, such as conversations, the use of onomatopoeia or a question, or beginning with a quotation (correctly punctuated, of course).

➔ Restating the topic in the first paragraph and referring to it in all subsequent paragraphs.

➔ The use of any literary device.

➔ The use of strong, active verbs, especially in descriptions.

➔ A topic sentence and a concluding sentence in each of the four to five paragraphs.

➜ Indented paragraphs (although in most states—because the writing is considered a rough draft—students can earn the highest score without indenting at all if the paper is otherwise superb), correctly punctuated quotes, and the use of compound and complex sentences.

➜ Any "$100, big, juicy" vocabulary word that appears in the paper.

➜ A strong conclusion that wraps up the essay or narrative.

➜ A theme that threads itself through the paper (such as a reference to a bird, a simple metaphor, or a repeated image).

➜ And, most importantly, the use of nitty-gritty detail. Point out every use and non-use of it you can. When a general statement is made and not followed up with detail, ask your students to supply that detail. For example, the statement, "I hate my sister because she messes in my room," is not considered nitty-gritty detail; but to say, "I hate my sister because she messes in my room, plays my CDs, takes my stuffed animals off the bed, tries on my clothes, and sneaks a peek in my diary," is nitty-gritty detail. (See **Activity #1** under **Writing Middles with Elaboration, Nitty-Gritty Detail, and Down-and-Dirty, Nitty-Gritty Detail,** in **Step Three**, page 97.) The more examples you read to your students (especially the younger ones), the better the chance is that they will learn to elaborate in their writing.

Analyze Anything Written

So that your students get the idea that all writing can be analyzed (not just essays and narratives written for test practice), I suggest that you and your students, as a brief, oral exercise, analyze anything you come across. Examine each piece for the elements that make writing (even poems) good or mediocre. Marcia Freeman wrote a book, *Listen to This: Developing an Ear for Expository* (Freeman, 1997), with great expository *and* persuasive examples you can analyze. It is designed to be used at any level. This little book proved to be a very valuable resource in my classroom since adult expository or persuasive writing is often difficult to come by. Marcia takes the five traits of writing (see page 56, **The Basic Criteria for Scoring the State Writing Assessment Test**, at the end of this step) and analyzes each short piece of prose or poem for you.

I found (don't know where) and modified a sample scoring sheet (see the next page) to help students analyze in detail anything written, including poetry and ads. I think you will find it useful.

Writing to be analyzed _____

Your name _____

EVALUATING ANYTHING WRITTEN

Function of Writing: _____

Organization Used: _____

Beginning:

    Hook: _____

    Topic Statement: _____

A Few Nitty-Gritty, Supporting Details in the Middle:

    1. _____

    2. _____

    3. _____

Lively Writing and Figurative Language Used:

    Strong, Vivid Verbs: _____

    Great Vocabulary Words: _____

    Literary Devices: _____

    Other Lively Writing: _____

Zinger at End: _____

Necessary Tools for Scoring

To make things easier for you, I have included four tools you might need. The first is the **Basic Criteria for Scoring the State Writing Assessment Test**, which has the required domains reduced to their basics. You can make copies to post in your classroom and for each student to keep close at hand as he or she writes.

The second is for your eyes only. It is a **Six-Point point Modified Holistic Rubric**. I used a précis of the basic Florida rubric since it is on a six-point scale and breaks down the requirements into smaller increments than states which use a four-point rubric. Some of the words in the rubric have been changed for clarity. These are the official criteria for Florida, sent to my district by the Department of Education in Tallahassee, Florida, but almost all other states use the same or similar criteria, no matter how they assign the scores. If your state does not use a six-point rubric (and most do not), you certainly can get a copy of the official scoring criteria from your English supervisor.

Following the detailed rubric, you will find **Lesson Plans for Practicing Scoring**. Change them to fit the needs of your students and your teaching style.

The last (and most important) is a page that contains two **Focused Analytical Score Sheets**. You will need one of these sheets for each student for each essay or narrative he or she scores or writes. In this way, you can score by domains (as most states do these days). When you use these sheets, you also let your students know specifically where they have problems so that they can learn from their mistakes. I used these same sheets for years, drastically shortening the time I spent grading papers while giving valuable feedback to my students.

The Basic Criteria for Scoring
the State Writing Assessment Test

1. Focus

Essay or narrative presents and maintains a clear main idea, point of view, theme, or unifying event. It sticks to the topic and genre. There is no extraneous information. It sticks to the purpose.

2. Organization

Essay or narrative shows a definite plan or development. It has a clear beginning, middle, and end. There is a logical relationship of ideas (they flow) and use of paragraphing and transitions. It reads well and makes sense.

3. Supporting Ideas

There is ample support with lots of nitty-gritty detail, examples, reasons, and arguments. Details are credible and thoroughly explained. There is consistent elaboration in the middle of the narrative or essay. Vocabulary beyond the basics for the grade level is used.

4. Conventions

This includes mechanics, capitalization, spelling, word usage, sentence structure (must vary types of sentences), and use of action verbs. There are no fragments.

5. Style and Voice

The paper shows voice (individuality), flair, passion, pizzazz, use of literary devices, and choice and arrangement of words that create a distinct style. There is good vocabulary, and the paper is not formulaic.

Six-Point Modified Holistic Rubric

0 Points

Either the student did not write at all, the writing is totally illegible, or the writing is totally off the topic.

1 Point

The writing may be only slightly related to the topic. Fragmentary or incoherent listing of related ideas and/or sentences may occur. Little, if any, development of support and/or organizational pattern is apparent. Limited or inappropriate vocabulary frequently obscures meaning. Gross errors in sentence structure and usage may impede communication. Frequent and blatant errors may occur in the basic conventions of mechanics and usage, and commonly used words are misspelled.

2 Points

The writing is related to the topic but offers little support. Little evidence of an organizational pattern may be demonstrated. Development of details may be erratic, inadequate, or illogical. Vocabulary is limited, inappropriate, or vague. Gross errors in sentence structure may occur. Errors in basic conventions of mechanics and usage may occur, and commonly used words may be misspelled.

3 Points

The writing demonstrates an awareness of the topic but may include extraneous or loosely related material. The paper may lack a sense of completeness or wholeness. Some support is included but may not be developed. An organizational pattern has been attempted. Vocabulary is adequate but may be limited, predictable, or occasionally vague. Most sentences are complete. Knowledge of the conventions of mechanics and usage is usually demonstrated, and commonly used words are usually spelled correctly.

4 Points

The writing is generally related to the topic with adequate support, although development may be uneven. The paper exhibits some sense of completeness or wholeness. Logical order is apparent, although some lapses may occur. Word choice is adequate. Most sentences are complete. The paper generally follows the conventions of mechanics, usage, and spelling.

5 Points

The writing focuses on the topic with ample support and has a logical structure. The paper conveys a sense of completeness and wholeness. The writing demonstrates a mature command of language, including precision in word choice and variation in sentence structure. With rare exceptions, sentences are complete except when fragments are used purposefully. The paper generally follows the conventions of mechanics, usage, and spelling.

6 Points

The writing is focused, purposeful, and reflects insight into the writing situation. The paper conveys a sense of completeness and wholeness with adherence to the main idea and a logical progression of ideas. The support is substantial, specific, relevant, concrete, and/or illustrative. The paper demonstrates a commitment to and an involvement with the subject, has clarity in the presentation of ideas, and may use creative writing strategies appropriate to the purpose of the paper. The writing demonstrates a mature command of language with freshness of expression. Sentences are complete except when fragments are purposefully used. Few, if any, conventional errors occur.

(From an older rubric put out by the Florida Department of Education; changed for clarity here)

Lesson Plans for Practicing Scoring

Beforehand:

1. Run off many copies of the **Focused Analytical Scoring Sheet** located on the following page.

2. Make overhead copies of at least three examples of essays and/or narratives for each score your state gives on the test.

3. Run off class sets of many examples (mixed scores) of essays and/or narratives. Be sure to include at least three examples of each score from 0 to the top score in your state. Put numbers (Sample # 1, etc.) on top of each example.

4. Make sure that you divide your class into heterogeneous response groups of four students.

Lesson:

1. Teach the five components of a good essay.

2. Teach the scale of scoring—high, medium, low.

3. Show at least three examples of each score on the overhead. Have students read them and, as a class, score them with you writing on the overhead on a copy of the scoring sheets that follow this page.

4. Divide students into groups of four. Pass out copies of three more papers, one high, one medium, and one low. Ask each group to read each paper and score it on another score sheet (as a group). Do this several times until students are comfortable with scoring on their own. After each session, debrief the students by discussing and analyzing why each example deserved its score.

5. Do the same with more examples, either copied (one set per student) or on an overhead transparency, but this time have students grade them individually. Middle- and high-school teachers can gradually move to using the real rubric as their students grow more comfortable with scoring.

6. Now students are ready for the next step, **Step Three**.

Focused Analytical Score Sheet

ON THE CD

Focused Analytical Score Sheet

Focus   High_____   Medium_____   Low_____
   On the topic?   Restates topic or Key Words each ¶
   No unrelated information   Connection among paragraphs

Organization   High_____   Medium_____   Low_____
   Beginning, middle, end?   Transitions?
   Pattern of organization (¶'s)?   Beginning and end sentences each ¶

Support   High_____   Medium_____   Low_____
   Extended main ideas?   Similes and other devices?
   Nitty-gritty detail?   Examples?
   Specific language (great vocabulary)?

Conventions   High_____   Medium_____   Low_____
   Spelling?   Capitalization?
   Punctuation?   Usage?

Style   High_____   Medium_____   Low_____
   Pizzazz?   Flair?
   Voice?   Not Formulaic?

   TOTAL SCORE: HIGH   MEDIUM   LOW

Focused Analytical Score Sheet

Focus   High_____   Medium_____   Low_____
   On the topic?   Restates topic or Key Words each ¶
   No unrelated information   Connection among paragraphs

Organization   High_____   Medium_____   Low_____
   Beginning, middle, end?   Transitions?
   Pattern of organization (¶'s)?   Beginning and end sentences each ¶

Support   High_____   Medium_____   Low_____
   Extended main ideas?   Similes and other devices?
   Nitty-gritty detail?   Examples?
   Specific language (great vocabulary)?

Conventions   High_____   Medium_____   Low_____
   Spelling?   Capitalization?
   Punctuation?   Usage?

Style   High_____   Medium_____   Low_____
   Pizzazz?   Flair?
   Voice?   Not Formulaic?

   TOTAL SCORE: HIGH   MEDIUM   LOW

Step Three

Teach Students to Plan and Write Good Essays and/or Narratives with the Required Elements

I always told my students to put their arms out in front of them. Then I asked them to imagine two walls descending from their arms. These walls, I told them, were the required elements of a narrative or essay. In between those walls, they needed to be themselves, to express their individual voices, to write with pizzazz and flair, and to keep the walls from closing in and making a boring essay or narrative.

Step Three describes the "walls," the "structure," and the nuts and bolts of the narrative or essay. While you will find some suggestions in this step to avoid formulaic writing, it is in **Step Four**

that you will find a plethora of ideas for what students can do to zing back and forth in between those walls to find their voice.

Please note that all the ideas and activities in this step have been classroom-tested again and again by me with my students and also by other teachers all over the country. You may use a few or all of them, depending on the level and the needs of your students.

The last part of this step is using the 220 writing prompts/topics, organized into four main types of prose—descriptive, expository, narrative, and persuasive—and available on the CD. Within each category of prose you will find even more specific divisions such as "favorite" and "problem/ solution" under expository, for example.

Most states do not specify what kind of expository, persuasive, descriptive, or narrative writing prompt they will have on the test, but the divisions I made allow you to focus specifically on the types in which your students need more practice. Also, since states' choices and nomenclature of required genres vary, you can pick and choose the prompts to use that you think best exemplify the topics your state will provide on the actual test.

In fact, some of the 220 topics were all actual pre-2000 prompts on tests in several states. Others have shown up as official prompts after the previous edition of this book appeared. No, I do not have any inside information. It's just that there are only so many topics that are generic enough and clear enough to use. In addition, many states recycle the better prompts.

Differentiating among the Genres of Prose

Before students learn what constitutes a good narrative piece or descriptive, expository, or persuasive essay, they need to be able to recognize each of the different genres from a prompt alone. One of the dangers that students of any level face on the writing assessment test is reading an expository or persuasive prompt and mistakenly writing a narrative instead of an essay. Thus, it is imperative to teach students to recognize what kind of writing they are being asked to produce in any given prompt.

Pre-planning for a narrative and for an essay of any type are approached differently, and an essay is definitely a different animal than a narrative. Of course, in states where only one type of writing is required for the test, your job is easier, but even beyond the test, students need to know the difference.

In most states, those of you who teach fifth grade or above need to prepare your students to write some sort of an expository, descriptive, or persuasive essay as well as a narrative. You also need to make sure that your students know the difference among these four genres. One of the dangers middle- and high-schoolers face on the writing assessment test is treating a persuasive essay as an expository one (explaining the topic rather than arguing a side of it). This is a common problem. The difference between expository, descriptive, and persuasive essays is not as clear as between any type of essay and a narrative piece. Interestingly, my state twisted a narrative prompt used with the fourth grade into an expository one for the eighth grade several years later. They did the same in reverse as well. Confusing.

I offer three activities that other teachers and I have found useful to teach students the difference among the four types of writing they may be expected to produce on the state writing assessment test. The first two activities are simple and require very little preparation on your part although students tend to enjoy the second one more. The third activity is more complicated, but it is worth the trouble because after students master the concept, it can become an extremely effective literary tool. And, after you and your students practice **Activity #3** on page 64 a bit, it also can become a spontaneous, thirty-second activity every time you read anything in class as part of an assignment.

First, though, your students will need to know about each type of prose you are asking them to identify:

Descriptive writing. Descriptive writing is just that, a pure description (no action or explanation) of a scene. The scene can be anywhere. The object of descriptive writing is to paint a "word picture" vividly enough that the reader can "see" what is being described. Really good descriptions go beyond the visual aspect and describe the place, scene, or object from other senses as well, such as what might be heard at the place being described.

Expository writing. Sometimes confused with descriptive writing, expository writing explains how or why something happened or clarifies why you feel a certain way. It can be "how to do something," "this is how they did it," or "this is why someone feels this way"; or it can explain "why you like something," etc. It could be proposing solutions to a problem as well. Or, it could be a response to something written (such as literature or a quotation). Expository writing always explains and elaborates or clarifies a main premise which usually is found in the first sentence or paragraph.

Narrative writing. Narrative writing tells a story (or part of one). The key to narrative writing is that it is a series of events that happen or are told in chronological order. This happened, then that happened, then this happened, and so on. Narrative writing can be personal (true story) or imaginative (fictional) or a combination of the two. Narratives usually begin as fact and develop into fiction. They have a definite beginning and an end.

Persuasive writing. The key to persuasive writing is that the writer or speaker is trying to convince someone of something. Usually the persuader is arguing his or her point. Direct address, too, often is found. This occurs when the author or a character directly says the name of the person whom he or she is trying to convince. Several arguments are usually given to try to persuade the reader of the writer's point of view.

Activity #1: The Hat Trick

This activity involves a hat (or a small box, basket, or any small container), a copy of the prompts listed on the CD, a pair of scissors, and two minutes a day for practice.

Beforehand:

→ First, make a copy of the prompts that pertain to your students from the **220 Practice Prompts** on the CD. For example, in Florida, eighth-graders are tested only on expository and persuasive essays (different types of each), so an eighth-grade teacher in Florida would copy all of the expository and persuasive prompts and throw in only a few of the descriptive and narrative ones just to add a level of difficulty.

→ Then, take the copy of the type of prompts you want, cut out all the prompts individually, fold them up, and place them in the hat (or box). (FYI: you will be using these cut-up prompts again in another exercise to practice elaboration.)

Procedure:

→ Daily, after the Caught'ya (see **Bibliography**) or as a starter at the beginning of a period, ask a student to draw one paper from the hat. Have that student read the prompt out loud. Then elicit from your class the type of prompt *and* the key words that helped them in their identification. Discuss why it is a certain type of prompt and how they would go about writing it.

Key words:

→ **Descriptive:** describe; sense words

→ **Expository/clarification/informative:** explain; clarify; give reasons; propose solutions

→ **Narrative:** tell; story; recount what happened

→ **Persuasive/point of view/argumentative:** persuade; give point of view; convince; argue

---

Although you probably should do no more than two or three prompts a day (to keep the activity interesting), it is a good idea to do this activity at least three times a week for several months or until your students make no mistakes for a week.

Activity #2: Identify types of writing while writing and scoring

This can be done as you complete the paragraphs in **Step One** and the scoring in **Step Two**. First, in **Step One**, you assign your students to write a strong, vivid-verb paragraph; you also can require that they write the paragraph in a specific genre. Strong, vivid-verb paragraphs, as short as they are, can tell a story, explain something, convince someone of something, or paint a word picture of something. Before you begin requiring that an SVVP be a narrative or an essay, you need to make certain that your students understand the difference.

Second, as you and your students score each essay and narrative in **Step Two** of this book, you also can ask your students to identify the type of writing they are reading. In the same vein, using the examples in the last section of this book, pick one to represent each type of writing. (The score does not matter as long as it is identifiable as one of the four genres.) Read these four examples to your students and ask them to identify the type of writing.

This activity can be done for an entire class period as you pick essays and narratives at random from the back of the book, or it can be used as a mini-lesson at the beginning of the day or period as you read only a few randomly chosen essays or stories for the class to identify.

Activity #3: Identify types of writing in various passages

While it sounds daunting to pull different parts of books that illustrate each type of prose, it actually is quite simple. And, once you begin looking, the passages will leap out at you. Within the narrative books and stories that we read to our students or require them to read, examples of all the types of prose writing can be found.

There are expository passages when the author explains something. Persuasive passages occur when a character tries to convince another character of something. The author uses descriptive passages when he or she describes the scenery or a location, and, of course, you find narrative passages when the narrator relates the part of the story that is not covered by dialogue.

This activity is effective with *any* piece of reading material you happen to be using in your classroom, even a poem or a history text. To give you examples, I pulled five books from my shelves, perused them briefly, and came up with the following passages. In 1999, when I picked the passages from *Harry Potter and the Sorcerer's Stone* for the previous edition of this book, I deliberately had not yet read the book so that I could check out and illustrate how easy it is to find a passage in a book for the purpose of this exercise.

Beforehand:

→ First, pick a book, preferably the one your students are currently reading as a class or being read to by you, or one like *Harry Potter* that is very popular with your students and read by most of them.

→ Then, skim the book yourself and find brief examples of the four types of prose—descriptive, expository, narrative, and persuasive. This may sound difficult, but, once you begin doing this, you can't stop!

➜ Next, type up your own examples and/or make copies of the sixteen examples below. (To keep yourself legal, be sure to put the title of the book, the author, and the page number by the quotes when you make the copies.) Run off a class set of these examples.

Procedure:

➜ First, pass out copies of the excerpts and initially, as an entire class, identify the type of writing in each passage. To make it easier for students, it is a good idea to group one example of each type as I have done. (See below.)

➜ When students are comfortable identifying the four different types of writing, give them another set of examples, divide the class into groups (making sure that each student has a "job," like reader, runner, leader, and recorder, to keep the group on task), and ask each group to identify the types of writing in the passages.

➜ Once the group decides the type of writing in each passage, the recorder records the answers along with the reason for the group's decision. When all the groups have completed the exercise, discuss the answers as a class.

➜ The next step is to ask students to do the same on their own, without the help of their peers. Again, when all are finished, discuss the answers with the entire class so that students can argue their points.

➜ After students become adept at recognizing the types of writing, this activity can be continued all year for reinforcement. You can do this orally without any advance preparation. Simply identify passages as you come across them. With your students, read and discuss the reasons for the decisions. This can become a game with your students to see how many examples of the four types of writing they can find in a given chapter.

Sample passages:

➜ Listed below are short excerpts from five well-known books. After the passages, I have included a key to help you since the line among persuasive, narrative, and expository is sometimes blurred. If you disagree with me, you may be right. After all, even the powers-that-be who decide the topics that will be used on the test once chose an obviously expository topic for the fourth grade and called it a narrative.

From *Winnie-the-Pooh* by A. A. Milne

    A)   Once upon a time, a very long time ago now, about last Friday, Winnie-the-Pooh lived in a forest all by himself under the name of Sanders.
       One day when he was out walking, he came to an open place in the middle of the forest, and in the middle of this place was a large oak-tree, and, from the top of the tree, there came a loud

buzzing noise.

Winnie-the-Pooh sat down at the foot of the tree, put his head between his paws and began to think. (p. 2-3)

B) "I have just seen Eeyore," he began, "and poor Eeyore is in a Very Sad Condition because it's his birthday, and nobody has taken any notice of it, and he's very Gloomy — you know what Eeyore is — and there he was, and..." (p. 76)

C) Little soft clouds played happily in a blue sky, skipping from time to time in front of the sun as if they had come to put it out, and then sliding away suddenly so that the next might have his turn. Through them and between them the sun shone bravely; and a copse which had worn its firs all the year round seemed old and dowdy now beside the new green lace which the beeches had put on so prettily. (p. 45)

D)   PLAN TO CAPTURE BABY ROO

1. General Remarks. Kanga runs faster than any of Us, even Me.
2. More General Remarks. Kanga never takes her eye off Baby Roo, except when he's safely buttoned up in her pocket.
3. Therefore. If we are to capture Baby Roo, we must get a Long Start, because Kanga runs faster than any of Us, even Me.
4. Another Thought But, if Pooh was talking to her very excitedly, she might look the other way for a moment.
5. And then I could run away with Roo. (p. 93-94)

From *Charlotte's Web* by E. B. White

A) Twilight settled over Zuckerman's barn, and a feeling of peace. Swallows passed on silent wings, in and out of the doorways, bringing food to their young ones. From across the road a bird sang, "Whippoorwill, whippoorwill!" (p. 62)

B) Life in the barn was very good—night and day, winter and summer, spring and fall, dull days and bright days. It was the best place to be, thought Wilbur, this warm delicious cellar, with the garrulous geese, the changing seasons, the heat of the sun, the passage of swallows, the nearness of rats, the sameness of sheep, the love of spiders, the smell of manure, and the glory of everything. (p. 183)

C) "It was a never-to-be-forgotten battle," said Charlotte. "There was the fish, caught only by one fin, and its tail wildly thrashing and shining in the sun. There was the web, sagging dangerously under the weight of the fish. ...There was my cousin, slipping in, dodging out, beaten mercilessly over the head by the wildly thrashing fish, dancing in, dancing out, throwing her threads out, fighting hard. First she threw a left around the tail. The fish lashed back..." (p. 103)

D) "It's cruel," replied Wilbur, who did not intend to be argued out of his position.

"Well, you can't talk," said Charlotte. "You have your meals brought to you in a pail. Nobody feeds me. I have to get my own living. I live by my wits. I have to be sharp and clever, lest I go hungry. I have to think things out, catch what I can, take what comes. And it just so happens, my friend, that what comes is flies and insects and bugs. And furthermore," said Charlotte, shaking one of her legs, "do you realize that if I didn't catch bugs and eat them, bugs would increase and multiply and get so numerous that they'd destroy the earth, wipe out everything?" (p. 40)

From *Harry Potter and the Sorcerer's Stone* by J. K. Rowling

A)   He brought Harry a hamburger and they sat down on plastic seats to eat them. Harry kept looking around. Everything looked so strange, somehow. (p. 86)

B)   "Not Slytherin, eh?" said the small voice. "Are you sure? You could be great, you know, it's all here in your head, and Slytherin will help you on the way to greatness, no doubt about that—no?" (p. 121)

C)   Harry had never imagined such a strange and splendid place. It was lit by thousands and thousands of candles that were floating in midair over four long tables where the rest of the students were sitting. These tables were laid with glittering golden plates and goblets. At the top of the hall was another long table where the teachers were sitting... (p. 116)

D)   "This," said Wood, "is the Golden Snitch, and it's the most important ball of the lot. It's very hard to catch because it's so fast and difficult to see. It's the Seeker's job to catch it. You've got to weave in and out of the Chasers, Beaters, Bludgers, and Quaffle to get it before the other team's Seeker, because whichever Seeker catches the Snitch wins his team an extra hundred and fifty points, so they nearly always win.... A game of Quidditch only ends when the Snitch is caught, so it can go on for ages..." (p. 169)

From *Watership Down* by Richard Adams

A)   Fiver seemed to grow even smaller as he flattened himself on the hard earth. "I'm a fool to try to argue," he said miserably. "Hazel—dear old Hazel—it's simply that I *know* there's something unnatural and evil twisted all round this place. I don't know what it is, so no wonder I can't talk about it. I keep getting near it, though.... I tell you I'll have nothing to do with the place..." (p. 79)

B)   The primroses were over. Toward the edge of the wood, where the ground became open and sloped down to an old fence and a brambly ditch beyond, only a few fading patches of pale yellow still showed among the dong's mercury and oak-tree roots. On the other side of the fence, the upper part of the field was full of rabbit holes. (p. 1)

C)   When she had gone, Bigwig felt desperately tired and lonely. He tried to hold in his mind that his friends were not far off and that he would see them again in less than a day. But he knew that all Efrafa lay between himself and Hazel. His thoughts broke up into the dismal fancies of anxiety. (p. 297)

D)   Fiver hopped out on the road. He looked round for a moment and then made his way to the nearer end of the bridge. Hazel followed him along the verge, keeping close beside the rail on the upstream side. Looking round, he saw Pipkin close behind. In the middle of the bridge Fiver, who was perfectly calm and unhurried, stopped and sat up. The other two joined him. (p. 265)

From *I Know Why the Caged Bird Sings* by Maya Angelou

A)   The missionary ladies of the Christian Methodist Episcopal Church helped Momma prepare the pork for sausage. They squeezed their fat arms elbow deep in the ground meat, mixed it with gray nose-opening sage, pepper, and salt, and made tasty little samples for all obedient children who brought wood for the slick black stove. (p. 19)

B)   Later Mother made a broth and sat on the edge of the bed to feed me. The liquid went down my throat like bones. My belly and behind were as heavy as cold iron, but it seemed my head had gone away and pure air had replaced it on my shoulders, Bailey read to me from The Rover Boys until he got sleepy and went to bed. (p. 67)

C)   Momma said, "Dentist Lincoln. It's my grandbaby here. She got two rotten teeth that's giving her a fit. ... She had this toothache purt' near four days now, and today I said, 'Young lady, you going to the Dentist.'" ...
        "I know, Dentist Lincoln. But, this here is just my little grandbaby, and she ain't gone be no trouble to you... Seem like to me, Dentist Lincoln, you might look after her. She ain't nothing but a little mite. And seems like maybe you owe me a favor or two... I wouldn't press on you like this for myself but I can't take No. Not for my grandbaby. When you come to borrow my money you didn't have to beg. You asked me, and I lent it." (p. 160)

D)   The wind blew over the roof and ruffled the shingles. It whistled sharply under the closed door. The chimney made fearful sounds of protest as it was invaded by the urgent gusts. (p.128)

Key to sample passages:

Winnie-the-Pooh
A) Narrative—telling story of a walk ("Once upon a time")
B) Persuasive—arguing that Eeyore is in a "Very Sad Condition"
C) Descriptive—describing the sky and the forest
D) Expository—explaining how to do something (capture Baby Roo)

Charlotte's Web
A) Descriptive—describing the scene at twilight on the farm
B) Expository—explaining why life in the barn was very good for Wilbur
C) Narrative—telling the story of Charlotte's cousin and the fish
D) Persuasive—Charlotte is trying to convince Wilbur that she has to kill flies

Harry Potter and the Sorcerer's Stone
A) Narrative—telling the story of Hagrid and Harry when they first met
B) Persuasive—the Sorting Hat trying to convince Harry to choose Slytherin
C) Descriptive—describing Daigon Alley
D) Expository—explaining how to play Quidditch

Watership Down
A) Persuasive—Fiver is trying to convince Hazel that something is wrong
B) Descriptive—describing the field where the warren lay
C) Expository—explaining why Bigwig is tired and lonely
D) Narrative—telling the story of the rabbits on the road (sequence of events)

I Know Why the Caged Bird Sings
A) Expository—explaining how the ladies made the sausage
B) Narrative—telling the story of what Mother and Bailey did for Maya
C) Persuasive—Momma is trying to convince the dentist to help Maya
D) Descriptive—describing the wind and its sounds

The Composition of What Students Will Write

A standard essay can be expository, descriptive, or persuasive. A story is a narrative whether it is fiction or not. Some states may have changed the nomenclature of the essays by breaking them down into more specific topics for the writing tests. For example, instead of the word "expository," they use "expressive," "argumentative," "response to literature," "informational," etc. This does not affect the basic requirements that make up a good essay or narrative. No matter what you call it, an essay is an essay and a narrative is a narrative, and all forms of prose have basic components that must be included.

Definitions of the genres

Narrative. A narrative tells a story based on a real or imaginary event or recounts a personal or fictional experience. It should include specific detail to liven up the story. It requires a beginning, a middle, and an end of some kind that wraps up the story. Dialogue is a good idea, and the narrative should be less structured than the essays. The idea is to tell a coherent story in chronological order that is interesting, provides good detail and description, clearly expresses the writer's voice, is imaginative, and does not contain extraneous side stories. The key to a narrative is to have consistent chronological order with inner detail and voice.

Expository/explanatory essay. An expository essay instructs, gives information, or explains something, such as why one particular year was your best school year. It also can clarify a process, such as making school rules, or define a concept like "beauty." The support in the middle of this essay should provide specific, nitty-gritty examples or should relate an incident to further clarify or explain the topic without straying from it. Voice also is important. The author is explaining, not arguing or taking a side. An expository essay also can be a response to literature, to a question, or to a quotation.

Persuasive essay. A persuasive essay tries to persuade the reader to support the writer's point of view or argument; for example, "The school year should be extended by ten days." The specific details necessary in the middle of this essay must support the writer's point of view or argument. In a persuasive essay, the writer needs to come up with some good evidence in the form of examples or detailed reasons to make his/her point, being careful not to stray from the argument at hand. The writer needs to constantly keep in mind that he/she is not explaining the topic but arguing a point of view. It is a good idea to use direct address and a person's name as the writer gives his/her arguments. A strong voice and detailed, persuasive arguments are very important.

Descriptive essay. Whether or not your state requires your students to write descriptive essays, it is a good idea to practice writing them anyway. I always required my students to write descriptive essays or paragraphs because description is an integral part of good writing and absolutely necessary for a good narrative. I brought in out-of-the-ordinary objects (like those orange candies with bumps, statues, vases, a bizarre plant, etc.) and asked my students to write a description of those objects. Since I also taught one French 1 class for many years, I was lucky enough to possess quite a few rather large reprints of paintings by the Impressionist artists. These also were extremely useful to evoke good descriptions.

In the few states that include a descriptive essay on the test, the required elements vary from state to state. Some states encourage the use of all five senses to enhance the description. Most states, however, require a visual description from different focal points of the object or place to be described. In other words, the writer should describe the object or place from different angles or focal points. This should be done so vividly that the reader clearly can picture the object/place being described. Other senses may be used and can even be the focal point of a paragraph (sound, for example) to enhance the visual, but the visual image must be maintained throughout. A descriptive essay is not telling something or explaining anything or relating anything. It is, purely and simply, a description of a place, thing, event (most difficult), or person.

In a descriptive essay, students may be directed to describe such things as a kitchen, a place where many people gather, a storm, or any object or place common to all children but usually not a person. Each of the three supporting paragraphs in the middle of the essay should be vivid, strong-verb descriptions of one focal point of the object or place. For example, to describe a season such as fall, a student might take the different focal points of the trees, the leaves, the ground, the weather, the sounds of fall (keeping the visual in mind), or the overall panorama. To describe an object, the writer might want to describe the front, the back, and then the sides or instead tackle the appearance, the colors, and the shape of the object. In other words, divide the place or object to be described into three focal points.

In a state that encourages sensory descriptions in addition to the visual, that same description of the fall scene, for example, could have each of the supportive/descriptive middle paragraphs showing what fall looks like, what it feels like (weather, etc.), and what it smells like (wet leaves, and so on). A writer really could get into fall sounds in the woods, the swishing of leaves under feet, and the stillness of cold weather.

There are four key things to remember in writing a descriptive essay:

→ Take two to four focal points of the object or place and describe each one in one of the middle paragraphs;

→ Use strong, active verbs;

→ Keep the essay in the third person (avoid the use of "I"); and

→ Never use the words "reason" or "because" since you would be clarifying or explaining rather than describing.

To sum it up, the expository and persuasive essays take one point of view and expand on it. The narrative tells one story. The descriptive essay describes one object, person, or place. Neither the essays nor the narrative should jump from topic to topic or switch from one genre to another.

Procedure for learning the components

I have found no humorous or clever way to teach the basic elements and composition of the different types of prose. If you do, please let me know. (My e-mail is janekiester@comcast. net.) As you already know, standing in front of a class and telling students something as complicated as what belongs in an essay is like trying to talk to the wind in the trees. Even if students have the information in their notebooks or copy it down, that is not going to get that "boring" information into their heads.

I suggest using a time-honored tradition of teaching—repetition *ad nauseum* in every different manner possible until students get the idea. Then, using brain-based teaching techniques, let the ideas percolate in their heads by letting them participate in their own learning. In other words, no one, no matter how bright he or she is, can listen and absorb any information for more than ten minutes without needing time for the brain to let the information filter through like flour through a sifter, a cup at a time.

Here are a few ideas to vary the drill:

➜ Go over the components of one type of essay (or a narrative) orally with the class several times. Then, pair up your students and tell them that one of them is "orange" (or a number or an animal or anything) and the other is "blue" (or anything that would appeal to your class). Ask "orange" to explain the components of that type of writing to "blue" and "blue" (who has the definition and components in front of him or her) to fill in the gaps. Then reverse the exercise with "blue" doing the explaining and "orange" filling in the gaps (with the information in hand). This can be repeated with all the genres.

➜ Again, go over the components of one type of essay or narrative orally with the class. Make sure your students' desks are clear. Ask a student to come up to the board and, with the oral help of the class, try to write the components on the board. This can be repeated with the different types of writing.

➜ Go over the components once again with your class. Make sure the desks are clear, and divide the class into groups of five or six. Call out a type of writing, such as "expository essay." Give students time to talk it out in their groups. Then, when a group thinks they can define the required elements of an expository essay, quiet the class and call on them to list the components out loud. If they are wrong, call on another group, etc. You can keep score.

➜ Write the names of each of the four types of writing on slips of paper, one per slip, and make four or so copies of each. Go over the components once again with feeling. Divide your class into groups of four. Give each group one of the slips of paper. That group then discusses and writes down the elements of that one type of writing. Each group in turn shares the results with the class.

I'm sure you can think of other ways to make sure the needed information is repeated enough times to put it into your students' heads. I heard somewhere that people need things repeated from fifteen to sixty times before they can learn it. And, the older we get, the more times we need things repeated. This is good news for our children. I always kept this in mind as I taught any new vocabulary word, concept, or grammar rule.

> **TEACHING NOTE:** *Although in the following descriptions of essays and narratives I say "four to six paragraphs," in most of the states where the writing test is considered a rough draft only, actual indenting is not absolutely necessary for a high score.*

The Basic Essay

A basic essay of any kind has between three and six paragraphs. The number does not have to be exact, but at least four paragraphs are usually necessary for an effective essay. As students write their essays, no matter whether descriptive, expository/informative, or persuasive, they should keep in mind the characteristics of good writing.

It is extremely important to do the following:

➜ Keep to the topic at hand. Do not stray or go off on a tangent. Do not turn a persuasive or descriptive essay into an expository one or vice versa. Either convince, explain, or describe, but don't mix the three.

➜ Use great vocabulary. You want to show that you have a good command of words that is above and beyond what the average student your age knows. Word choice is very important. Use good, strong, vivid verbs.

➜ Organize yourself well. Never make a statement that you do not back up or support. Develop that support well.

➜ Use a good quote, even if you make it up.

➜ Use transitions—the more interesting, the better.

➜ Do not be afraid to argue or develop a side of a topic with which you disagree. Do not be afraid to make up something. You will probably dislike the topic given to you on the actual test. It is important to learn to quickly cluster several ideas to see which one you can substantiate with enough support or detail to compose a good essay. Sometimes in a persuasive essay you may find that the point of view you easily can support with convincing arguments will be the point of view with which you disagree. Go for it. Be a "devil's advocate." On the actual test, you will be evaluated not on what your opinion is but how well and how passionately you support the stand that you take.

Components of a Good Essay

It is important to learn the components of each part of an essay. The following is a précis. Note that these components follow (in paragraphs instead of sentences), the same pattern as the strong, vivid-verb paragraphs.

Introduction:

➜ Begin with a good "grabber."

➜ Restate the topic and define it.

➜ State some good arguments (persuasive), explanations or reasons (expository), or focal points to describe (descriptive).

➜ Conclude with a transition sentence that leads into the next paragraph.

Middle paragraphs:

➜ These paragraphs are the body of your essay.

➜ Use a transition at the beginning of each paragraph or at the end of a previous one to link ideas. Indent if you can. Try to be different and not use the dull and formulaic "first," "next," etc.

➜ In each paragraph you develop one of your arguments, explanations, or focal points as fully as you can, restating the argument (persuasive), explanation (expository), or object of description (descriptive) and then expanding on it with really specific examples or evidence to support it.

➜ This is the most important part in the grading of the state assessment test. The judges are looking at how well you support the broad statements you make and how excited you sound. The more nitty-gritty detail you use, the better. Do not be boring. Boring = low score.

➜ Each paragraph could use an introductory sentence and a concluding sentence (details in the middle). Do *not* do this if it will make your paragraphs boring or repetitive.

→ The middle is the part where it is important to use spectacular vocabulary and to show a good knowledge of words. Use strong, vivid verbs.

→ A little well-placed humor and creativity definitely add to the quality of the paper and make it yours. Your essay should sound like you and not like a machine. Whatever the topic, let the reader feel your passion and excitement even if they are not your true feelings.

Conclusion:

→ This is where you sum everything up and leave the reader remembering you.

→ Restate your topic in words that are different from those in the introduction. Think of an original way to do this. Do *not* just repeat the topic.

→ Summarize some of what you said in the middle.

→ Draw a one-sentence conclusion.

→ End with a "zinger" that makes the reader think or smile.

→ Do not use the words "in conclusion."

The Basic Beginning, Middle, and End of a Narrative

Beginning:

→ Begin with a "grabber" to hook your reader.

→ Describe scene.

→ Introduce characters.

Middle:

→ Develop the story with at least one specific incident or happening.

→ Keep your happenings in the correct order of time.

→ Include descriptions.

→ Here is where your action takes place.

→ A conversation might work well here.

→ This is a good place for a simile or two or even a bit of humor.

End:

→ Bring the story to a close, referring to events in the story for continuity.

→ Wrap it up with a satisfying ending, a zinger, or a humorous comment to leave your reader with a feeling of completion.

Detailed Elements of a Basic, Short Narrative

A basic narrative must contain a definite beginning, middle, and end. Paragraphing isn't as important as the chronological order of events in the narrative. The narrative format is based on telling a story in a logical order, with passion, and with a clear progression from beginning to end. Dialogue and details add to the quality of the narrative, as do descriptions of the scene.

Remember the following as you write your narrative:

→ Keep to the story you are telling. Do not stray or go off on a tangent. Do not tell a story within a story.

→ Make sure that the events in your narrative happen in chronological order. Do not skip around in your telling of the story, jump from one event to another, or suddenly change the scene.

→ Use great vocabulary. You want to show that you have a good command of words that are above and beyond those the average student your age knows.

→ Use dialogue or other creative writing strategies somewhere in your narrative.

→ Use similes and strong verbs to enhance descriptions.

→ Make sure that you include enough detail to make your narrative interesting to the reader and keep him/her hooked.

→ Write with a clear voice. Pick whether you want to write using "I" or the third person (he or she), and stick with it.

→ Tell your story with flair so that the reader gets interested and wants to know what is going to happen next. Don't bore your reader.

→ Make sure that you draw your narrative to a reasonable end. Do not leave your reader hanging or your narrative sounding unfinished.

Four Tips to Help Students Keep to the Prompt (Focus)

Tip #1: Restate the topic carefully and creatively

In most states, if a student does nothing but write one paragraph in which he or she restates the topic, he or she will earn a score of at least a 1. Thus, it is of extreme importance to teach your students to restate the topic, at a minimum, in the first paragraph, assuming you can get them to indent. You can do this very easily by giving your students topic after topic and asking them to practice restating it. I ask my students to go one step further.

There is what I call, "the gifted hole" into which many bright students stumble. Their minds usually do not focus on one thing, but on many things at once. Sometimes they can write a word (any word—usually a noun), and a flood of ideas comes to mind. Unfortunately, when writing their essays or narratives, they often go off on these tangents and make the most egregious error they can possibly make on a writing test—they get off the topic!

To prevent this, it is a good idea to teach *all* your students to restate the topic in some fashion in every paragraph of the essay or narrative. This could be using one word only! In this way, the writers not only remind the reader of the focus of the paper, but, more importantly, they remind themselves not to stray from its path.

Now, restating the topic in each paragraph has its own hazards—boredom and formulaic writing. You do not want your students to keep writing, "Another reason that spring is my favorite season is..." or "My next argument why students should wear uniforms is..." This rings the death knell of high scores in most states. If students bore the scorer by this type of dull, uninspired, formulaic repetition, they will earn a boring, low score for their monotonous and lackluster paper.

Tip #2: Use key words

So, how do you restate the topic without boring the reader and writing a lifeless, bland essay or narrative? The answer is "key words." If students can find the one or two key words in a prompt and somehow integrate them into the middle of the text of each paragraph, they will avoid dullness. By the way, whenever one of my students wrote as the first line of each paragraph, "Another reason my eighth-grade year is my favorite year..." or the like, I drew a nose by the sentence when I scored the paper.

In International Sign Language, a nose symbolizes "boring." This sign consists of twisting your right index finger gently back and forth on the exterior right side of your nose. I taught this sign to my students at the beginning of the year, and we used the symbol as needed. (Of course, some class clown always put his finger inside his nose...) I sometimes saw students wrinkle their noses themselves as they wrote, then go back and erase the offending line. One student, when she received her graded paper with a nose by the middle part bemoaned her grade saying, "I know. I know. I forgot the 'woo woo factor.'" In other words, she *knew* she had written a formulaic paper.

She asked for a chance to rewrite the paper with more pizzazz. Of course I was delighted to let her do so.

In each prompt, one can find the one or two key words that need to be woven into the text of each paragraph. In a narrative, it is usually the last word or the word that follows "about a." In a descriptive essay, it is the thing being described. In an expository essay, it is the topic being explained, plus the word "why" or "reason." In a persuasive or point-of-view essay, it is the word "convince" or "persuade," plus the word that is the crux of the essay.

Examples of key words in prompts. In the following partial prompts (of which I have stated only the meat of the topic), the key words are bolded.

Descriptive:

➜ Describe the place where you go to find **peace** when you are upset.

➜ Describe your favorite **food**.

➜ Describe the most beautiful **scene in nature** that you can imagine.

➜ Describe a place where you can have **fun**.

➜ Describe your favorite **season** (or the name of that season).

Expository/Explanatory:

➜ Explain what the traits are that make a **good friend**.

➜ Explain why your **favorite season** is your favorite.

➜ Explain some **solutions** to this environmental problem.

➜ Explain why eating **healthy foods** is important.

➜ Explain why you think it is important to **learn to read**.

Narrative:

➜ Imagine that you were a pioneer, and tell a story about a time when you traveled on a **wagon train** that was pulled by horses.

➜ Tell a story about what was in that **bag** on your teacher's desk.

➜ Tell a story about what was on the other side of that **door**.

➜ Tell a story about a day in which **everything went wrong**.

➜ Tell a story about what would happen if you were your **favorite character** in your favorite book.

Persuasive:

→ Do you think the **drop-out age** should be raised to 18?

→ Should **homework** be eliminated on weekends?

→ Convince your reader to adopt your **suggestion** (or name suggestion).

→ Should **uniforms** be required in public schools?

→ Convince your parents to allow you to have this **pet**.

To practice finding the key words, I suggest using the "hat trick" activity explained in the first section of this step (page 63). Print the **220 Practice Prompts** from the CD. Then find the type of prompt you wish to use and cut out appropriate topics. Fold them and put them in a "hat" from which your students will draw. I suggest doing only one or two a day so this does not become hackneyed. After a student draws a prompt, ask the class to ferret out the key words in that topic and perhaps to supply a few details that might be included if they had to write a narrative or essay on that subject.

When your students cluster or write a narrative or essay, ask them to identify the key words. Do this until they can find them on their own. For a while, ask your students to circle the key words in their writing. This will make them aware of their use. Don't be afraid to use the nose...

Tip #3: Use direct address to write persuasively and keep it persuasive

When faced with a persuasive prompt, many students make it expository instead. There is a simple solution to this problem: teach students about direct address. If language arts/English teachers use Caught'yas (see **Bibliography**) to teach grammar, mechanics, and usage, then I can assure you (because I used them with my students for 24 years) that, by October or November, students will be able to understand, identify, correctly punctuate, and use direct address. Of course, there are many other ways to teach direct address. Once your students have mastered this art, they are ready to improve their persuasive, argumentative, and point-of-view writing.

In my state, the writing assessment test is administered to fourth-, eighth-, and tenth-graders. In the eighth and tenth grades, students are given either an expository (of any kind) or a persuasive prompt. They do not know in advance which type of writing they will be required to produce on the day of the test. Half get a persuasive prompt. Half receive an expository one. Most other states also include a narrative prompt as well or require two separate prompts.

Traditionally, test scores on the expository and narrative writing are higher than those for the persuasive. However, once I began requiring that my students use direct address (and after they knew how to do so) whenever they wrote persuasively, the scores of those students who wrote to the persuasive prompt scored higher than their peers with the expository one. Why?

Well, as you know, children and young adults just *love* to argue. They argue amongst themselves, with us, with their parents, with everybody. This is the nature of children, especially the ones who are at the rebellious age. It is one of children's delightful traits—to question everything. My strategy has been that if I could teach my students first to recognize a persuasive prompt, then to use the simple tool of direct address, and finally to practice using that tool in their writing, they could tap into their love of arguing and produce some really fine essays.

Once students have mastered those first two tasks, we teachers can move to the next step—requiring that they use direct address when writing persuasively. I invited students to argue with me orally, addressing me by name and trying to convince me of something or other.

> "Mrs. Kiester, please don't use spit on the overhead to erase the Caught'yas. It's disgusting."

> "Please, Mrs. Kiester, don't assign homework over the weekend. We have *so* much homework in other classes."

> "Oh, I beseech (word learned in Caught'yas) you, Mrs. Kiester, let us go write outside today."

I'm sure you get the idea. After arguing with you orally as a class, your students (with you writing on a graphic organizer on the overhead) painlessly and inadvertently produce a detailed plan. You then can give them some similar prompts and instruct them to plan and write a persuasive essay on their own. When you do this, first require students to address you and use your name. (I required no fewer than five uses of direct address in each essay.)

After this "teacher-directed practice," you can branch out and instruct students to argue, in a persuasive essay, of course, with the administration (in a letter), with their parents, and with various other adults who have power over their lives. They revel in being allowed to vent!

One wonderfully bright and creative young lady in my class wrote a persuasive letter to her father (a colleague of mine), asking him to let her have a traditional, pungent Christmas tree instead of their usual, live, Florida cedar tree that doesn't smell. (Her father preferred the live kind of tree that could be planted in the yard every January.) I urged this student to show the letter to her father. She did. On Christmas morning, she found in her bedroom a cut, odoriferous tree which originated from farther north.

Students can write letters to the principal arguing for various privileges. A few of my students even got their peers to sign their essays as a petition. Every once in a while, students were granted their wish—like being allowed to sit with their friends at lunch again instead of sitting at tables assigned by homeroom. If students experience the power of effective persuasive writing just once, they will be hooked on the genre forever.

Tip #4: Master the problem/solution and quote analysis prompts

There are two types of prompts which are being used more and more these days on the writing tests—those asking for a problem/solution expository essay and those that deal with an adage or quote. These two types of prompts can be deadly if students are not used to dealing with them.

I'm sure in future years, states will come up with even more ways to confuse and challenge our students on the writing test. For now, let's address these two.

Problem/solution:

➜ It is in the nature of people (especially when panicked on a writing test) to skip words as we read, our eyes focusing on one or two words that appeal to us like "love," "money," "lottery," "problem," "environment," "pollution," etc. Let's look at this problem/solution prompt:

> **Writing situation:** There are many pollution problems in the world today such as trash dumping, dirty air, contaminated oceans, and polluted beaches.
> **Plan:** Think of one pollution problem that particularly bothers you. Now think of some possible solutions to this problem.
> **Writing directions:** Write an essay to propose some solutions that might help solve one of the pollution problems that faces our world today.

This prompt looks innocent and fairly easy. In fact it is one filled with land mines at every turn. Children look at the word "pollution" and think "smoke" or something similar and write all the bad aspects about that. Or, they glom onto the word "problems" and want to write about two or three pollution problems that they perceive. They ignore the words *one* problem" and write about several. They ignore entirely the word "solutions," which is a key word in sticking to the topic in this essay. After all, it is a boring word that makes them have to think...

Another pitfall in problem/solution prompts is that if students even read or absorb the word "solutions," they see "solution" in the singular instead of "solutions" (plural). In their essays, these students talk about various problems and maybe (if we're lucky) one small solution to one of the problems. If no other instruction takes place, or if someone does not spoon-feed them and interpret the prompt, most students, if presented cold with a prompt like this one, will write about two or three pollution problems that bother them and never discuss one possible solution.

So, what is the solution to the problem/solution essay?

➜ Find as many examples of problem/solution prompts as you can. Some are included in the list of prompts on the CD. I'm sure you can make up more if needed. Put up one of these prompts on the board or overhead. Make your students copy it. Then, together, read the prompt three times, pointing out the word "solutions" each time. Your students already should know how to identify the key words in a prompt. They just have to realize that it is "solutions."

➔ After doing this at least five times, take one of the prompts, put it on the board, read it out loud and stress again the word "solutions." Together with your students, come up with at least three possible solutions for the problem, more if you can. Don't fuss with the nitty-gritty details of the solutions at this point. That can be taken care of later (see page 96 in this step).

➔ Brainstorm solutions with your students again and again with different prompts until you acclimate them with glomming onto the word "solutions" instead of "problems." Propose common problems. Ask students for at least three solutions to each problem you propose. You need not even put up a prompt. Any problem that requires a solution will do. For example:

"I have a problem of overhead pen smudge marks all over my hands (show hands). Class, can you give me some solutions to this problem?"

"Your mother locked her keys in the car. Can you think of some solutions to her problem?"

"Your brother or sister locked him/herself in the bathroom. Can you think of some solutions your parents might try to get him/her out?"

"You need more money to buy something you want. What are some solutions to your problem?"

➔ The idea is to make the word "solutions" appealing *and* to get your students accustomed to seeing the word "problem" and then "solutions" immediately after. In the previous situations you are using the word "solutions" instead of "solve." You also must get your students used to coming up with more than one solution to a problem. Posing silly problems or ordinary problems that your students and their friends might encounter make it even more fun.

➔ Put a prompt on the board or overhead and ask students to plan (but not write) an essay. Walk around the room to make sure that each student is proposing solutions in his/her essay plan instead of listing three problems. In this way, you can give immediate feedback.

➔ Finally, I suggest you put up prompts, make students plan the essay, and walk around the room checking the plans until all of your students get the idea. *Then*, assign a problem/solution prompt and require your students to plan and write the essay. When you score the essays, you can note the students who still don't understand the concept of one problem/many solutions and work with them if you can while the rest of your students complete some other assignment.

Quote prompts:

➔ Then there are the really difficult prompts that many states are including in their writing tests these days—the quote as a starter. For example:

    Writing situation: John Donne said, "No man is an island." Think about what he meant by that adage.

    Plan: Now, think of how this adage could apply to your life and the experiences you have had.

    Writing directions: Write an essay to explain the quote, "No man is an island," in terms of your own personal experiences.

To make matters worse, most states now require students with learning disabilities to take the test. Worse still is that they score these students' essays the same way they score the essays of students without dyslexia or other learning disabilities. Most students with learning disabilities cannot process from a quote to its meaning and then to applying it to their own lives. Many students without learning disabilities have the same difficulty. This makes it so easy for a student to lose focus and get off the topic.

So, what do you do with this type of prompt? How do you train your students, with and without learning disabilities, to keep to the topic and not go off on a tangent or flounder?

The biggest problem with the quote prompt is getting students somehow to think about what the quote really means. This is difficult as children tend to take things literally. So, I suggest the old, tried-and-true method of repeating something (even a process) enough times that your students get the idea.

To this end, find a list of simple quotations and aphorisms. There are many sources out there, many books with lists of quotes on any subject you desire. It always is a good idea to ask your students to bring in a favorite one or one that they and their parents like.

With list in hand, first as a whole class, take a quote or aphorism, read it, and discuss its meaning in everyday terms. Do this as many times as it takes for your students to get the idea of the transfer from quote to common sense. When your students begin to get the idea, put them into groups of three or four, give them a quote, and ask them to figure it out. Discuss the results with the class. Finally, of course, you can challenge each student to come up with a simplification of a quote. Again, share and discuss the results. Here are a few examples to get you started.

"All that glitters is not gold." (John Dryden)
Things that look as if they might be really great can turn out to be crap.

"A stitch in time saves nine." (American proverb)
If you attack a problem early, it may not become a big problem.

"When handed a lemon, make lemonade." (Gwendolyn Brooks)
When bad things happen, turn them into something good.

"Life is like a box of chocolates." (Forrest Gump)
You never know what is going to happen next.

"A cloth is stronger than the threads from which it is made." (Richard Nixon)
The group that works together can do more than each person in the group can do by him/ - herself.

"This above all: to thine own self be true." (Shakespeare)
Do what is right for you, not what you think others want you to do.

"My life is my message." (Gandhi)
It is what you DO in life that is the most important.

I'm sure you get the idea. In truth, the original intent of the quote may be lost, but if it makes sense, a more modern interpretation will do just fine.

Now, the process of taking a quote and applying it to your life is a higher-order thinking skill of the highest order! Several processes are involved, so you have to break it down to the manageable. Put a quote or aphorism on the board. Ask students to translate. Write the "translation" on the board.

Then begin taking it to the next level. With the simple interpretation of the quote or aphorism in front of them, hold a discussion with your class on how they can find examples from their own lives to illustrate the meaning of the quote. Do this as many times as it takes so that it becomes easier for your students to make that leap.

Once you see the light bulb dawn on many of your students' faces, take a plan form and do the same thing in writing: simple meaning ➜ three examples from life that they can apply to explain that meaning. When your students are comfortable planning in a large group, have them do the same thing in small groups as you walk around the room to see the results. Of course, the final step is to require students to do this individually.

If you have students with learning disabilities, or your students just don't get the idea, you can repeat the entire process as many times as it takes. One thing that really worked for me was to find out what a child liked to do and tell him/her to use that to give examples to interpret a quote. You can, for instance, always find an example in a sport like football to explain just about anything. A good example would be: "A cloth is stronger than the threads from which it is made" ➜ The football team must work as a team if they wish to win. Then, of course, you proceed to the nitty-gritty examples about, say, a time when the team didn't work together, everyone wanted to hog the ball, and they lost.

Teaching the Useful Devices

The use of great, non-traditional **transitions**, original **grabbers** (first sentence to "grab" the reader and interest him/her), and effective **zingers** (ending the narrative or essay with a "bang" so that the reader does not forget you) makes essays and stories more personal, interesting, and less formulaic. These are part of the voice of the writer. These also are part of the secret to getting your students to earn those higher scores.

Most states expect the use of some transitions in the essays as well as in the narratives. They look for the flow of the piece. Transitions make it clearer to the reader that the writer is sticking to the topic. They establish a definite organizational pattern and make the essay or narrative more coherent. The use of these connective devices, however, should not be boring or repetitive. Encourage students to be creative and not stick to the traditional "first," "second," "third," and "finally," which do *not* promote flow. That is the "kiss of death" for a high score.

You will find a list of some transitions, grabbers, and zingers at the end of this section, but first let me share a few tips on how to get your students to use the "good ones" in their writing.

Tip #1

With classes in which the majority of students have learning disabilities or are reluctant or below-level writers, just getting one transition out of them seems like an impossible task. I suggest singing the "boring" transitions. Yup, singing them. Students learn the lyrics to many songs. Why can't they learn the basic transitions by singing them? If you choose to do this, you will want to use a simple tune that all will recognize and that fits the words. I like "She'll Be Coming 'Round the Mountain." Sing it enough and your students will learn the boring transitions so well that they will use them when they write. Once students are able to use these boring, stilted transitions comfortably, you might be able to get them to use the effective and non-formulaic ones. You never know… Here are the lyrics to the transition song, but feel free to wing it.

> **To-pic sentence, first, next, then,**
> **Finally, and a con-clu-sion.**
> **Topic sentence, first, next, then, fin-ah-lee hee,**
> **And end with a con-clu-sion. Yee Haw!**

Tip #2

As for the more complicated transitions, you sometimes can get students to "fall in love" with them. A bunch of my students just loved to use "to commence with" at the beginning of any essay they wrote. Another batch always managed to use "talking about _____." They rarely used "in conclusion." (I forbade it anyway.) They really liked to be individualistic. "Consequently" was one of the favorites. How did I get them to use these more interesting transitions?

I told my students that they never would buy an article of clothing without trying it on to see if it fit. The same is true for transitions, grabbers, and zingers. You have to find some that work for you and feel comfortable enough to use fairly naturally. (Very few people use transitions naturally, even English teachers.)

For a while, every time students wrote an essay, I put three transitions next to the prompt. Students were required to use those three transitions—one for the beginning, one for the middle, and one for the end. They complained, but when I changed the transitions with each essay, they got the idea of what I was trying to do. After "trying them all on for size," students were allowed to pick and choose which transitions on the "acceptable list" they wanted to use.

Being "bulletin-board challenged," I liked to put up boards that (except on the day of the writing test when I had to take them down) could stay up all year. My bulletin boards never were high-class ones, but they got the point across. On one, I put great transitions, grabbers, and zingers along with strong, vivid verbs. Students could look at the bulletin board as they wrote. They also kept a copy of the list of useful devices in their notebooks for reference.

Tip #3

Just like the transitions, students need to try on grabbers and zingers for size. But, you may want to do it in a slightly different way from the transitions. You'll need to begin by having students memorize them. Chanting them while making appropriate hand gestures (like hands up for "shocking statement") works well. For "humorous," you can say "Ha, ha, ha." I'm sure you can figure out a rhythmic chant that your students will like. Once they learn the grabbers, you can do the same thing with the zingers. Then, your students are ready to begin using them.

You can put a different grabber up on the board when you assign a strong, vivid-verb paragraph or an essay and require that your students use that particular type of grabber, trying it on for size. Younger students usually stick to questions, but they are capable of using most of the other grabbers as well.

A good exercise (which also works to get quality beginnings out of your students) is to cluster and plan only the two to four main reasons for four possible essays (one a day). For the purpose of this exercise, it is best to use an expository topic like "Explain why _____ is your favorite _____." Favorite season of the year works well to start since there are four of them. Then students plan the main points only for each season. (This also helps train them to take a stand with which they do not agree and to try to look at a prompt from all angles.)

Once they have the two, three, or four main reasons why a particular season is their favorite, students can write the introductory paragraph for each season. (I suggest clustering and writing only one a day.) For each introductory paragraph, you can require a different "grabber," letting your students try them all. When you have required your students to use all the types of grabbers you want them to try, turn them loose to use their personal favorite. You can do the same thing with the zingers and concluding paragraphs.

Transitions

      Transitions are supposed to link parts of a narrative or essay. They can come at the beginning or end of a paragraph. The use of transitions at the end of a paragraph is more sophisticated and usually shows the link between that paragraph and the following one much more clearly.

Interesting transitions

Speaking of _____ (refers to previous topic)

Talking about _____ (again refers to previous topic)

And so it follows that,

Moving on from _____, we come to _____

In view of the fact that,

Taking into account that,

Other useful transitions

Similarly	Likewise	Thus
As compared (contrasted) to	In addition	As a result
Simultaneously	Concurrently	Owing to
As stated above	On one hand	Thanks to
Consequently	On the other hand	Because of
As a final point (argument)	In conclusion	Afterwards

Standard, boring transitions (but better than none at all)

First	Second	Third	Next
Then	Another	Finally	

Types of Grabbers and Zingers

Grabbers are designed to wake up the reader by grabbing attention and startling him or her enough to be curious about reading the rest of the narrative or essay. Zingers are supposed to "goose" the reader by letting the writer's voice come through loud and clear.

"Grabbers" to begin essays or stories with

Question

Quote

Brief dialogue

Shocking statement

Something humorous

Onomatopoeia

String of pearls (series of three participles)

Anecdote

Exclamation!

"Zingers" to conclude essays or stories with

Question

Quote

Original simile

Humorous statement or joke

Shocking statement

Come back to theme

Using Great Graphic Organizers (Clusters)

Now that your students can write a good paragraph, know how the officials score the essays and narratives, can differentiate among the different types of writing, know what comprises a good essay and narrative, are aware of some useful devices, and know what poor essays and narratives look like, they are ready to begin writing the essays and stories themselves.

First, however, they need to know how to plan. As good English teachers, we know that good writing usually is preceded by good planning. (Of course, there are always a few exceptions.) Planning is especially important for the state writing assessment since so much of the score depends on the details and the organization of the paper.

On the other hand, clustering (pre-planning) can be dangerous since most writing tests are timed, and some students spend way too much time planning and do not leave enough time to write the essay or narrative. I have watched eighth-graders try to write a rough draft in the clustering, not leaving enough time to finish writing the actual essay.

However, planning beforehand, besides improving the quality of writing, greatly helps young pupils and students with learning disabilities. It gives them something familiar and rote to do and affords them the time to ruminate on how they are going to tackle the assignment. In other words, drawing a familiar graphic organizer while contemplating what to write lessens the deer-in-headlights panic and the I-don't-know-what-I'm-going-to-write gulp at seeing the topic.

Thus, we need to teach our students the art of quick-but-well-thought-out planning that organizes their thoughts in as few words and as little time as possible. To this end, if students can organize their planning by using a particular type of graphic organizer, we can help them along.

TEACHING NOTE: *I use the terms "graphic organizer" and "cluster" interchangeably in this book.*

All English teachers know about graphic organizers. There are a lot of them out there. Some of them are better for students who find putting ideas on paper difficult. Students for whom writing comes easily might find other organizers more effective. Since everyone learns differently (and some of us are "right-brained," others in the middle, and still others "left-brained"), we also think differently and organize our thoughts differently. This can be a problem in a classroom with thirty or more different thinking styles.

So, how do those of us who teach writing solve this dilemma? We can require the use of a great graphic organizer and train our students from the beginning of sixth grade on to use it without even thinking every time they begin to write an essay. I guess what I'm suggesting is a sort of Pavlovian response training in that our students are on automatic pilot—see topic, read topic, draw organizer, fill out organizer, and write.

Two Theories

Here are two different theories about coming up with that great graphic organizer, and, depending on how they are implemented, both work well.

Theory #1. This theory can be extremely effective or detrimental, depending on the graphic organizer and how it is used. It is a very simple principle. The teacher, grade, or entire school picks one particular graphic organizer. *All* students in that teacher's classes, grade, or school use that one organizer and no other.

Using a school-wide organizer is fantastic and especially effective for students with learning disabilities and those who don't process easily since they don't get frustrated or confused by being exposed to a myriad of graphic organizers. It frees them from having to make a choice. They just draw the old familiar one on their paper. Then at least they have a way to organize their thoughts. If the school chooses a good organizer that allows wriggle room for the good writers yet is structured enough for the weaker ones, it works.

If the organizer is too limiting, however, it restrains the better writers but helps the weaker ones. If it is too complicated, the weaker writers flounder while the good ones soar.

Theory #2. This is the theory that I applied in my classroom. I believe that we all think differently, so I liked to introduce a variety of graphic organizers, require that students try each one at least once, let them pick the one that suited them best, and then ask that they stick with that one until it became automatic.

Of course, this theory works best if it is begun in the grades previous to the one in which students are tested. In that way, students uniformly use that same organizer for years in every class. When they take the state writing assessment test, they have used the same organizer for at least a year and a half, and it is as familiar as their favorite pair of jeans. The majority of English teachers at my school preferred to use a different organizer, so I began the year with my students trying out and picking their favorite. While they used it for only three and a half months before the writing test, they had little trouble with it.

The big advantage (besides better, more organized writing) of using a familiar graphic organizer is that when students take your state's writing assessment test, they immediately turn over the plan sheet without thinking and automatically begin drawing their chosen organizer. This gives them time to analyze and process the topic, to calm down, and to plan and write without panic. It even stimulates thoughts to churn and produce details, etc. as the student continues to draw and see the blank spaces. They have a tool that has worked for them in the past, a familiar "Linus blanket," inspiring confidence.

What to do with the theory you choose. To help you, whichever theory you espouse, I have included one organizer for narratives and four organizers for essays on page 94. Three I found, one I modified from an existing one, and one I invented. Remember, there are a myriad of graphic organizers out there to choose from. Please note that although they are set up for a five-paragraph essay or narrative, *students need not conform to that*. These organizers are *not* designed to limit students or to make their writing formulaic. They merely are a tool to plan. You can add segments to the caterpillar cluster or to any of the others or, conversely, you can take away parts of an organizer. We do *not* want formulaic papers!

The **first organizer** is the same as the cluster used to plan the strong, vivid-verb paragraphs. It is best used with a narrative but works for essays as well. This organizer is best for your right-brained students since it allows them to think first, put the ideas down as they occur, and plan the order later. Since a blank copy of this organizer has been included in **Step One**, it has been filled out for you in this step for illustrative purposes.

The **second organizer**, in case you haven't seen it yet, is the hand (dubbed "Edward Scissorhands" by my students). It was given to me by a third-grade teacher at a conference. I took it back to my classroom, told the students that they probably wouldn't like it as it was used by third-graders, and required that they use it anyway on their next essay before rejecting it out of hand. (Ha! Pun intended.) More than half the class chose it as their all-time favorite organizer. They loved tracing their own hand before writing, and they loved making the "scissorhands" part.

The **third organizer** (the tried and true one) was the most popular one among my students before I introduced them to "Edward Scissorhands." It lays out an essay clearly yet differs from an outline or other organizers because it allows some "wriggle room" for right-brained students to move their ideas around or number them afterward. Left-brained students can use it rigidly, planning the order as they write.

The **fourth organizer**, the caterpillar, I devised for students who found it difficult to plan and an onerous task to write and also for students who have to write summaries (as was required briefly in several states). It looks simpler to those students who become stymied when confronted with anything that looks complicated. It also has "weird" appeal. Elementary-age students especially like this one. Although, as with the hand organizer, you never know what will appeal to your students...

The **fifth organizer** was designed by Cathy Callahan at Marco Island Charter Middle School. I include this blank copy since this flow chart organizer is more complicated. You might want to let students first use this printed copy several times before they begin to draw the organizer on their own. I wish that I had found it while I still actively taught as I think it would have worked well with some of my students.

I suggest that you search out there for other graphic organizers to try. I even found a wheel that has at least a dozen of them from which to choose. Now let's start planning!

Clustering for the narrative—topic clustering

For the narrative essay, students have the added problem of inventing a story that dovetails with the prompt they are given. Usually students do not like the prompt and cannot think of a story idea off-hand. They need to learn to do so quickly, using their own experiences or past practice narratives. You can train them to use the same form of clustering as they did when planning the strong-verb paragraphs. However, this time they will use the cluster to *find* a topic.

In order to show students how to cluster to find a topic, teach them to take the basic theme of the prompt (like the bag for the prompt about the wriggling paper bag left in the classroom, a theme used twice on the fourth-grade test in Florida and in other states as well). Then, if they cannot immediately come up with an idea, quickly cluster around it until they do find one. Here is an example.

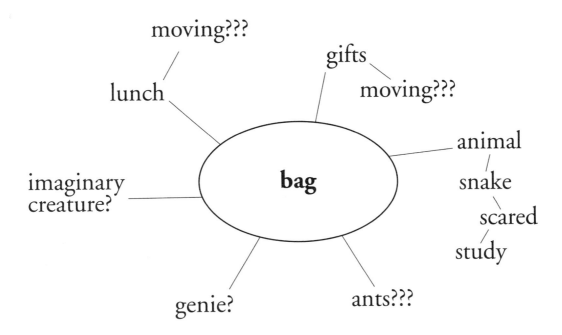

Note that the writer decided to have an animal of some sort in the bag. This was the topic he/she could pursue in the essay. No more than five minutes should be spent on this cluster since the student will need to cluster further to develop and organize his/her narrative. You probably will want to cluster for a topic with your class at least five times as a whole group while you direct and model the thought patterns necessary to come up with a topic in this manner. You will have to supply the prompt. (You can use the **220 Practice Prompts** on the CD.)

Then, after you have clustered story ideas as a whole class, divide students into pairs and assign them a narrative topic. (Again, feel free to use the practice prompts I provided.) Students do not write the narrative at this point; they only come up with the idea for one. Next, have your pairs share their ideas for the prompt. Repeat this procedure until you feel that your students are ready to try to cluster for ideas on their own.

This is the point at which you bring out your timer. Working individually, students should cluster and, in five minutes or less, come up with an idea to a prompt you supply. Practice with your students until they can do this. After each session, it is a good idea to share your students' ideas since this will put more plots into their minds for possible future use. One of these ideas may just come in handy on the day of the test!

Now your students are ready to plan the actual narrative. For this, they can use the same cluster form they used to find their idea. How you use that same cluster to plan the content of a narrative is described in the next section. No more than five to seven minutes should be spent on this cluster or outline.

Clustering for the narrative—content clustering

Once students have a topic for the narrative essay, they need to make another plan for the organization and order of ideas for their narrative. This can be done in many ways, but the following works very well for most students.

Students cluster in the same bubble form they used to find the idea for their narrative. The big bubble in the middle is the idea. The smaller bubbles surrounding it contain the main events that will occur in the narrative. The roots that extend from those bubbles are the details and planned conversations that will enhance the event listed in the bubble. As in the cluster for the strong-verb paragraph, the smaller bubbles in this cluster need to be numbered to organize the order of events in the narrative, an element that is so important for a good score on this type of paper. Here is an example of the content cluster for the topic about finding a paper bag with something wriggling in it on the teacher's desk. Note the numbers, which tell the order of the paragraphs.

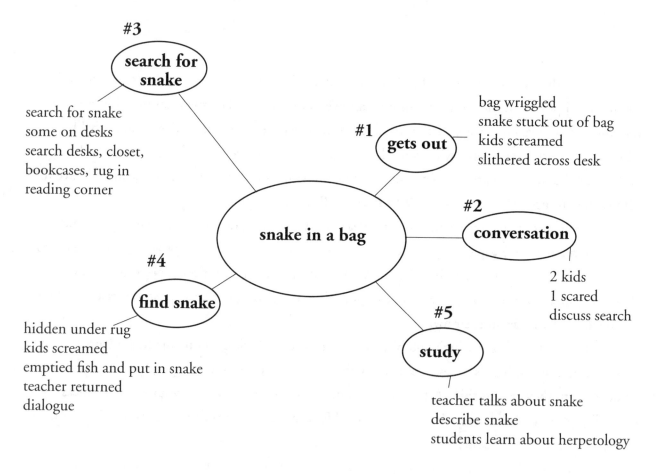

Keep in mind that at this point students are not writing the narrative, just planning it. As before, it is always good to model the planning as a whole class, then have students plan a topic in groups and then in pairs, and finally have them plan individually.

Clustering for the expository/explanatory, descriptive, and persuasive essays and narratives

No matter which graphic organizer you or your students choose to use, you will find that the form itself does the organizing.

You will want to run off many copies of whatever organizer you choose. You will need them for practicing planning alone as well as for the planning that precedes the writing of the actual practice papers. Eventually you want students to draw this plan on their own since, on the day of the actual test, they will be provided with a sheet of paper with one side lined and one blank on which to draw a cluster.

First, introduce a topic (prompt) and teach students to plan out their essays or narratives. Your resource teacher or your county coordinator for English may have given you a number of practice prompts to use. If not, use the ones from previous years' tests or some of the ones from the **220 Practice Prompts** on the CD.

Another source of prompts is a brainstorming session with your fellow teachers. Just come up with some general topics to which students can relate. High-school teachers can ask their students to brainstorm with them to come up with a good list.

Put the topic (prompt) on the board and pass out a copy of the chosen graphic organizer, one per student. These organizers work with all grade levels (although the caterpillar is more suited for elementary-school students). Instruct your students to write the essay topic in the center of the hand, in the box or triangle at the top, or in the head of the caterpillar. Into the three fingers, boxes, or segments in the middle go the ideas that will be developed to support or to give details to the main topic. In the "scissorhands," four spaces in each of the bottom boxes, legs of the caterpillar, etc., students should write specific, related, supporting details or examples (depending on the type of essay) to develop the more general idea in the middle box above it.

You may want to start by doing this together at least four times with four different prompts (two of each kind of essay that will be tested) before turning your students loose to use this form of clustering on their own. Tell them to use words, not complete sentences. This is a plan, not a rough draft of the essay. Please note that, at this stage, no essays are being written. Students will do that later. Now they are getting used to planning.

After practicing planning as a large group, students are ready to plan in smaller groups. Divide your class into groups of four and assign at least another two or three prompts to use for planning purposes in the small groups. After this practice, students should be ready to plan and write essays on their own.

Graphic Organizers (available full-size on CD)

Content Cluster

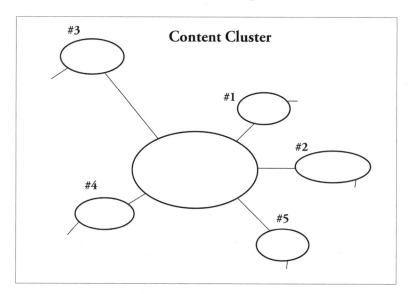

#3

#1

#2

#4

#5

The Hand

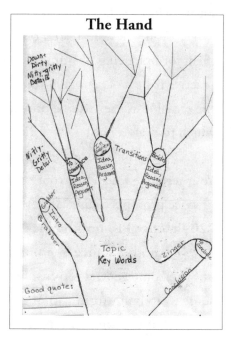

Tried and True Organizer

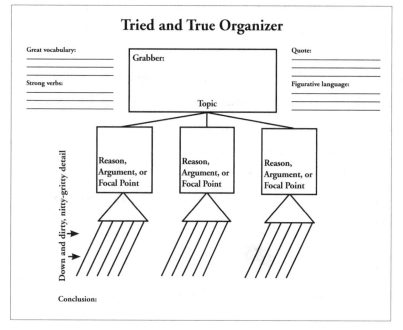

Great vocabulary:

Strong verbs:

Grabber:

Topic

Quote:

Figurative language:

Reason, Argument, or Focal Point

Reason, Argument, or Focal Point

Reason, Argument, or Focal Point

Down and dirty, nitty-gritty detail

Conclusion:

Blank Flow Chart Organizer

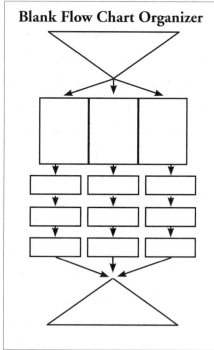

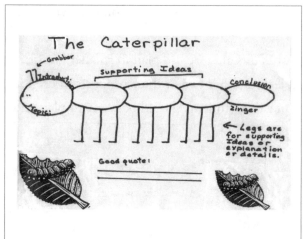

The essay clusters are simply a tool for you to organize your essay. You can have whatever number of paragraphs you want. Be creative.

Writing Beginnings with Flair

Now that your students know what constitutes a good essay or narrative and how to plan one, they need to begin the actual writing process of producing a well-written, top-scoring paper. To begin this process, it is a good idea to start with the beginning—the "grabber." This is the first thing that a reader sees in a paper. This is the "hook" that makes the reader want to continue reading the piece.

I tell my students that this is a vital part of good writing and thus helps them earn high scores. Without that scorer's initial interest, that student's essay or narrative will read like the thousands of others the scorer has read that day. It is important to "wake up" the reader, to make that scorer gasp and shout out loud in the hushed quiet of rustling papers being read, "Wow, folks, I have a live one here!"

This actually happened when I was helping score our county-wide writing test for seventh-graders. A sweet young teacher just jumped up and said, "Wow! I've got a great one here!" An official scorer once told me that she had experienced the same thing. It gets boring reading the same formulaic thing over and over.

To achieve the goal of sinking that initial "hook" into the reader requires practice. Thus it is a good idea to hand students a topic, such as the common expository one, "Explain why your favorite season is your favorite." An excellent practice is to take such an uninspiring topic and make students write an introductory paragraph for each of the four seasons, espousing that each one is, indeed, the student's favorite season. Then instruct students that each introductory paragraph must begin in a different way.

I would list some of the "grabbers" on the board:

➔ Begin with a brief conversation.

➔ Begin with a bold "wake-up" statement.

➔ Begin with an appropriate quotation (made-up or a real).

➔ Begin with a brief narrative episode that leads into the topic.

These are the simpler "grabbers" to use, but there are others you can ask your students to use. (See page 87 in this step.) Students get to pick which season to put with which type of "grabber," but you will notice that fall almost always gets the onomatopoeia.

The rest of each introductory paragraph must restate the prompt cleverly (see **Tip #1** on page 76); somehow creatively indicate the three explanations, arguments, or focal points that would be developed if the essay were being written; and conclude with a sentence that wraps it all up in a nice bow and perhaps leads to a theme that could be continued in the rest of the essay. All this must be done cleverly, not in a boring, rote fashion, such as, "The three reasons why I like spring the best are…"

This same practice can be done for a narrative. After the "grabber," (and you can ask students to write four different grabbers for the same narrative topic), students must launch into the beginning of their narrative, making sure that they restate the key words in the prompt (see **Tip #2** on page 76).

I like to repeat this exercise at least four times with different topics/prompts (you can use the ones listed on the CD). Students save these first paragraphs so that when they write the entire essay or narrative, they can use one of them to begin it. In having to look through their folders and re-read their introductory paragraphs, students get used to the idea that they must begin their writing in an interesting way.

You also can use the **Evaluating Writing** sheet on page 100 in this step which asks students to identify the "grabber."

Writing Middles with Elaboration, Nitty-Gritty Detail, and Down-and-Dirty, Nitty-Gritty Detail

So, what is "nitty-gritty" detail? Simply stated, it is giving specific incidents or examples that support any statement that you make. Nitty-gritty detail is the bane of most writing teachers' existence. In other parlance it is called elaboration. And, to make it even harder, very few universities have courses in how to teach writing, so most of us have no formal training and have to wing it ourselves, a tough task.

Teachers from grades one through twelve have told me of their struggles to eke details out of the majority of their students. Students do not elaborate for a number of reasons: 1) They simply don't know how; 2) They are lazy writers; 3) They can't get the details and pictures that are in their heads down onto the paper when they write; and 4) They just don't process the idea that they need to provide word pictures to flesh out their writing. They know where the narrative or essay is going but can't convey that to their readers.

Whatever the reason(s), the following activities may help. Elaboration is the key to good writing and higher writing scores. In all states that conduct a writing test, a student cannot get anything but the lowest score without elaboration. I called elaboration "nitty-gritty" detail because my students could relate better to that term. And, I called it "down-and-dirty, nitty-gritty" detail when they elaborated on the elaboration by giving specific examples.

Actually getting students to produce nitty-gritty and down-and-dirty, nitty-gritty detail in their writing? This is not an easy task. While some books on writing include worksheets on the subject, I tend to shy away from them. Worksheets never taught my students anything that they retained and understood profoundly enough to carry over into their writing. I liked to teach by practice, repetition, and example. Here are four activities that proved effective to inveigle students to elaborate.

Activity #1: Extracting detail using books and student papers

First, you can use examples from any reading selection you have on hand. You can find nitty-gritty detail in a book as simple as *Winnie-the-Pooh* when Pooh, for example, talks about the bees. Look in any book. Details abound.

In more sophisticated reading material or literature, finding nitty-gritty detail is even easier. I'll never forget Maya Angelou's detailed picture (in *I Know Why the Caged Bird Sings*) of life for an African-American child in the 1930s in Stamps, Arkansas, with examples galore to illustrate her point.

Examples from previous students' papers also can be used to show nitty-gritty detail. A prime example that I found in a student's essay is "My sister messes in my room." This statement has little meaning without some details, some examples of exactly how her sister messes in her room. What, in fact, does "messes in my room" mean?

The student continued after her topic sentence, though, to provide a little nitty-gritty detail to support her basic thesis that her sister "messes in" her room. With a lot of encouragement (not to mention duress), this student finally added enough nitty-gritty detail into the paragraph so that the reader would have a clear picture of how her sister "messes in" her room.

Example:

→ **General detail:** "I would like to be Melissa for one day because she is an only child, while I have to deal with a sister who messes in my room."

→ **Nitty-gritty detail:** "My sister plays with my CDs, gets into my closet and tries on my clothes, takes my stuffed animals from my bed, and reads my diary."

→ **Down-and-dirty, nitty-gritty detail:** "When my sister comes into my room, she throws all my CDs on the bed so she can look through them and play some of them on my stereo. This includes my precious _____ CD. She goes into my closet, pulls out my favorite tops (including my newest red one), tries them all on, and then throws them on the floor when she is done. Then she takes every one of my stuffed bears off the bed and throws them on the floor. To top it all off, she goes under my bed where I hide my diary, takes it out, reads it, and then blabs all my secrets to my mother."

Other good student examples of elaboration can be found in the last section of this book where you will find ninety narratives and essays written by students in grades four, seven, eight, and ten. Read your students the nitty-gritty detail in the high-scoring ones. Example #7 of the expository sample set titled "Book" is a good one to use. In this superlative essay, the student supports almost every statement he makes. For example, he says he likes the book because "the action never stops." He then goes on to include his down-and-dirty, nitty-gritty detail. "There is trickery as Napoleon manages to change the basic rules of the new farm and treachery as he gets rid of Snowball." He could have said, "There is trickery and treachery." This would not be down-and-dirty, nitty-gritty detail. He gets into the plot of the book with examples to illustrate his point. That is good elaboration and good writing.

To illustrate the point even further, take any of the "telling, dead-verb" sentences on the worksheets in **Step One**, and ask your students to provide some examples and details to illustrate that topic sentence. Essentially, if you have used this book step-by-step, you already have taught your students about nitty-gritty detail when they wrote all those strong-verb paragraphs! That is exactly what strong-verb paragraphs are—elaboration (nitty-gritty detail) about a topic ("telling") sentence. Down-and-dirty, nitty-gritty detail just carries it one step further. But, there is a caveat here. A few students get carried away and ramble on for paragraphs. You will need to draw the line in those cases.

> *TEACHING NOTE: To help with practice in locating detail and other things in any passage that students read, you can provide them with a sheet to fill out as you read (see the Bibliography for Marcia Freeman's book with this idea). My students enjoyed analyzing poems, essays, etc. using that simple form. They worked first in groups and then individually. Sometimes, with the form on the overhead, we analyzed a selection orally as an entire class. On page 100 in this step, you will find an example of the Evaluating Writing sheet to use in evaluating essays. You can, of course, modify this evaluation device and leave out the parts you don't wish to emphasize at this point in time.*

Activity #2: The Hat Trick—again

Besides pointing out examples in the books your students read, in student examples, and in the strong-verb paragraphs, you can play games to elicit the desired details from your students. Print the prompts from the CD. Cut them up. Put them in a box or a big hat, and mix them up. Ask a student at random to pull a topic from the hat. After the class has determined what type of writing is required—narrative, expository, descriptive, or persuasive—elicit from that child (and, subsequently, the class) one of the scenes, explanations, focal points, or arguments that could be used when writing a paper from this topic. Then ask for detail to support that scene, explanation, focal point, or argument.

For example, if the student pulls the topic "Explain whether you prefer living in a large city or a small town," elicit first the type of writing. (It is, of course, expository.) Then go on to ask for a choice between small town or big city. Let's say your student picks big city. Now elicit one reason why he/she chose the big city. Maybe the student would say, "Because there are many things to do in a big city." Now you have your topic sentence from which to work.

At this point, I liked to place my hand, palm up, in front of me and curl my fingers back and forth as if inviting more and more detail (or like using the symbol for the Italian word "Ciao"). This hand motion was my signal for students to get busy providing detail about a topic sentence. As long as my fingers were curling, students needed to keep providing more detail.

For the above topic, you would want your students to come up with nitty-gritty detail of exactly what things you can do in a big city. "Big cities have many skating rinks where you can ice skate or roller blade, lots of theaters for a wide choice of movies and plays to see, and even ramps for skateboards." I don't let my students stop there. I go on and elicit at least five more down-and-dirty, nitty-gritty details (such as which movies and plays) that could come from that one simple sentence about the "many things to do in a big city."

This exercise will work with any of the **220 Practice Prompts**. It is a good idea to do *no more than* one or two a day over a period of several weeks. Students will soon get the hang of it, and you will find that the elaboration carries over into their writing.

Activity #3: Use actual student papers to elicit detail

If your students need even more practice with elaboration, here's another activity that brings the point home. Take your students' essays or narratives. As you read them, write down any "telling," unsupported topic sentences. You will soon have a long list. Type them up in a font large enough to be seen from an overhead. After pointing out to your students that these examples are from their own papers, elicit the nitty-gritty and down-and-dirty, nitty-gritty details that were lacking in the original papers. No student need to know from whose papers the examples come. The class as a whole must suggest details and examples.

You can carry this one step further. Read one of the "telling" sentences you took from your students' writing. Write it on the board or overhead. Group your students and ask them to write at least five nitty-gritty details to support it. When they are comfortable doing this in groups, repeat the exercise, requiring students to work individually.

Activity #4: Students need even more practice?

Have each student select an essay, preferably one that they wrote themselves. Then, using a graphic organizer of your choosing (see page 94), instruct them to try to fill out the plan sheet, especially the bottom part in which they list the nitty-gritty details. If they cannot find any details in the essay or narrative to list there, ask them to think of some appropriate examples and then rewrite

Title _____

Name _____

Class _____

Evaluating Writing

Function: _____

Organization (paragraphs, order, etc.): _____

Beginning "Grabber": _____

      Statement of Topic _____

Explanations, Focal Points, or Arguments:

      1. _____

      2. _____

      3. _____

List 4 of the Supporting Details: _____

_____

Lively Writing and Figurative Languages:

      Strong Verbs Used: _____

      Great Vocabulary: _____

      Literary Devices Used: _____

      Other Lively Writings: _____

Interesting Part of Ending: _____

_____

the paper, putting in the elaboration they neglected to put in the first time they wrote it.

If all else fails, go back and repeat **Step One** of this book, and have your students write more strong-verb paragraphs.

Writing Endings with a Bang

Students tend to peter out towards the end of an essay or narrative. Their conclusions often leave something to be desired. And, in narratives, what teacher hasn't encountered a simple "the end" as the entire conclusion?

I told my students that the ending is just as important as the beginning. They must really end with a bang! They want that official scorer to stand up and say, "Wow! This is really good!" They also wanted to keep me (who had to read 1,200 to 1,500 essays between August and January) from being bored. Boring and formulaic essays without a clear voice do not earn high scores from me or from the scorers on the official writing test. The kiss of death in my class was for a student to find a nose beside his or her conclusion. That was the signal that a rewrite was in order.

Learning to practice ending with a bang or a "zinger" is more difficult than getting students to begin with a "grabber." This is where a well-placed quote works well. A good ending conversation might not be amiss either. Ending with a question also is good. In fact, anything that works well as a "grabber" works equally well as a "zinger."

Remember: This is your final chance to leave a lasting impression. Chose your closing words wisely!

Activity #1: Practice writing endings

For practice, read, give students a copy to read, or put on the overhead a narrative or essay that lacks a good ending (*not* one of your students' efforts). Students, in groups or individually, must then write the end, coming to a satisfying conclusion that brings the story full circle in a narrative or gives closing statements and very briefly restates (in a different manner) the main points in an essay. Students must then elaborate on this and come up with a final bang or "zinger" that leaves the reader laughing, wondering, or otherwise engaged.

For this exercise, since you don't want to use your own students' narratives or essays, copy a few examples from the ones in the last section of this book and take off the last paragraph. You should repeat this practice until students can write satisfying and interesting conclusions.

Activity #2: Using response groups

If you have working response groups in your classroom, as I did, you can ask the groups to take four pieces of writing, one from each member of the group, and as a group, rework the endings on each paper until the group feels that they are good. This consensus method works extremely well. Since all papers are being critiqued and corrected, no one student feels singled out.

Again, as in practice for the introductory paragraph, you could use the **Evaluating Writing** sheet on page 100 in this step. This sheet asks students to find the "zinger" in a piece of writing or literature.

A Blitz of Writing

Now that students can plan an essay and a narrative, write a good introduction, use transitions, produce nitty-gritty detail, and create an ending with a bang, it is time to write!

Weekly plan

My students and I spent three to four weeks following these plans.

Monday. Put a prompt on the board or overhead. Invite students to read the prompt silently and contemplate it for a minute. Give students forty-five minutes (or whatever amount of time your state allows for the writing test) to cluster and to write their essay or narrative. You may need to provide students with one of the graphic organizers for the first few times they write. They will soon be willing, and indeed prefer, to make one on their own just as they will have to do on the actual test. Encourage this practice.

For scoring purposes, do not let students put their names on their papers. Instead, assign each student a number. It is a good idea to use the number in your gradebook that is by each student's name. This will make it easier for you to record the results.

While your students write, you can finish scoring the previous day's or class's essays or narratives. Encourage students to be enthusiastic and write with pizzazz. When time is up, pass out a copy of the **Focused Analytical Score Sheet** (on page 59 in **Step Two**), and have students attach one to each paper.

Tuesday. Students get into groups and score essays or narratives, writing "high," "medium," "low," or "zero" plus the reasons why in the upper left-hand corner of the back of the folded Focused Analytical Score Sheet. Any questions can be referred to the teacher. Students can be asked to score them blind, score their own papers, or score in a consensus with their writing response group. For more detailed feedback, high-school teachers may want to have students score on the six-point rubric (even if your state uses a different one). Discuss results.

Wednesday. Same as Monday.

Thursday. Same as Tuesday.

Friday. Same as Monday.

> **TEACHING NOTE:** *After you have scored at least five essays or narratives for each student, you probably will be ready to scream, and your eyes will be crossing. So that you don't have to continue to score every paper your students write, or when you reach the point that you can't stand to score another paper without suffering from extreme nausea at the very thought of it, try the following. When students have completed and scored two or three essays or narratives, have them pick the one they think is the best and hand it to you to score. In this way, you have to grade only one out of every two or three. This makes the scoring more manageable. Also, in requiring students to score their own papers before handing them in to you, you are asking your students to take the final step and actually analyze their own papers without any crutches at all.*

You should plan to have students write at least fifteen essays or stories before the actual day of the test. Don't flinch at this point. The grading is not hard or time-consuming. Read on...

Grading All Those Essays and Narratives You Assigned

Collect each set of completed papers. Scoring is neither difficult nor time-consuming if you do the following. *Remember that each official scorer of the actual test takes only one to two minutes per paper. You should do the same.* Marking up a paper for grammar, mechanics, or usage or correcting mistakes is a useless, time-wasting exercise. Use the guidelines set out in **Step Two**. In fact, you might want to keep the book open to **Step Two** as you score.

Now, just as your students did in **Step Two** when they practiced scoring, use the **Focused Analytical Score Sheet** (page 59) already attached to each paper to score it holistically. Use the high-medium-low or your state's rubric if you wish to be more specific. Problems can be pointed out by putting checks in the appropriate places on the score sheet (which saves time) and circling the appropriate problem, just as your students did in **Step Two**. For example, if a paper lacks good vocabulary, you circle the words "specific language (great vocabulary)."

As in **Step Two**, scores can be assigned by circling "high," "medium," or "low" at the bottom. You then fold over the scores sheet and staple it closed so that students cannot cheat when they themselves score the paper. I usually scored the papers first simply because I collected them at the end of the period (or writing time in elementary school) and had time to score them while the next class was writing. In that way, the papers can be returned to the students the next day when it is *their* turn to score.

TEACHING NOTE: *Do not be afraid to score your students' essays. Scoring on a high, medium, low scale is very easy after you have read a few papers. Also, do not be intimidated by the large number of practice papers you have to grade. In my two-day workshops, I ask the teachers to score ten to fifteen essays or narratives in approximately the same number of minutes. While my students wrote the essays, I (and most of my colleagues as well) could score more than 400 essays a week and not take a single paper home! Scoring holistically is a lot different from regular paper-grading. You are only skimming each paper, not reading it thoroughly. It should take less than a minute per paper to read. You are looking for an impression, not a detailed analysis. If it takes you longer than one minute per essay, your skimming skills might be rusty.*

After you score the papers, the next day in class review the criteria for scoring in each of the five elements that should be included in a good essay or narrative. Hand out the papers, telling students that if they get their own, they should hand it to someone else. If you have several classes, you could use the papers of a different class. With numbers instead of names on the papers, no one will know whose paper he or she is scoring. Each student should have an example to score.

You also could divide the class into groups of four and have the groups collectively score the papers that each student in that group holds. Walk around the room to arbitrate disputes or resolve problems. Elementary-school teachers may be able to suspend reading groups for a week in order to do this. After all, students *are* reading. This would increase time spent writing and practicing for the test (which also improves writing). Students learn to read by writing.

After each scoring session, hold a discussion. Ask students to expose the stapled scoring sheet to see the score you gave the paper. Discuss any glaring differences between your scores and those of your students by scoring the paper once more via consensus of the class. After grading about five papers in this manner, students are ready to analyze and score a few of their own efforts.

TEACHING NOTE: *On a 6-point scale, "high" is equivalent to 5 or 6, "medium" is equivalent to 3 or 4, "low" is equivalent to 1 or 2, and zero is the same as "unscorable." On a 5-point scale, "high" is equivalent to a good 4 or 5, "medium" is the same as a 3 or 4, and a "low" equals a 1 or 2. On a 4-point scale, "high" is a 4, "medium" is a 3; and "low" is a 1 or 2. Of course, if your state uses domains and double scores, you will have to adjust accordingly.*

Using writing response groups for scoring. Some years, I used writing response groups (four students heterogeneously grouped by competency in English and grouped together for most of the year) to score their own papers. Each student in a group read his or her own essay to his/her peers, and the group debated and then decided the score. Since the response groups were used to working together and used to each other's writing, there was little insulting going on.

If students can handle them, writing response groups are very effective as students learn more quickly from participating in scoring their own essays with peer help. Keep in mind, however, that this works best if you have a particularly amiable group of students who work well together and who, for the most part, take each others' writing efforts seriously.

I do not recommend using this method if your students will make fun of each other's writing. Instead, you can hold the whole-class discussion of the results after both you and the students have scored their papers and after students have seen the scores assigned to their papers.

Now that your students know the walls that bind them, they are ready to fill the space between those walls with their own voice, style, pizzazz, and flair.

220 Practice Prompts (on CD only)

The suggested prompts come from a variety of sources. Some are actual test topics from various states. Others were written by other teachers or by the former Alachua County Supervisor of English, Mary Ann Coxe. Still others came to me by word of mouth via students regarding practice test prompts they encountered over the years. I wrote most of the remainder to use with my students.

Whatever the source, these practice prompts are included here to be used to cluster, to write, to practice topic recognition or produce nitty-gritty detail, or to discuss as possible types of topics that could appear on the real writing assessment test.

Since these prompts work for all grades, you will wish to make the actual wording of the prompts more specific for the third/fourth and seventh/eighth grades and more general and open-ended for the tenth grade. You also may wish to simplify a prompt or make it more sophisticated depending on your students. Some may not be appropriate for your grade level. Pick and choose from among them.

Some of the prompts offer alternative versions for younger students since many states recycle topics from elementary to middle to high school, changing the wording a bit. Since different states present the prompts in different formats, I have reduced many of the topics to their basic content, the part that tells the students about what they are to write.

When you use one of these prompts, expand it to fit the usual format your state writing assessment test uses, or your students may be confused when they see the long introduction and instructions on the actual test. Some states even include a story, essay, or picture that sets the scene for the topic. Remind students that usually the last sentence of the prompt actually tells them what to write. Some of the following prompts are equivalent to those last sentences on the actual test.

Other prompts are wordier and try to mimic actual test questions.

Please note that although the following prompts are, by necessity, generic, you will find that the potential pitfalls that usually occur with actual test prompts are amply represented. The most obvious and potentially dangerous (score-wise) of these pitfalls is the one in which a prompt asks for one part to be explained but mentions other parts. For example, "There are many environmental problems that plague our world. Pick one of these problems and propose some solutions to it." Or, "If you could pick one item of your school's dress code to change, what would it be? Write an essay to convince your school's administration to change that item." Many students see the words "environmental problems" or "dress code" and get off the topic by writing about a bunch of problems or argue about the dress code in general.

You will notice that I have included more expository and persuasive prompts than narrative or descriptive ones. Since most states require that students at all the grade levels that are tested compose an expository essay, I have included many more examples of this type to give you a broader choice. Also, since the persuasive/argumentative essay is often the hardest to write and usually the type students score the lowest on, more prompts of this type are included. There are 40 descriptive, 75 expository, 45 narrative, and 60 persuasive prompts.

Good luck on the actual test, and good writing!

NOTE: On the CD, each genre (descriptive, expository, narrative, and persuasive) is in a separate file for easy access.

Step Four

Teach Students to Write with Voice, Great Vocabulary, Passion, Flair, Pizzazz, and from Another's Point of View

This step is all about making good writing better. It is about getting those coveted highest scores on the writing tests. It is about putting the icing on the writing cake. It is about making the reader sit up and pay attention to what the writer is "saying." It is about making a piece of writing different from the "average." It is about adding things to a piece of writing that make it stand out and grab the reader and wring some emotion out of him or her. It is about what Nancy Keese, a Pennsylvania teacher, calls "the freedom within the structure." And, it is about what keeps an essay or narrative from being formulaic and boring.

I mentioned at the beginning of **Step Three** the "walls," or required elements, that my students had to put into their writing—the nuts and bolts that make an essay or narrative a coherent piece. As long as the "walls" were in place, my students zinged back and forth between the walls with passion and verve and whatever else they could include that would make their voice loud and clear. **Step Four** suggests a plethora of ideas that your students can use. Mine used them with much success, resulting in many top scores on the writing test. I know your students will find the same success while discovering their own writing voices.

Instilling Voice in Writing

A writer must find his or her voice in order to write well. Voice is difficult to define because it varies from person to person, but it includes the author's choice of words, elaboration and details, word pictures with sensory detail, attitude, and how the writing is constructed. Voice is what makes a book funny or sad or frightening or poignant. Voice is what enables you to recognize the writing style of a particular author even though you don't know why you recognize it. For example, anyone who knows me well could read one of my books (with my name taken off) and know that I wrote it. I write the way I speak. I use strong verbs. I digress with examples and personal experiences. I use a plethora of big words. I paint pictures of my students. I never (well almost never) split verbs. I use parentheses a lot, etc.

One student of mine wrote with such passion and such voice that, several years after I had taught her, when she was in high school and I was a judge in a writing contest, I had to disqualify myself because I recognized her style of writing after reading only one page. (Names had been removed from the papers, and no teacher could be a judge for the grade level he or she taught.) Later, when we revealed the names of the winners (and she was one of them), I knew that I had been right to disqualify myself. Her style was so unique and personal with descriptions of nature so real that you felt as if you were there, and her writing voice was so strong that I could still recognize it after several years!

Voice is what made the last example of the elementary writing on page 37 in **Step One** so different. It is funny. It is clever. It definitely is not boring. Can't you just picture the group of three or four third-graders giggling and snorting and wriggling with delight as they wrote that? Without voice (otherwise known in my classroom as "pizzazz," "flair," "passion," and the "woo-woo factor"), an essay or narrative falls flat and reads as cardboard tastes.

So, how do you entice your students to find their writing voices? Instilling voice in writing is not something that can be done quickly. But, children of any age (I include adults in this) definitely can have a distinctive voice that comes through. In this section, I proffer five activities that will begin your students on the path to finding their own voice. I list two books on voice by Nancy Dean in the **Bibliography**.

Activity #1: Choose your words carefully

Concentrate on **Step One**—writing strong, vivid-verb paragraphs—to narrow in on word choice. Word choice, or diction, is extremely important in finding your voice. Writers need to find vivid words that convey a picture. The verb "is walking," for example, does not give the reader a clear picture. The verb "struts" does. This is word choice, and it begins with the use of powerful, "showing" verbs.

In the same vein, using vivid adjectives and adverbs (other than the trite "mad," "sad," "pretty," "glad") also is vital to finding your voice. The shout isn't *loud*, it is *ear-piercing*. The kid doesn't just think chocolate is *good*, he considers it to be *delicious* or *tasty*. These are fairly simple words that convey a wealth of meaning by being specific, not just generic.

If you do Caught'yas or study vocabulary with your students, you will find many adjectives and adverbs for your students to play with as they write. You might want to make a word wall with a separate space for verbs, adjectives, and adverbs. This will take "mad," "sad," "pretty," and "glad" out of students' vocabulary.

Activity #2: Wax poetic

I assume that you read to your students. We are never too old to listen to a good story. As you read, point out vivid vocabulary that leaves a picture in the reader's mind. Poems are a good source of the succinct, vivid use of words. In a poem, the author has to convey an image or an idea in as few words as possible. Thus, in a good poem, every word is fraught with meaning. Read poems you know your children would enjoy; pick a word from the poem that conveys a lot. Write it on the board. Discuss what feelings or images come from that word. I'm sure you can find books of poetry that are appropriate for your grade level.

Activity #3: Describe and draw

Take your students to various places around the school or to a nearby park if you have one, and ask them to write a description of that place. Require that they use sensory words like "smells like," "sounds like," etc., as well as good adjectives to describe the feeling they get in that place. Encourage your writers to paint a picture of that place with words, a picture vivid enough that the reader can picture in his or her head what is being described. You also might want to have students as a group come up with a list of vivid adjectives that they could use to describe the place and then require that they use those adjectives in their descriptions.

Then there is always the ever popular "Describe a monster" writing assignment in which each student draws a monster using prescribed geometric shapes (squares, triangles, etc.) and colors. Once the students have drawn their monsters, they write a description of it and make it as detailed as possible. (Of course, they must hide their monster drawing from the view of their peers.) Next students exchange written descriptions and attempt to draw the monster being described. Finally, students share the drawings to see how close the reader was able to come to the picture. Even if your students have done this activity in previous grades, they never grow tired of it. Their descriptions just get clearer and clearer.

Activity #4: Write with a purpose

Voice also expresses the purpose of the writing. Start an argument with your students about something they can feel passionate about—doing away with P.E., making them sit in alphabetical order at lunch, requiring that they have school on Saturday (or all summer), etc. You know what will get your students impassioned. Then ask them to write a letter to the person with whom they wish to argue and make their opinion known with passion, details, and imaginative arguments.

Activity #5: Tone up

Voice also expresses an identifiable tone. Your students certainly recognize your tone when you really mean business or are angry. All I had to do was lower my voice to a deadly, monotone one and fold my arms over my chest, and my students sat up and paid attention. This was my "angry" tone. My teaching partner, Kren Kurts, used "The Look."

There are many different tones to writing. The tones are as varied as our emotions—anger, humor, love, sadness, fear, disgust, etc. To help foster use of tone in writing, you can point out various emotions and tones that the authors used in the books you read to your class.

For example: If you read *Charlotte's Web,* you can point out Wilbur's happiness at finding a friend, his disgust at Charlotte's killing bugs to eat, his disdain for lazy Templeton, his fear of dying, his subsequent elation at Charlotte's scheme, his sadness at Charlotte's impending death, etc. As you can see, in one simple book, lots of emotions are expressed by the words and actions and demeanor of the characters. And, the more sophisticated the book, the more examples you will find. Try Shakespeare!

To teach tone, you also can assign topics for paragraphs (or essays and stories) that will help your students write with a particular tone. A few possible topics are below.

Anger:

→ Write a letter to someone who has done or said something to you that made you angry. (Do this one after lunch.) Express your feelings.

→ Think about a time when you were *really* angry. Try to remember how you felt. Now write about that time and sound as angry as you felt.

Humor:

→ Write a funny story using the starter: It all happened when I fell down on my behind right in front of the principal.

→ Think of your favorite joke (or quote). Write a funny story around it.

Love:

➜ Think of someone you love a whole lot. Now write a letter to that person to tell him or her how you feel. Feel the love in your heart as you write.

➜ Do you know how when you really love someone, your heart kind of feels as if it is swelling up? Try to think of a time you really felt lovingly about someone or something (like your pet), and just write to tell me about that person or thing.

Sadness:

➜ Write about someone (this includes animals) who was close to you who died. Make your reader feel your pain at your loss.

➜ Tell me something with enough sad detail that it will make me cry.

Fear:

➜ Write a Poe-like story to scare your classmates. Be sure to use suspense. Imagine, for example, that the classroom is haunted...

➜ Everyone has something that scares him or her. It could be bugs or thunderstorms or a dark room at night or a dark closet or anything. What is your scary thing? Explain it and try to capture your fear.

Disgust:

➜ What does a cockroach sound like when you squish it? What does it look like? Write a disgusting picture of this squished roach.

➜ If someone in class threw up all over the floor, it would be disgusting. Can you write to describe the sound, sight, and smell of it? Try to express how you feel as you describe it. Try not to throw up yourself...

The rest of the information mentioned in this step are merely the tools and building blocks that a writer may choose to use to find his or her voice. All of them are important for improving writing and subsequently raising writing test scores dramatically.

Conventions

I'd like to get this out of the way first as it is a necessity in writing but can be difficult to teach so that it carries over into students' writing. I only can recommend what I used successfully with *my* students—Caught'yas. See the **Bibliography** for my Caught'ya books. I was able to teach everything I needed without using boring grammar books. My kids loved doing the Caught'yas because the "boring stuff" was taught using a funny story that was long enough to last all year and was designed to appeal to students.

Incorporating Superlative Vocabulary in Writing

Do you teach vocabulary in the traditional manner—require students to write the word, part of speech, meaning, and a sentence (which usually is using the word incorrectly)? Then, do you test your students and see that most do very well on the test? How long do your students retain those words? Do you find that they use them in their writing?

Well, mine certainly didn't when I taught vocabulary in the time-honored way. So, I invented, borrowed, and stole (just kidding) some ideas to help my students remember the vocabulary I was trying to teach them and to put those words into their permanent memories. Once these words were put in their permanent memories, students could call them up when needed to use in their writing. No, they didn't learn *every* word taught, but they did learn enough to use more superlative vocabulary when they wrote.

Students find that big, succulent words can be fun to play with and can give them power when they use them. The key is that if the teacher makes learning something "cool," kids of all ages will *want* to learn it.

Almost all of my students always adored the words "a plethora of" as they could never remember whether "a lot" was one word or two, but they had no difficulty with the former, and they loved the sound of it. Other words that have caught my students' fancy over the years are "dulcet," "a dearth of," "pulchritudinous" (which sounds like something a cat hacks up), "comely," "obese," "loathe," "abhor," "blithe," "egregious," "puerile," "pugilist," and more. Many students, in fact, became true "wordaholics," always trying to find a new, "cool" word to use or searching for one the meaning of which I did not know.

The use of great vocabulary should be its own reward, but being a realist, I always gave my students extra credit (two points for each word, up to ten points) for each outstanding vocabulary word that was correctly and aptly used in their writing. Some students considered this to be a personal challenge, and I had to tone them down if their writing began to sound too stilted. I worked with those students to bring their vocabulary use to a more natural degree. But, what a delightful problem!

There is, however, one thing to keep in mind as we teach new vocabulary to our students.

Whether the words be from the Caught'yas, from a list in a traditional vocabulary book, from your own beloved list, or from the literature you read, it is very important to separate the learning of vocabulary from traditional schooling. To that end, I recommend highly that you rarely (if at all) give any formal vocabulary tests. I have found from experience that they are a pointless exercise anyway—the diligent students will memorize the words and promptly forget them after the test; the otiose ones won't even try to learn them temporarily.

Instead, use informal vocabulary drills—a daily game or challenge. Rarely did my students look up the definition of words individually. Instead, they completed that tedious exercise using "silly sheets," (see **Activity #2** on page 114) in groups, in a mass class effort, or in a contest to see who could find the meaning first—much more fun. We made "word walls" and a "word ceiling" with great abandon.

Included in this section are some of the tricks and activities I found to be successful. My former students (and their high writing scores) can attest to that. Besides, they are fun! And, shouldn't learning new words be fun instead of drudgery? Enjoy them with your students.

Activity #1: Word(s) of the Day

Put one or two difficult but fun words on the board. They can come from any source. I used the vocabulary in the Caught'yas and words I pulled from the literature we read, and I chose words that could be substituted with simple synonyms. For example, "comely" for "pretty," "odious" for "horrible," "egregious" for "really bad," etc. Post each day's word(s) prominently in your classroom, and use them in your parlance as often as you can. "My, what a comely hairdo you have today, Mary." To help put these words into your students' permanent memories, I suggest utilizing a kinesthetic technique that was designed for students with learning disabilities but works for all, including adults. Instruct your students to write the word of the day on their arm with a finger. My students called it their "spelling finger." Then repeat the word and its meaning rapidly at least ten times. Go from word to meaning and then from meaning to word.

If you can get the cooperation of your administration and fellow teachers, it is even better to have a "word of the day" for the entire school. With one word circulating around your school all day, students will learn it. Remember, in order to put something into your permanent memory, it needs to be repeated from fifteen to sixty times, depending on your learning curve (and your age). Imagine a student being asked the meaning of "egregious" by several teachers, the principal, and the vice-principal while walking the halls or eating lunch. You will be amazed at the fun students have learning one word a day in this fashion. They know that no one is going to test them. They know that it is done in fun. They learn a word with which they can stump their parents or siblings that evening. Try instituting a "word of the day" in your school.

Activity #2: "Silly sheets"

These are just a sneaky way to get students to write the words and meanings so that they can study from them if they wish. A French teacher at the local high school came up with this idea. It works well to teach vocabulary in *any* language.

Most of my students found the use of "silly sheets" to be so effective for learning vocabulary that, independently, they applied the idea to *any* vocabulary they had to learn in other classes. What is even more amazing is that students are *still* e-mailing and writing letters to tell me that, in high school, college, and even in medical school, they continue to use "silly sheets" whenever they have to learn a list of something, be it vocabulary, chemical formulas, dates, or bones in the body.

So, what on earth is a "silly sheet"? While the concept is very simple, explaining it in words without an actual demonstration is a challenge. You may need to read the following description at least two times in order to get the image in your head. Try to make one as you read.

"Silly sheets" are self-study tools that slowly eliminate words which one already can define. They force students to go from word to meaning *and* from meaning to word. Even if they don't use the sheets as intended, this tool works since, in order to make a silly sheet, students have to write or go over the meaning of the words orally at least six times.

How to make a silly sheet:

➔ Have students take an ordinary piece of lined paper and place it flat in front of them. They fold the paper in half length-wise to make a crease, and then lay it unfolded and flat in front of them again. Next, they fold in the sides (again length-wise) so that they meet at the crease in the middle of the paper. This should look like a double shutter. There will be two outside "shutters" on which to write.

➔ Instruct students to write the vocabulary words on the left side of the closed "shutter," one on each line of the paper. (They can fit only as many words as lines on the front of that closed left "shutter.") Then instruct students to copy the meaning of each word onto the right side of the closed "shutter," opposite the appropriate word. (If you ask that they look up the words, have them do it in groups to lessen the pain.)

➔ Now, divide students into pairs, each student with his or her own "silly sheet." One student in each pair hands his "silly sheet" to his or her partner. (The partner who receives the "silly sheet" puts his or her own sheet away for the time being.) The partner who has the "silly sheet" systematically asks his or her classmate the meaning of every word on the list. If the student who is quizzed does not know a meaning, the partner with the "silly sheet" highlights (or circles) the words missed and tells his or her partner the meaning. The students then reverse rolls.

➔ Using his or her own "silly sheet," each student studies the highlighted or circled words and their definitions. **Alternative**—Divide students into pairs and have them drill each other.

➔ Here comes the hard part. Instruct students to open the right-hand shutter that has the definitions written on the outside. The left-hand shutter remains closed with the words still visible. The definitions no longer are visible since the inside of the right shutter still is blank.

➔ Without peeking at the definitions, students now test themselves and attempt to write the definition of each word on the list on the open right side. When they have written as many definitions as they can, they circle or highlight the blank space of any definition they did not know.

➔ Next, students close both shutters and once again look at the outside right shutter where all the meanings are complete. They then copy the definitions they did not know in the highlighted blank space or circle on the inside of that shutter and (ideally) study the words they missed.

➔ Finally, here comes the true challenge—going from definition to word. Tell students to open the left shutter, thus concealing the vocabulary words. They should now have the full sheet open in front of them with the meanings written on the right side. Instruct students to write the appropriate vocabulary word in the space to the left of each definition.

➔ On the inside of the open "silly sheet," students highlight or circle the empty spaces where they could not supply the vocabulary word to match the given definition.

Activity #3: "Dictionary days"

This is a simple activity that works incredibly well to put great vocabulary words into your students' minds so permanently that they use them in their writing. My students begged to have frequent "dictionary days" because they enjoyed them so much! My colleagues, who did not hold "dictionary days," swore that their students learned the words by osmosis!

Give your students a vocabulary list (any list of great words will do). Then you are ready to begin. Here's how it works.

After students look up the meaning and part of speech of all the words on the list (individually or in groups), ask each student to pick out one word they would like to teach to their peers. Write down each student's word in your gradebook as you do not wish to have two students choose the same word. (One year two students fought over the word "puerile." Kids really get into this activity with a passion.)

A few days before "dictionary day," ask students to plan how they will teach their word and what they will wear to illustrate its meaning to the class. It is a good idea to ask them to do this in writing. Students must think of a clever way to teach the meaning of their word so that their peers will remember it. They also must figure out a way to illustrate the word in their dress and make a large card with the word printed in large letters.

A good example would be how a student dressed for "puerile." She wore her hair in pigtails, dressed like a small child, acted very childish, and carried a borrowed doll. Across her chest in big letters blazed the word "puerile."

Another imaginative student cut his parents' bushes and draped himself in them. The word he put on his green cap in big letters was "bracken," but he could have used "foliage." The student who picked "carnage" used make-up to draw bloody cuts across her face. Another carried a placard proclaiming the end of the world and the word "apocalyptic."

The child who taught "flabbergasted" made her hair stand on end in large clumps and wore a surprised expression on her face all day. The usually talkative student who chose the word "mute" did not say a word all day and communicated by way of note!

A child who taught "perplexed" cut out puzzle pieces, wrote "perplexed" on each one, and taped them all over his clothes. The student who chose "resonant" wrote "echo" all down his arms. One clever (and very lazy) student chose the word "languid." He got one friend to hold a sign with "languid" written on it and another friend to hold his signature sheet. As for him, he slumped lazily in a chair. You will be amazed by how creative your students get.

On the designated day, in addition to wearing clothes and a large card with their word written on it to illustrate the meaning to their class, students also carry a piece of paper (or tape one to their back) on which they have numbered from one to forty (or more if you wish). They must wear their word all day and teach it to, as well as get the signatures of, students you have in any of your classes during the day. They teach their word and get signatures at lunch, in between classes, and in your classroom that day. You can spend the entire class period teaching words and getting signatures.

It is a good idea to warn your colleagues in advance. Since at my school, students changed classes, fellow teachers jumped into the spirit of the day and used the words that they saw emblazoned on my students' bodies. The dean always got into the activity at lunch and pointed out the words and definitions of particularly creative children. All in all, it can be a fun day for all, and everyone learns new words.

Give three grades—one for creativity (a "C" if you have to help the child make his or her costume the morning of "dictionary day"); one for getting the required number of signatures; and the third as a test grade. For the latter, you can simply walk around the room the day following "dictionary day," lists in hand, and ask students who signed the sheet for the meaning of that word. It is a good idea to ask three students per list. If all three know the meaning, the student whom the list belongs to gets an "A." The average test grade usually is an "A+."

Activity #4: Create vocabulary games

Using the words from any vocabulary list you provide, ask students to invent a game to teach the word. Students can work in pairs to make their games. They may invent new games or use an old game board (like Candy Land) for their game. The key is that, before a player is allowed to move, he/she must draw a card with a vocabulary word on it and give the definition. The makers of the game must provide a master list with the words and definitions so that whoever is playing the game can check to see if he/she is correct. The maker(s) of each game also must include directions and all the pieces required for playing.

It is a good idea to spend two to three class periods playing the games. Students like to play each other's games as well as their own.

Activity #5: Disguise drills as games

These six games really are disguised drills and are based on the concept that we need things repeated many times to memorize them. Play these games often enough, and students will learn the words. They are meant to be played for five to ten minutes at a time at the end of a period or before lunch when the students are restless. When my students knew that they were going to play a vocabulary game for five minutes or so at the end of a period, they grew wings and halos because they knew that how diligently they tackled the work or paid attention that period determined how long they got to play the game.

I'm sure you can think of other drills that are easy to implement and disguise as games. If you come up with one and would like to share it with your fellow teachers around the country, please send me the directions, and I will include it in a future book with lots of credit to you as the inventor. Contact me via e-mail at janekiester@comcast.net.

Old-fashioned vocabulary bees:

→ Instead of a spelling bee, hold a vocabulary bee! Line students up against the wall and, in turn, quiz each student on one of the words you have been learning. I suggest only one modification to allow *all* students to experience success: if a student misses the definition, he or she simply goes to the end of the line but is not eliminated from the bee. (Any student who misbehaves, however, can sit down and write the words and meanings.)

→ After everyone has been asked a word and you have arrived at the students who missed the words the first time around, again quiz those students who were sent to the end of the line. But, this time, give them words that you are *certain* they know. If they falter again, give non-verbal clues to help.

→ When I did this, after a quick round or two, I then switched and gave the meanings, and the students had to provide the words. But, when I reached the students who had missed the word (when I gave the definition) and had gone to the end of the line, I switched and gave them the word, asking for the meaning. No student, even the most astute ones, ever caught on that I was doing this. In this manner, no student feels unsuccessful.

Circle of meanings:

➜ Originally this was an activity used in social studies and was called the "circle of knowledge." I saw no reason why it wouldn't work with learning vocabulary as well. There is a trick to this, however, so that your weaker students don't get picked on more than the others.

➜ Divide your students into groups of ten or twelve (so that there are no more than three groups in the class). Each group picks a name, a leader, a recorder, a scorekeeper, and a word keeper.

➜ Hand each group the same list of big, "juicy" vocabulary words (ten to twenty words on the list). Less is more...

➜ Ask each group to look up the meaning and part of speech of the words and then drill each other until they "learn" them. They then pick ten of the words they want to learn "really well." The group studies these words. You will have to check each group's words to make sure that there are few or no repetitions of words among groups. You can, of course, simply assign words to each group.

➜ Now students are ready to play the game. Set up three desks in front of your room. Each group's leader brings the list of ten words and meanings his or her group chose and sits at one of the desks. I liked to post each group's name on the desk. Hand each student a seating chart.

➜ The leaders ask students in other groups, in turn, to define a given word. If the chosen student in the first team to be quizzed cannot give the correct meaning, his/her team receives no points, and the leader who asked the word quizzes someone in the next group. If the student in this latter group does not know the answer, the word goes to someone in the team of the leader who asked the word. If the chosen member of the leader's group cannot correctly give the meaning of the word, his/her team loses a point!

➜ It is very important to keep this game fair and not let your students constantly pick on the weakest learners in the class who still may not know the meanings. In order to instill perfect fairness in the game, I give a copy of my seating chart to every student. As a student is called upon to give a definition, everyone puts a check by that student's name. No leader may call on that student again until all the members of his/her group have been called on to supply a definition. We sometimes played until each student in the class (including the leaders) had been called on at least twice.

➜ Play progresses with a point given for each correct answer until all the words have been asked. It is a good idea to ask leaders to have back-up words in case students really get into this or you goofed when checking the groups' words and there is duplication.

Reach the teach:

→ This is a simple, no-frills game that takes only a few minutes a day and can be played for weeks until your students tire of it or learn the words. Start by putting two masking-tape lines on the floor, one behind the other, with enough space for you to stand in front of them.

→ Pick a volunteer, anyone who raises a hand. Write that student's name on the board and make a mark by it on your seating chart.

→ This student comes to the first masking-tape line you have put down on the floor and picks a peer to challenge. You make a mark by the name of the second student on your seating chart.

→ Both students stand side-by-side with toes on the far line (the second masking-tape line you put down). You stand about two steps in front of the second line and face the students.

→ From your list, choose one word (check it off) and say it out loud. (You may give the definition instead and ask students for the word in return. It is good to vary it.)

→ Students vie to be the first to say the definition or provide the word. The student who first voices the definition steps up to the second line. You say another word or definition. The student who first voices the correct answer moves either up to the second line or to you to share a "high five." Hence the name "reach the teach."

→ Repeat the procedure until one of the two students "reaches the teach." The losing student goes back to his/her seat with applause from the class. Put a mark by the winning student's name on the board to indicate a win.

→ Now comes the complicated part. The winner selects the next contestant from the rest of the class. First the winner must choose from students whose hands are raised who have not yet had a turn in the game. (Your seating chart of checked names will discern who may or may not be chosen at this point.) If no one raises a hand to challenge, the winner then chooses the next "victim" from among students who have not yet had a turn in the game. This ensures that no one hogs the game and no weaker student gets tortured more than once.

→ Each winner may challenge only three people before retiring as a "vocabulary champion." I gave "vocabulary champions" a token prize, and they retired in honor until the next game (which occurs after every student has had a chance to compete). This allows you to have many "vocabulary champions." The notations on the board enable you to remember who the current challenger is in each period (if you have periods) and how many times that student has won.

Throw the bug (or any other small stuffed animal):

→ This simple variation of a drill has no winners, but students enjoy it for the simple element that is different—if a student correctly gives the word or definition, he or she gets to choose the next "victim."

→ Take any list of words for which you want to teach the definition. Get a small bean-bag animal.

→ Pick a student by eye contact. Throw the bean bag animal to that child. Then say one of the vocabulary words or the meaning of one, depending on which you desire. (It is a good idea to mix them up.)

→ If the student says the correct definition or word, he or she gets to choose the next "victim" and throw the bean-bag animal to another student. If a student misses the definition or word, he or she must throw the bean-bag animal back to you, and *you* get to choose the next "victim."

TEACHING NOTE: *You may have to gently remind students to give everyone a turn to be a "victim." Any student who misbehaves, of course, or throws the beanbag too hard is out of the game and writes the words and meanings instead.*

Quizmaster or Eggspert (or something similar):

→ Once again, this is a drill in the disguise of a modified Jeopardy game with buzzes and lights. Whichever version you use, you line up your students with an equal number behind the stations or buzzers or buttons. Ask for a word or a definition. One of the students buzzes. If he or she is correct, that team gets a point. If not, ask the word or meaning again. Then, the next row moves up.

→ If you or your school can afford it, find one of those Quizmasters in a catalogue or on the Internet. You will want to get one that has at least six stations. The cost, however, usually is too much—between $400 and $700. Your school or district already may have one, so ask around. I found one that had been made by a parent for the Math Department! They shared. Another teacher said she found one unused at the county office. You might get lucky.

→ There is a cheaper version of the Quizmaster called Eggspert with six stations (buttons to push). It is available from Learning Experiences at www.learningexperiences123.com (item EI7880).

→ As a super-cheap, no-frills version, some teachers buy eight of those bells used in shops and hotels to get someone's attention. They have these little buttons on top that depress to make a short ring of the bell. I preferred to have my students call out "ANNNNHHHHHH" (or something like that) in a nasal tone. All the bells sounded alike, but each of my students had a distinct voice. Besides, using voices is even cheaper!

→ Either way, you have to do without the lights, but how do you know which student rang his or her team's bell or "mouth-buzzed" first? Well, instead of lights, you can use student spotters. Choose different student spotters each time. For fairness, put one student on either side of you to listen and watch to see who "mouth-buzzed" first. It also is a good idea to use masking tape (if your custodians don't object) to mark the eight spots on the floor.

The Rassias Method:

→ This is another simple drill based on the idea by John Rassias, a Dartmouth professor, who had to invent ways to teach young people languages for the Peace Corps. Students don't like this one as much as the other games, but it is fast-paced and very effective. In 1967, Dr. Rassias's idea was that the faster students had to come up with the meaning of a foreign word, the better they knew the word and its definition in English. The same applies for English words and definitions.

→ Before staring this game, warn your students that they must pay attention to you as you will not call their names but instead will use a finger to point to them. They will have one second to think of the word or definition (depending on which you provide).

→ Keeping a mental log of the students you call on to make sure you include all your students (the kids will keep you straight), point to a child sitting at a random place in the room and say a word (or the meaning of a word).

→ If the student gives the correct meaning (or word) in less than one second, move on to another student at random with another word or meaning.

→ If, however, the student misses the meaning or word, move to the person next to or behind or in front of that student, depending on how your classroom is set up. Keep pointing to and asking students the meaning of the word until someone gives the correct definition. The key here is to keep going in an orderly direction so that you can remember on whom you have called.

→ Keep pointing to students, repeating the word or definition for each student who missed the word until you return to the first student who was asked. Each of these students must repeat the definition after you say the word. This goes in rapid-fire succession. You point—say word—student repeats meaning—you point to next student, etc.

→ Follow the same procedure with a new word. This game can be played until the bell rings. There is no time limit and no winner.

Using Quotations

Once students learn to punctuate quotes consistently, using quotations or brief conversations in their essays and narratives is a natural consequence. And, because students (especially in the grade targeted for your state's writing assessment test) need to stockpile some "re-memorable" quotations to use, it is a good idea to introduce them to some good quotes they can put in their essays.

To this end, I began posting a "quote of the week" on a three-by-five-inch whiteboard bought for just that purpose. Students had to make a section at the beginning of their notebooks just for those quotes. We discussed each quote as it appeared, briefly analyzed what it meant, and talked about why it might be memorable. Sometimes I provided some biographical information as well.

Having a "quote of the week" soon catches on with students (and some of their parents). You will find that students begin bringing in quotes they or their parents found and liked. If you receive a lot of suggestions any given week, your students can vote on which quote to use for that week or a committee of students can choose the quote, sifting through the pile of suggestions.

Initially, though, the "quote of the week" does not, to say the least, excite students. They do not like copying the quotes even though there is only one a week, and they just don't see the point of the exercise.

As the weeks roll on, and some neat quotes appear, you will find that your students will begin to show interest. After being rewarded for using the quotes in their essays, students will wax even more enthusiastic. Eventually, they will begin bringing in quotes for you to use. Underneath the quotes my students had found, I always put the name of the student who had supplied it. *That* was popular, and students went out of their way to try to find really "rad" quotes so that theirs would be used as the "quote of the week."

Where does one find quotes that appeal to students? There are myriad book sources—too many to name. You might want to check some out on Amazon. There are great quotes in doctors' offices, in newspapers, in novels (a few really popular ones even came from a Harlequin Romance about a teacher!). Mark Twain and Benjamin Franklin produced hundreds of pithy remarks worthy of quotation. I subscribe to a weekly newsmagazine which has a section of memorable quotations. Once you begin looking, the quotes just jump out at you. I was not above quoting one or two of my own "famous" sayings (or those of a colleague) in order to encourage my students to come up with some original ones of their own.

While not required to do so, students memorized the quotes they particularly liked. An overall favorite was one I found on the wall in a doctor's office. A Mohawk Indian woman had said it to President Theodore Roosevelt. "When you have fished all the fish from the sea, when you have shot all the buffalo, when you have cut down all the trees in the forest, I hope you can eat your money."

Whenever my students received a prompt that had anything to do with the environment, many of them used that quote to illustrate a point or serve as a dynamite ending.

Another quote students latched onto was one by Mark Twain. "There is no difference between the man who chooses not to read and the man who can not read." When the county-wide practice prompt asked students to write an essay explaining why it was important to read well, three-quarters of my students admitted (with much pride) that they had used that quote somewhere in the essay!

The year the "quote of the week" became a part of my curriculum, the average of my students' scores on the state writing assessment test went up a notch! After the test, student after student came to tell me what vocabulary and quote they had used on the test. They were so proud. Neat!!!

Memorizing Poetry to Use in Writing

Poetry that students memorize (and therefore "own") also can be stockpiled for use as quotations—only this time the quotes are useful and memorable lines from poems. For that reason (and several others), for more than thirty years I required my students to memorize classical poems. The idea came from the traditional British education system. In 1962, I spent my senior year of high school in England and attended a British school where my English, French, and German teachers each required us to memorize and then recite classical poems in front of the class.

More than forty years later, I still can recite (if anyone ever is interested) poems by Goethe (in German), Verlaine (in French), and Shakespeare (in English), among others. While it isn't a marketable skill, memorizing classical poems in school really can be useful to lessen the fear of public speaking.

Since our students (even at a very young age) memorize all kinds of awful lyrics to songs, they certainly can give a little brain power to memorizing poems by poets like Emily Dickinson who offers some memorable lines and metaphors. Therefore, you can pick poems that you like yourself and then require your students to memorize and recite them in front of the class.

Rather than proceeding in the traditional British fashion of making students copy a poem and then memorize it on their own, it is better to memorize each poem together as a class. It proves fairly painless and students, especially the struggling ones in drop-out prevention classes, delight in the effortless ease with which they memorize the poems.

Years later, visiting students informed me that at high-school parties attended by my former students, they enjoyed reciting in unison the poems they had memorized in middle school. Others "complained" that even after graduating from college, like me, they couldn't get one or more of those poems out of their heads.

What did we do? I told them about "Kiester's sure-fire, secret, rock-star, study method of successful memorizing." Actually, it is a method used by professional singers that I discovered in my youth when I was a folk/rock singer in the San Francisco area in the 1960s. (I must add that I also was a graduate student at the time.)

To stand up before a crowd of people and sing that first song totally unnerved me until a performer with much more experience imparted the secret of erasing the "first-song jitters." Essentially, the method is to repeat and repeat (even after you know it well) the first song you plan to perform so that when stage fright turns your mind to mush, your mouth belts out those words anyway. Once you successfully get through the first song, the jitters evaporate. Piano teachers have used this method for eons with their young students—repeat a piece often enough, and you can perform it in your sleep.

The moment the bell stops ringing, you and your students recite the current poem you (or they as a group) have chosen. At first, say the poem a line at a time with students repeating each line after you. Then, when a bunch of them start murmuring the lines twice (once with you and once with their peers), stop saying the poem line in the repeat-line-repeat fashion, and just recite the entire poem *with* the students. Do this daily for about a month.

Reinforce this with homework. Now I am not naive enough to believe that students will voluntarily do homework for which there is no accountability, but there is a devious way to catch the interest of most children and young adults. You can give the homework assignment, "give up an ad for English." Students make an additional copy of the poem they currently are memorizing. Then they discuss which TV ad they detest the most and why. Each student then writes down his or her most despised TV advertisement on the top of the extra copy of the poem.

Next, students are supposed to tape that second copy of the poem near the TV set at home. I challenged my students to read the poem (or recite it after they had memorized it) *every* time that TV ad came on. The kids had a grand time, driving their parents batty. For the most part, the parents were delighted to hear their child recite a poem by Langston Hughes or Emily Dickinson although they reported that they tired of hearing it again and again.

You veteran teachers know that there's always a student or two who will find a loophole in any assignment. Each year, there usually is at least one student who (truthfully sometimes but not so truthfully most of the time) maintained that he or she *never* watched TV. Since TV watching in *our* house ended at six p.m. on school nights and was limited on weekends, clearly some parents do nix television. Of course, there is an answer to this protest.

You can ask those students who "never watch TV" or who "do not have a TV in their homes" to announce to their families that their crazy English teacher insists that they recite (or read) this poem every night before taking a bite of supper. My students reported that the nightly recitals at the dinner table drove their parents nuts. Kids of any age love this! Many of those who did admit to watching television also instituted the poem recital at dinner just for torture purposes.

Ignore the motives; just enjoy the results. You will find that students will permanently memorize classical poems painlessly and quickly. It is helpful to keep repeating the poem daily in class even after every student already has memorized it. Keep up the repetition so that the poem enters students' permanent memory banks and will be able to recite them forty years from now.

From tracking the number of times I repeated a concept that I wanted my students to learn, it became obvious that students with learning disabilities sometimes require things to be repeated a hundred times. Like the piano recitals where, when the piece departs the mind from panic but the fingers keep on going from practice, the majority of students easily recite the poem in front of their peers on the day of the "test." Students will have repeated the poem so many times in the six weeks prior to the test that the words come almost involuntarily. During this "test," I asked each student in turn to stand up at the podium and recite the poem. Of course, some people suffer from stage fright to varying degrees.

To allay nervousness and fear, those extremely tense students can clutch onto a friend for comfort. Some really nervous ones can be allowed to turn their backs to the class. One of my students, a dancer, felt better reciting her poems while doing a split. It seems that she had practiced them in that position. You also can provide non-verbal clues to jog a panicked child's memory of a word. No one will object as the panic was always obvious on that student's face.

And, what do you do for the child who shakes and turns pale and looks as if she is going to vomit on the floor? Tell the class that they can talk to each other quietly while that student recites the poem close enough for you to hear above the din. By the third poem of the year, that student usually is confident enough from past successes to recite the poem in front of his or her silent peers. Ninety-five percent of the students received an "A" on the test. After all, the purpose of allowing these bizarre variations was for students to experience success.

I asked those few who did poorly to tell me the truth for research purposes (and for the chance for a re-test with only ten points off)—had they ever said the poem at home? They almost always replied in the negative. Conclusion: repetition works!

We memorized a poem about every six weeks or so, requiring me to choose six poems for each grade level taught for each year. Which poems to choose? Those I loved, of course, but I also read many other poems to my students so that they could have a say in the choice as well.

I recommend that you begin with poems you love, then get your students excited, read poetry to them just for fun, and let them pick some that *they* like (with the requirement that they had to be written by classical poets such as Emily Dickinson, Langston Hughes, Robert Frost, Walt Whitman, Gwendolyn Brooks, etc.). Someone always wanted to do Poe, but his poems are too long. Twenty-four lines in a poem was a good length limit. It was important that *all* my students experienced success, and keeping the poem length to a minimum helped guarantee this.

The biggest thrill, of course, is to hear your students falling in love with and reciting your favorite poems and complaining that they "just can't get that poem out of their head." Once students thoroughly memorize a poem, they "own" it and can call lines and phrases up at will. With a little encouragement, your students will use those lines and phrases from the poems in an essay as a quote or literary reference. If they do this on the state writing assessment test, it almost certainly will improve their scores.

Threading a Theme

Threading a theme is one of the most sophisticated (and difficult) skills to use in writing. It must be skillfully done (and not forced), or the essay or narrative will be stilted and illogical. Your good writers probably can learn to do this with a little prompting and practice if the topic they are writing about lends itself to a theme. But, they will not be able to do it consistently.

To thread a theme throughout an essay or narrative, first you need to find one. It could be an idea, an emotion, a word, a short phrase, or a brief question that dovetails with the topic of the paper. It can be as simple as the word "smell" when the topic is about lunchroom food or "Tinker Bell" when the topic of a narrative includes flashing lights or magic. It can be an allusion to ballet (or any sport) woven through almost any personal narrative. It can be as simple as the use of onomatopoeia like "click" in an expository topic. It could be the word "computer" in almost any essay or imaginative narrative that has to do with technology. It could be the repeated question "Why not?" or "What if?" It could be a bird metaphor. The list is endless. The problem is coming up with a theme that sounds natural and can be threaded through a short piece of writing.

In novels, threading a theme or idea is easier as you have more plot or points through which to work. Dickens, for example, is known for his theme of poverty. Every novel he wrote touches on it. Victor Hugo always threaded in or based his novels on social agendas such as unfair imprisonment of people. J. K. Rowling threads many less broad themes. Harry's scar always is mentioned. Friendship among Harry, Ron, and Hermione is an important theme as is the responsibility and rules of using magic. In *Charlotte's Web*, of course, the theme is the web itself and friendship.

Threading a theme in a short essay or narrative of fewer than three pages entails using that word, short phrase, idea, or brief question repeatedly in the writing, in almost every paragraph. My students who were capable of threading a theme used very simple ones. Remember the young lady who wrote to convince her environmentalist father (who refused to have a cut-down tree for Christmas) to buy a real tree for the beautiful forest smell? She used the words "forest" and "aroma" throughout her essay, and every paragraph had something about smell.

Unfortunately, there is no easy way to teach threading a theme into writing. And, because the majority of writers are not capable of doing it, you can't do a class assignment. Instead, after explaining about threading a theme, you can issue a challenge to your good writers (privately, of course).

First, find some examples of a narrative or essay that use the technique, and read them to the class. I suggest using Marcia Freeman's book *Listen to This: Developing an Ear for Expository* (Maupin House, 1997). The essay on page 106, for example, about the use of big words, uses all one-syllable words. The poem on page 76 begins most lines with the same phrase. On page 41, the word "silk" is used in almost every paragraph. There are other examples as well in that book.

Next, *you* tell the students what theme to thread throughout a particular essay or narrative. For example, let's look at the essay topic, "What is your favorite time of the year? Explain why." You could challenge your good writers to use the symbol of the season they pick—heat for summer, leaves for fall, snow for winter, and flowers for spring. If the topic is something like, "Convince a friend to move to your town," you could challenge your students to use the question "Why not?"

Then I suggest that you also meet with your better writers in a small group while the rest of the class is otherwise occupied. With that small group, you could name a topic (the one they will write next) and elicit possible themes from the group, getting students to think of some on their own.

Finally, the only other thing I can think of is to practice, practice, practice. None of my students, even my most sophisticated writers, could consistently thread a theme throughout everything they wrote. But, the skill, once mastered, is a valuable one that dramatically improves writing and helps to earn the highest scores on the writing test.

Taking Different Viewpoints in Essays and Stretching the Truth in Narratives

Writing from a different point of view in essays

Often, when someone (even professional writers) writes on a given essay topic, it is difficult to expand and elaborate on that topic. Or, the writer feels strongly one way or another, but support for that point of view is hard to come by. We all have strong feelings which we express when we write. It is difficult enough for adults to write from a point of view other than their own. With children, the problem is compounded because they feel it is so important to express *their* side of an issue.

A prime example occurred in 1993, the first year of the writing test in my state. The eighth-grade persuasive topic asked students to argue whether the school year should be extended by ten days. Not surprisingly, an overwhelming number of students tried to argue against extending the year. In discussions with my students after the test, most conceded that they could have more easily thought of better arguments to support the other point of view, especially since the topic suggested extending the school year by only ten days.

That year, the persuasive scores were significantly lower than the expository scores, probably due to the fact that most students (including mine) who got that topic wrote what they felt, not what they had persuasive arguments to support.

The following year, a similar topic was given, but this time my students (as well as students of other teachers) were ready to take either side of the argument before they wrote. In fact, many students confided after the test that they heartily disagreed with what they had written but had taken the point of view that they could better support with more convincing arguments. After all, they had heard the adults in their lives use those arguments time and time again. Students' scores on the persuasive essay rose considerably that year.

The problem also is similar for expository essays. It is a fact of life, I think, that students will detest the prompt they get on the test and not wish to "waste their time" writing about it. Warn students of this, and then repeat this homily many times so that, hopefully, on the day of the test, they will say to themselves, "Gee, this isn't such a bad topic." They just have to learn to "keep their cool" and write away! Read on for a few ideas about how to train your students to take an "unpopular" stand.

The first thing you have to do is convince your students that no one who knows them or their school and no one who matters to them is going to grade the writing test. Only adults they never are going to meet are even going to see the paper. And, as you know, adult opinions don't count.

Once you convince your students that it is OK to take a view that their peers would disagree with, you can talk about taking the side on an expository or persuasive essay that could be easily supported with detail, regardless of whether the students agreed with that point of view. This is a hard concept for young people to grasp. They have to get away from the typical knee-jerk reactions which often get them into trouble in real life as well as in the essays they write. To that end, we teachers must accustom them to take whichever side of a topic they can support the most convincingly with the most details.

Activity #1: Arguing both sides of a persuasive essay. This activity will help your students organize their ideas and convincingly write to support both sides of an argument for a persuasive essay.

Begin by having the entire class (in a whole-class discussion) come up with arguments to support an unpopular topic, such as to lengthen the school year, require uniforms, put girls and boys into separate schools, or require alphabetical seating in all classes or assigned seating in the lunchroom, etc.

Write the arguments on the board. Then, using those arguments, cluster the popular point of view with your students. Cluster the opposite side as well in order to show students that the important thing is not which side they take but that they attack the topic from the side they can support best, whether they agree with it or not.

After clustering both sides of several topics in this manner at least three times, give students another unpopular topic like "Should homework be assigned on weekends?" or "Should school uniforms be required?" or "Should students be allowed to wear hats (or whatever is forbidden at your school)?" I'm sure you can think of many. You also can ask your students to suggest some ideas.

Then divide students into groups of four, and assign half of the groups to find support for the unpopular side and the other half to find support for the popular one. Discuss the results. It is a good idea to do this several times so that all students experience both sides. Switch sides on the same prompt.

Next, assign another topic and ask students, individually this time, to plan both sides of the topic. Discuss the results as a class (which side they could support the best). It might be a good idea to time your students as they plan since you don't want them to get into the habit of spending too much time planning. Ten minutes per side of the topic should be sufficient. At this point, students are not writing the essays. If you have enough transparencies, have students put their plans on them and share them, using the overhead projector. It helps students to see their peers' ideas.

Finally, assign prompts and tell students which side to take. This time, they are to plan and write essays. Vary the tack. Sometimes make students write the unpopular opinion and other times make them argue the side they, themselves, would probably naturally choose.

Activity #2: Writing from a different point of view in expository essays. For students to be able to look at an expository prompt and write from the angle they can support (rather than the one they personally agree with), you will need to change their thinking. To be able to do this, students will need to cluster and write the same prompt from several different angles. You can tell them which angle they are required to take. You may not be popular sometimes, but when students can weigh different viewpoints on a topic (especially the ones which use the word "favorite") and decide on the one they can best support, writer's block often disappears. This activity will help students accomplish that goal.

Take the prompt which asks students to explain why their "favorite season" is their favorite season. Ask students to plan an essay for each of the four seasons. They are not to write the essays at this point, only plan them. It will take several days to come up with all four plans.

In pairs, students look at all four plans and pick the one (regardless of which season) that shows the most detail. Students then write an essay using that plan.

This can be repeated with any prompt where the students must make a choice. You will need to make a list of at least four choices on the board.

Here are some typical prompts that ask students to make a choice:

➜ If you could trade places with anyone for a day, who would you be and why?

➜ If you could go anywhere, where would you go and why?

➜ Think of a place you like to go. Explain why you like to go there.

➜ Any prompt that asks students to pick a favorite of something—favorite sport, season, toy, subject, pastime, thing to do after school, etc.

Taking a true story and expanding it into fiction for narratives

The only way to get students to do this is to give examples, make them practice, and convince them that all writers start with a kernel of truth (like finding a web in a barn with a pig for *Charlotte's Web*) and expand on it, stretching that truth into a story.

Try these tips:

➜ Take any event that happens in your classroom or school. It could be an assembly, a fight (horror), a tornado that is nearby (happened to me), a field trip, a wasp (bird) that flies into the classroom, a big cockroach that scurries across a desk (or the floor), etc. Orally with your students, go over what really happened. Then (with you taking notes at the board) elicit embellishments from your students. In other words, take a true event into the realm of fiction by adding to it. Do this a few times with different subjects. You will have lots of ideas and notes on the board. If you wish, you then can ask students to write a narrative using some of these embellishments.

→ Have students make a list of memorable events in their lives. Then ask them to write events and details they can add to embellish those true stories. Finally, they can write a story using a combination of truth and fiction.

→ And, of course, you can write or tell a story of your own, informing students where and how you embellished the truth to come up with a good story that sounds as if it really happened (personal narrative). For example, I wrote a story about a pig who came to the back door of my house as I was leaving for work (truth). The end of the story was that the last time I saw the pig (Rosie—fiction), she was galumphing down the road just ahead of a police car that had its sirens blaring and lights flashing. One of the policemen in the car was leaning out the window shouting "Sooey." These two events were true and made a great story, but there was nothing that happened in between the two events to flesh it out. Everything I wrote in between the pig showing up at the back door and the police car incident was pure fiction (except wondering how my principal would react to my excuse for being late to school...). I'm sure you can think of some startling (and funny) events in your life that can be fleshed out with a little imagination.

Writing with Passion

No essay or narrative is going to be interesting unless it is written with passion and enthusiasm. It is good to start early, encouraging students to write with fervor (sounding a bit enthusiastic yourself at the thought). I liked to ask my students after each practice, "Now, who wrote that last essay with passion? Who threw his/her heart and soul into the paper?" A few hands of your boldest students invariably will go up (since this is a good thing to have done). You can then continue the brief discussion about how they felt as they wrote.

One of my former teaching colleagues, Tim McShane, stresses "passion in writing" to his students on a daily basis. His students obviously follow his advice since they score well on the state writing assessment. His theory is that without passion, there is no really good writing. I agree. The high scores are awarded only to those whose papers followed the few mandatory guidelines (the "walls") and then demonstrated verve and passion for the subject.

When *we* enthuse over something and show passion and excitement for what we are teaching, our *students* sit up and listen. It is the same for writing. Now, no one denies that the prompts for the writing test (which by necessity have to be very generic and thus boring) do not lend themselves to evoking any feelings of passion in the writer. However, students can be shown how to produce passion in their writing even when it is faked. They can become enthused about writing itself and learn to look at a dull topic with different eyes.

The following are some suggestions to encourage passion in writing:

➜ Read students' selections (from anywhere) that were written with passion and flair. Reading examples of passionately written essays and narratives to the class also can help raise enthusiasm for otherwise rather dull-sounding efforts. Good examples of peer writing efforts often can spark better writing than examples written by adults.

➜ Encourage passion in writing and note it when students demonstrate it.

➜ Submit student essays and narratives that demonstrate passion to whoever does the morning announcements. If students hear passionate writing written by their peers, they may try to emulate it.

➜ Be passionate yourself about writing. Read anything you have written that demonstrates passion for the subject.

➜ Hold a pep rally for writing. If you find that your students lack enthusiasm or cannot passionately get into their essays (this is especially true at the high-school level), a pep rally for writing is in order! Have students sit on the floor with you and talk about things that they could write passionately about. Have them visualize feeling strongly enough about the topic to be able to write passionately. Hold a real pep rally, complete with signs and chants. This works well in middle and elementary school, too. After all, they hold pep rallies for sports.

➜ On the day before the writing test, dress up and become a god or goddess for high scores. Be very dramatic. Spread "magic high-scoring dust" liberally, and pass out "magic mints" or little stars that remind students to show enthusiasm for an otherwise dull prompt. Get them excited! This activity has the added effect of making the test less frightening and intimidating by giving students a "talisman" to promote good writing (the mint or star). Believe it or not, this works well for high-school students as well as for the younger crowd. It was started at the middle-school level.

Writer's Pizzazz

The following pages contain a partial list of the pizzazz and flair that writers use to keep their readers hooked and interested. Some are simple to teach, and others will require much practice on the part of your students in order to implement correctly and effectively in their writing. These little tricks put passion and flair into writing and earn young writers the highest scores on the writing assessment tests.

Use the following pages with your students however you wish. I suggest that you introduce some of these devices through the use of Caught'yas, through the vocabulary games discussed previously, through reading examples in literature, and through frequent practice.

If you and your students have followed the four steps explained in this book, they will be on their way to higher scores on your state writing assessment test. If nothing else, the frequent writing practice, the exposure to many writing ideas, and the constant encouragement of an enthusiastic teacher will boost the writing of your poorest producers and incite your best writers to soar! The end result will be better writing fluency for all, and that, of course, is the true goal.

How a Writer Dazzles a Reader

anecdote — A story within a story to catch the reader's fancy

catchy title — A title that creates interest or arouses curiosity

dialogue — This can come in many forms, with or without a tag. It can be repartee (quick and witty), vernacular (the language of the people), or just an ordinary conversation.

figurative language — Literary conventions that add creativity and flair to writing. Here are some of the most common examples:

➔ **personification** — Giving an inatimate object the characteristics of a human being (The leaves danced in the wind.)

➔ **similes** — A comparison, usually between two unlike things, using "like" or "as" (The leaves moved like dancers.)

➔ **metaphor** — An implicit comparison, usually between two unlike things (The green ballerinas danced in the wind.)

➔ **alliteration** — Repetition of the same sounds, often at the beginning of words (The lovely leaves leapt from their lofty perch.)

➔ **onomatopoeia** — Words that imitate sounds ("Cough, cough," spluttered the sick child.)

➔ **oxymoron** — Words put together that have opposite meanings (jumbo shrimp)

foreign language — If a writer knows a bit of a foreign language, such as a commonly known phrase like "Hola," this can be very effective. All of us teach students for whom English is not their native tongue. This device allows them to use that to their advantage. They must, though, always translate into English.

grabber or hook — This is a way of introducing an essay or narrative that wakes up the reader, grabs his/her attention, and makes him/her want to read more. A grabber can be in the form of a question, a quick dialogue of some sort (usually untagged), onomatopoeia, a quote, etc.

humor — This can be a witty phrase, a short joke, a funny incident that is related to the narrative or essay, or anything that would amuse the reader.

literary allusion — Referring to commonly known books; this is always effective.

nitty-gritty detail — Detail can come in many forms, but no broad statement (for example, "I have a nice house") should be made without being followed by detail that lets you know about what is in the statement. This can be in the form of a brief story, a description, an anecdote, a list of attributes, etc.

painting word pictures — Strong, active verbs evoke vivid descriptions that paint pictures so clear, the reader has no trouble imagining those pictures in his/her mind. Victor Hugo and Charles Dickens were masters of this technique.

quotes — The use of quotes, whether from the author, from people the author knows, from memorized poems, or from well-known people, is always a good way to add pizzazz. ("The sun rose a ribbon at a time." — Emily Dickinson)

sensory words — These are words that elucidate writing. ("The tangy smell of pungent salsa permeated the room.)

"showing," not "telling" writing — This is a technique used to avoid vague statements like "The girl was frightened." Instead, a frightened girl is "shown" to the reader. For example: "The frightened girl quivered as her knees knocked together, her throat closed up, and her mouth lost all moisture. She could not even scream her terror."

sound words — Sound words can mimic any sound you hear. For example, "toot toot" for the sound of a tugboat or "thbbbth" for a "raspberry." These also are called onomatopoeia.

strong, active verbs — These verbs say "The cat sprawled in the chair" rather than "The cat was in the chair."

threading a theme — An idea, word, question, etc. that is woven throughout writing, such as the web in Charlotte's Web that is mentioned on almost every page.

unusual transitions — See **Transitions** on page 86 in **Step Three** for some excellent examples.

zinger — This is an ending that zings the reader so that he/she is surprised, provoked to think, or made to laugh or cry.

90 Examples for Scoring Practice

On the following pages are nine sets of examples: one set of narratives from a fourth-grade class at an elementary school in Gainesville, Florida; one set of expository papers from fourth-graders at an elementary school in Marco Island, Florida; two expository sets from eighth-grade language arts classes (one regular and one advanced) from middle schools in Gainesville, Florida; one set of descriptive papers from seventh-graders at a middle school in Brevard, North Carolina; one set of persuasive and one set of narrative examples from seventh-graders at a middle school in Naples, Florida; one set of persuasive essays from a "regular" tenth-grade English class at a high school in Gainesville, Florida; and one set of expository examples from the "regular" tenth-grade students at a high school in Naples, Florida.

I included four sets of expository examples because expository writing is the most common genre required of all grade levels (including exit exams). In addition, I wanted to have examples of some of the varied types of expository writing. For the narrative sets, I did not include any high-school examples because most states do not require narratives at the high-school level. Similarly, I only included two sets of persuasive writing because only a few states require this genre for elementary-age students.

The papers were typed basically as the students wrote them, egregious spelling errors and all. I did, however, remove all specific school names and replace them with "our school" or "my school."

Some of the classes from which I obtained examples did not contain any "advanced" students and included many for whom English was not their native language. I must tell you, though, that all the teachers who provided the samples had worked very diligently with their students to ensure that they wrote well. Thus, when reading through sets of papers from class after class to find examples for this book, I discovered that finding papers with the lowest scores was difficult. The students had learned well, even in the classes where there were no "advanced" students and the poorest writers had not been taken out to join a basic-skills class. Most of the papers I read were in the medium range with a fair number of highs to choose from.

I encountered two problems when choosing the samples that were on the persuasive topics. One was that students often mistakenly wrote an expository essay (although well-written), and, on the problem/solution essay, many students looked at the word "problems" and never got to proposing any solutions. Again, though, the results were fairly well-written. See pages 76-83 in **Step Three** for four tips to help your students avoid these problems.

All but the descriptive essays were scored on the low-medium-high scale. Those papers were scored on a scale of 1 to 4 and had been scored officially (from those days when teachers used to get back their students' tests for practice with future students—names removed).

All the examples are grouped by type of writing, not by grade. I did this deliberately to encourage you to use them all, no matter what your grade level. Good writing is good writing no matter how old the writer. And, as you know, some fourth-graders write better than some tenth-graders. In case you feel strongly about scoring only papers of the level you teach, I will tell you that within each genre, I did put the elementary examples first, followed by the middle- and then high-school examples. In both high schools, though, the more advanced writers are not in the "regular" classes, so all the papers from that level are from "average" or "below-average" students. A good number of these examples were written by students who were not brought up speaking English.

I was impressed with the quality of writing of the students and with the obvious hard work the teachers had put in to teach their students to write well!

No matter what grade level you teach, you can use all of these examples to teach scoring to your students, just as you can use all of the examples to improve your students' writing. I have found that the quality of most examples is surprisingly similar from grade to grade. The good papers are good, and the poor ones are poor. The poor fourth-grade samples are less sophisticated but no worse than the poor eighth-and tenth-grade ones. Similar spelling and grammatical errors occur in all three grades. In fact, one of the examples in the tenth-grade set is from a student I had taught in the eighth grade. He doggedly still was making some of the same errors he did when I taught him!

Please note that after each set of examples, you will find a section with the holistic score for each paper in the set and a brief reason for each score, as well as a domain score sheet where the holistic score has been broken down into domains. For example, a rather poor paper that received an overall score of "low" could receive a "high" under focus on the domain chart for sticking to the topic without any extraneous information.

To make it more realistic for you, I have mixed up the order of the examples so that high and low scores are not simply grouped together. After you have scored each example, you can find its corresponding score that my colleagues and I assigned to see how your grading compares. Remember, too, we teachers tend to score lower than the official scorers.

Do not be dismayed if you disagree with us. Judges do disagree. That is why there are split scores (like 4.5 on a 1- to 6-point scale) in some states—because each judge gave a different score to the same essay. When you score the papers, if you are consistently off by a level, go back to **Step Two** and read once more the required elements of each score. Of course, it is better to err on the side of scoring low because your students always can use more practice.

11 Descriptive Examples

> **NOTE #1:** On the CD, each genre (descriptive, expository, narrative, and persuasive) has its own folder with each sample set in its own file. Each student sample is on a separate page within the file to make it easier for you to print individual examples. As in the book, the rubrics and scoring analyses follow each set of student samples.

> **NOTE #2:** Although states no longer do this, these particular examples were scored in the mid-1990s by the official scorers in North Carolina and sent back to teachers. North Carolina required that descriptions be mostly visual and scores on a scale of **1** to **4**. This score does not include the conventions, which are scored separately. If your state uses a rubric of **1** to **5** or **1** to **6**, you easily can translate a **1** to a low score, a **2** to a low to medium score, a **3** to a medium score, and a **4** to a high score.

Topic for Sample Set: "Describe a place where you go to have fun so that your reader can picture it."

Example #1

Chirp, chirp, those are just some of the wonderful sounds that you hear at a fun place like the beach.

At the beach you can her the soothing sounds of the ocean waves hitting the ocean floor. When it is dark and silent outside, you can hear the ocean banging on the shore, it sounds like someone is shooting a rifle. You will be awoken by the yelling and screaming of kids on the beach. It sounds like you are at a big carnival. If you look out of your hotel window you can see all kinds of people running everywhere. Some are even playing vollyball or tennis but those aren't all the things you can do on a hot windy day at the beach. There are even sounds of birds singing. Birds are all different colors there like rainbow's floating high in the windy sky. The birds eat bread and seeds off of the dark brown sand.

The sand is rough like sandpaper, when you run on it with just you're bare feet. The seashells make it hard to walk on in some places. Beneath you're feet the sand feels cold from the ocean water, you can feel the sand comeing up between you're tired little toes. When you walk on the sand at night you have to watch out for the night crawlers, such as little birds, snails, and pincher's. If you stand on the sand close to the water it feels like you're flouting for a second.

The ocean floor is sometimes rough because of the jagged shells and rocks. If you go further out you can feel the smooth sinsation of the soft and smushy ocean floor. If you watch you can see big white looking fish jump out of the water, like something down there is going to eat them. There is sometimes dolphines further out in the ocean that jump up and scwigle like they've never scwigled before. The ocean tastes like someone just poored five million gallons of salt in the water. The ocean fills the hole air with the fragrinte of salt.

If you have never been to the beach you might want to think about going. It is a wonderful place to be and have fun at. If everyone who go's to the beach likes it I know you will.

Example #2

Aah, hey watch it, swish! These are all sounds you would hear if you went to Franklin Park. At Franklin there's a slide, merry-go-round, Jungle Jym.

In front of you when you first go to Franklin is the slide. The slide has a nice cool feeling on a hot summer day. The slide it's self is silver. But the ladder to climb up is a old orange-red color. The "waiting area" is a nice deep blue that makes you feel like going swimming. And the poles to the side are like royal blue hands lightly touching the ground. Yet the slide is so high up that it seems as if you could touch the baby blue cloudless sky. To your right though is the merry-go-round.

I like the merry-go-round the best (Ol' Rusty). Ol' Rusty he's the fast thing you have ever set on (if you've never been on a roller coster) and on him it seems as if you could go on forever and ever. I like Ol' Rusty's wooden seats they're about the color of a weather washed board. And the rust on the medal makes you just want to sit not spin. I love Ol' Rusty. I just wouldn't suggest anyone with a weak stomach to go on or you wouldn't have to worry about staying there much longer. Many people sit were Ol' Rusty's the fastest his middle. To the far back of the park is Jungle Gym.

Now Jungle Gym, he can be one of the most frustrating things you have ever seen. All the up's and downs. But hey he's eye catching. Jungle Gym has a red latter, blue latter, orange latter. Boy I even think he's got a green one. I think he's got five or six latters. He is very peculiar of who gets one him. If he don't like the child Gym will have him lost in a second. But if he like the child he'll let him get to the pole to slide down with no problem's at all. The pole is at the end of the Jungle Gym and is rainbow colored.

Franklin Park is one of the most exiting places to ever be but on the earth. From slides, to merry-go-rounds, and even a Jungle Gym.

Example #3

Have you ever been to a pulcurtudinous park that had a pool, a snack bar, and a ice cream truck that promenetly came at 3:32 p.m. Well I have and I want to describe it to you so you can understand it better.

Click, Clat, Click, Clat, Click, that's what you will hear about 12:00 pm if your wating in line at Franklin Park. As soon as you walk in the door you see a woman sitting in a chair behind glass saying one dollar kids, two dollar's adults. To your imediet left is the boy's bathroom. And to your imediet right is the girl's bathroom. The room the woman is in is a square room, you can walk all the way around it. On the other side of the woman is a snack bar it has Reesies, rice cryspy treet's, Snickers, Peps, Mountain Dew, life Savers, and Crunch Bars.

Blue water, cement suroandings, life gourd stands is what you will find if you go strait away from the snack Bar. It is and outside Pool about 9 ft deep in the deep end and about 3 ft deep in the shallow end. It has a rope with flotaition devices on it in the middle of the Pool. The Pool is surounded By a 6 foot tall fence.

About 3:32 pm every day you hear ding, ping, tong, and that meens the ice cream truck is coming so every body gets there money and rushes up the steps, out the door to catch the ice cream man. "Stop" the kids scream, and the ice cream man stops. Everyone is saying I want chocolate, I want strawberry. I want vanilia. And the ice cream man say's o'kay, o'kay one at a time, so everybody gets there ice cream and goe's back to the Pool to get cooled of agian.

In conclusion, go to Franklin Park to have the best time of your life in just one day.

Example #4

Splash! Many kids jump into the enormous lake at the Southside Park. Many people come here to have a great time. Some people come to swim in the lake, others to work out in the gym. People even come to go in the woods. All of the places are fun.

The lake is a great place to have fun. A whole lot of people can come to swim because the beautiful lake is about the size of three football fields. Standing from the fifty docks where the boats are boarded, you can see the ground because the water is so clean and clear. Across the lake from the docks there is a rope swing that is azure blue and brings you high into the air. About 20 feet away from the swing there is a rock that has water gushing over it. It is great to slide down into the chilling water. Above the rock is a tiny tree house that has a zip line trailing out of the house in the sky. The crimson sip line connects to a huge tree in the woods. The lake is a good reason to come to Southside Park.

As you walk into the woods, the oak trees tower over you. You may even see a doe prance across the path. the path is actually a 4-wheeling path. The dirt is always flying everywhere. At the end of the path there are horse stables. The path is also used for horseback riding. In the distance, between the oak trees, there is a wild creek. It glides smoothly over the rocks. Down stream a little there is a cabin. The cabin is in usually empty. Some people go in there to get away from everyone. Everyone loves the woods.

Out of the woods and across from the lake there is a gym. It is very noticable because the outside is neon yellow. The building is a dome and the roof is completly glass. Inside the gym there is a room for weight lifting. Every machine that is for building strength is there. Across the hall there is a basketball court. Many people come in to play games and build strength. If you might need a snack, there is a Subway down the hall. Beside the Subway there is a sauna. Many people go in there to get hot. A lot of people go into the gym to have fun also.

Many people come to Southside Park to have the time of their lives. I believe that it is a great way to have fun. You can go swimming, work out in the gym or go for a hike in the woods.

Example #5

Smash-Clash-Whing-Boom! Do you hear that? That's the sound of people having fun. To have fun you can go to a club, theampark, and the mountains.

My first reason is to go to a club. People go to clubs to dance around with people, hang out with friends, and to meet new people. People like to hang out with their friends at clubs because it's fun. You have the music, drinks, and people, so you can hang out with your friends and other people to. While your in the club with the music blasting, hangin out, you can also meet new people who could like things that you like to.

Second you can go to a theampark and have fun there too. You can go swimming, you can hang out, you can also do thing that you've never done before. For example you can go down a big slide in a innertube, slide down huge water slides, float down a river, go on a roller coaster, go on a big ship that flips around in circles. In a theampark you can hang out with friends and do every thing that I listed.

My final reason is that you can also go to the mountains and have fun. In the mountains you can go mountain climbing with family and friends, you can go bike riding on a mountain bike, and you can also go river rafting. All of these are fun. You can go river rafting on a big raft, you can go biking on a trail in the mountains, and you can go mountain climbin on a lot of mountains with a harness and rope. Taking a trip to the mountains is a lot of fun and you can spend that fun time with who ever you want to spend it with.

Now if you ever think about going some where to have fun and you go to a club, theampark, or the mountains, just thing of all the things I've said and have fun.

Example #6

Little kids running wild, people on the basketball court waiting to get a game going, runners working hard to get in shape, all of these things take place at one of the most fun places I know. The park. There are all kinds of activities, many different happy sounds, and beautiful sights everywhere in the park that make it a really cool place be.

When you first arrive at the park, the first thing you notice are all of the different sounds surrounding you. Many birds fly all around you, each singing a different beautiful song. Then you hear the happy squeals that the little kids make as their parents push them in the swing, or as they shoot down the slides. Splash! The next sound you hear are people cooling off by taking a dive into the refreshing pool with its blue crystal water. Another sound seems to be getting closer. It's the sound of a group of people's quickly moving feet racing around the park. Next, you hear the bouncing of basketballs and you hear the excitement of the players as they score a point. The sound of cars coming to pick up or let off their kids, is never far away. Now you hear the sounds of people playing music to get them pumped up for their day at the park. Wherever you are in the park, their are always many unique sounds to be heard.

After you've engulfed all of the sounds around the park, you can start to check out all of the fun things people are taking part in. To begin with, there are all different types of sports being played. Adults and children enjoy biking or running around the park. Basketball is also very popular. Ten or fifteen people of all ages run up and down the court trying to prove that their the best. Next you see a ball fly through the air and realize many people are playing football. As you progress through the park you see boys and girls in their bathing suits getting ready to take a dip in the cold refreshing pool. Some people don't prefer activities, and you can see many lounge on the grass as they come just to relax and hang out with friends.

The scenery at the park is gorgious. There are so many different plants and trees and many other exciting things to see. To begin with, you notice all of the trees and flowers of lots of different colors that spark up the park's looks. There are dogwoods just blossoming and little maple trees that have been freshly planted. Tall oak trees provide shade for people. Next are the flowers. Lilyies line the outside of the park.

So, in conclusion, the park is the most fun and exciting place I know. If you're ever bored, or tired of the same old thing, go to the park and embark on a exciting, and exhilerating day.

Example #7

I am going to tell you a little bit about where people go to have fun. Read along and I will tell you.

The first place I decided where people should go to have fun is the museum. the museum is a place where you can learn about and explore many different ancient creatures that lived long ago. For example dinosaurs romed the earth thousands of years ago. The other creature you can learn about is how big was the transisurous. The basic reason why you would want to go to the museum is because you can explore the adventures of the cavemen or you can find out how people realy existed on earth. The last but certainly not the least thing to explore is the aquarium things like the octopus. You could find out how the octopus realy did get those suction cups under his tentacles.

See so it as worth reading after all you probably want to go to the museum now dont you I know I do.

Example #8

The most fun place in the world to me is the Carnival. Because of all the rides, games, and shows there. As you continue reading I'll explain why.

When you first get there all you can see is rides. Left to right, right to left everywhere. The rides go around and around, upside down even sideways. With lights tons of lights piled on each ride so that each one glows in it's own special way. As the lights of blueberry blue, strawberry red, buttercup yellow, firey orange, and even violet purple swirl and twirl all around the rides making each and every ride look like a rainbow wrapped around them.

Second of all is the games. Games with spectacular prizes for each one. One of the most intriguing parts about the games to me is the people inside each one finding a different way to attract people like changing their voices but usually bigger prizes turn people on. Prizes like clover green giant stuff teddy bears fire truck red stuffed dogs. I even like the ones where you win real animals like gold fish or bunny rabbits.

Last but not least is the shows. Each one eye catching an pulchritudinous in it's own way. Shows like where people swallow fire. Amazing musicians, or even famous tatooed people. Each little show is great not a single one in the whole Carnival is dull or boring. Because if you watch then you would realize how unique and special each one makes the carnival look.

These few details are what makes the carnival look and be the most fun place in the world to me.

Example #9

There are many places where people go to have fun, but the one that is the best is Champion Park. The pool, basketball courts, and of course play ground all make it a fantastic place to enjoy yourself.

As you pull up to this park you will audamatcly see the basketball courts. They are black as night with baby blue lines that show where the free throw line is, three point line, and out of bounce is. Also they have four black, blue, and orange goals. the basketball courts are surounded with trees of all sort like pine, dogwood, and so on. The black top is very hard that when you fall you say, Wow, that hurt." It also leaves strawberrys and bruises on your knees.

As you turn to your left you will see a concrete stairway that has a black metel bar that you hold on to. It leads up to a gray wooden building that has two bathrooms and changing rooms. One for the girls that is on the right and one for the boys that's on the left. You will keep walking in and you will see a desk to your left that says, "Sign up and pay to swim." the desk has lockers behind it that have names of the lifeguards. As you walk about four feet from the desk you will see a blue sparkling pool that when you look at it, it makes your eyes water and invites you to dive in. It is three feet to fourteen feet deep. On the sides of the pool are two five feet lifeguard stands. They are wooden and painted red. Their are also two white divenboards, one tall and one short.

As you look to the right of the pool you'll see a playground area with two merry-go-rounds that are purple and blue that six people can ride. You will also see eight metel swings that when you swing on them you feel like you are going to fly off like a bird. there is also a gray wooden building that has six or seven picnic tables so that people can come and have lunch in the sun. The picnic tables are white and gray. They are also 5 ft by 3 ft long. The building is open on all four sides. It is a square shaped building. To the left of the building is a metel stick sticking up out of the ground, and about 7 ft away from it is another metel stick, and it is a game called horseshoes.

Now you can see why I picked this place to describe for you. Don't you think this is a great place to describe? Wouldn't you like to visit it so that you can see it for yourself?

Example #10

The place where I go to have fun is Carowinds. It has lots of games, music, food, and clothing. Also the rides are awsome too.

My first reason is that it has lots of games like throw a baseball and knock the pins down and you win a stuffed animal. there lots of clothing shops like the tweety shop it's cool it has lots of tweety's. The music is old fashion but ok it's not really bad. The food there is great it has seafood, old fashion food, and fast food.

My second reason is the rides there awsome. The vortex is sort of uncomfortable the seats are bicylce seats. It starts off slow and then go's really fast and go's upside down. The hurrier is ok it starts off really fast it makes lots of people sick. White water was really cool it go's up slow then flys down and get's people all wet. Plus the swinging ship was cool but it started raining and it wouldn't stop until about an hour later.

My conclusion is that it has lots of games, food, music, and clothing. Also it has awesome rides.

Example #11

Tell me! What do you think about when writing about a place where people have fun? I think of Malls. Hanging out with your friends, shopping for new kix/shoes, and the good food, which I will elaborate more on in the following lines, but not exactly in that order.

Hanging out not alone, of course, but with five of your friends in the mall is fun. The great big walls that are full of marble and cement and the smell of marble in the air keeps me coming back. The mall is like a enormously big grocery store. It's got all of your needs just with high and low prices. The mall floor is a purple and green design, white purple green. It smells like buble gum chewed and thrown away but still with it's flavory smell. Then when your hanging out and you start getting closer to the stores you was looking for, everything starts turning the color of that sports store, and therefore also smelling as if your already in the store and all of you are looking at the same thing, the Nike air max. The black and white shoe takes your breath away until that hunger starts setten in and you don't smell the store any more or the smelly gym sock smell or the cement marble and buble gum rolled into one, but the food cort which I will elaborate on more in the coming paragraph.

The food cort smells like Chinese food, Mc Donalds chicken nuggets and Sabarrow Pizza rolled into one. While your smelling all this you are getting hungrier than a full grown mama bear out of hibernation. Just then you and your friends decide your eating at Sabarrow Pizza. As your walking over the smell of pizza gets stronger like a person throughing up in one part of the room and then the other while all other smells seem just too be clocked out. While the look of the mall starts looking like a restaurant with red and white floor tile, pizza menus all on the wall and behind the glass on the counter where the pizza is made. We tell the lady what we want. She slides over on a plate to the cashier. She gives us a drink, and amount of money it is. Then were off to eat where ever we want. After we finish eating someone says, "I'm going to get a shirt." So we finish quick and set off for the Gap. Which I will say more about in the next paragraph.

The Gap smelled just like the food cort since it was right across from it. My friend was looking at the Ginco shirts and found a black one that said, "Not here not there but everywhere." The store was playing music from some unknown place. The walks were painted fushea and blue which looked cool.

Scores and Analyses

Example #1

Since spelling and mechanics errors are scored separately in North Carolina, this paper earned a rather **high score** of a **3.5** on a 4-point scale. It began with onomatopoeia and contained three clear, fairly well developed focal points (the beach sounds, the sand, and the ocean floor). It maintained a fairly clear visual picture throughout most of the essay, slipping only a few times. There is some detail like "little birds, snails and pincher's" and "jagged shells and rocks," but more could be used for a higher score. Vocabulary (though misspelled) was more than adequate. The similes add to the image. This paper probably did not score higher due to the occasional slip from visual to other senses that did not enhance what you could see ("the sand feels cold from the ocean water" and "the ocean tastes like..."), the need for more nitty-gritty details, and the lack of a lot of strong, action verbs.

Focus	Organization	Support	Style, voice	Conventions
High	Medium/high—beginning/end	Medium	High	High

Example #2

This is a good, solid **medium** paper. It received a **3**. It is organized with three focal points—the slide, the merry-go-round, and the jungle gym—but it lacks the nitty-gritty detail necessary for a higher score. It begins with a grabber, but the introduction is not fully developed. The writer also gets off the topic and inserts himself/herself into the paper ("I love Ol' Rusty. I just wouldn't suggest any one with a weak stomach..."). Vocabulary is lackluster, and while you can visualize the jungle gym, some of the other descriptions are not clear.

Focus	Organization	Support	Style, voice	Conventions
High	Medium/high—Beginning/end	Medium	High	High

Example #3

Although this paper begins with a question, attempts good vocabulary ("pulcurtudinous"), and has three clear focal points (the pool, the snack bar, and an ice cream truck), it lacks detail necessary for the reader to picture the place clearly. It is a **low-medium** and received a score of **2.5**. The lower score also probably was earned because the writer got off the topic and turned the essay into a narrative. There are few action verbs, the conclusion is also poorly developed, and the lack of transitions takes away from the clarity.

Focus	Organization	Support	Style, voice	Conventions
Medium/low	Medium—beginning/end	Low medium	Medium	Medium

Example #4

This paper is a typical **medium** and received a **3** from the official scorers. It is organized, begins with onomatopoeia, uses a few good vocabulary words ("crimson," "azure," "chilling"), and contains three clear focal points—the lake, the woods, and the gym. Transitions are cleverly used ("Out of the

Descriptive Sample Set — "A Place to Have Fun"

woods and across from the lake there is a gym."), but more strong, active verbs are needed. While the author paints a fairly clear picture of the park, the lack of nitty-gritty details probably kept it from receiving a higher score. For example, the writer talked about machines for building strength but went no further in describing them.

Focus	Organization	Support	Style, voice	Conventions
High	Medium—beginning/end	Medium	Medium	High

Example #5
This below-average, **low** paper begins well but fails to develop the topic and, at times, turns into an expository essay ("My first reason..."). It received a **2** on the test probably because it did not stick to the descriptive style of writing and because it lacks three focal points for one place. Instead, it talks about three places where the writer has experienced fun. The paper also lacks support and good vocabulary. What probably kept this paper from receiving a lower score are the small descriptions within the three middle paragraphs. Obviously, following the directions of a descriptive essay would raise this paper's score.

Focus	Organization	Support	Style, voice	Conventions
Low	Medium/low	Low	Low—formulaic	Medium

Example #6
There is no question that this is a **high** paper. It received the top score of a **4**. It is well organized and developed. The three focal points—the sounds, the fun things to do, the scenery—are well supported with nitty-gritty detail ("To begin with you notice all of the trees... There are dogwoods just blossoming and little maple trees that have been freshly planted. Tall oak trees provide shade..."). Vocabulary is excellent ("exhilarating," "engulfed," "refreshing"), and literary devices (onomatopoeia, similes, alliteration) abound. The author frequently uses strong verbs as well.

Focus	Organization	Support	Style, voice	Conventions
High	High	High	High	High

Example #7
This paper received a **1.5** and is clearly a **low** essay. The only thing that saved this paper from receiving a 1 or lower was the skimpy attempt at a description of the ancient creatures and the octopus that could be found in the museum and the obvious attempt at some kind of organization (a beginning, a middle of some sort, and a conclusion). The introduction and conclusion are dull. No interesting vocabulary or strong verbs grace the essay, and the reader cannot picture the museum at all. There are no focal points, transitions, or details to help.

Focus	Organization	Support	Style, voice	Conventions
Low	Low/medium	Low	Low	Medium

Descriptive Sample Set — "A Place to Have Fun"

Example #8

While this essay is obviously higher than the previous one, it is only a **low-medium** essay that received a score of **2.5**. There are three focal points—the rides, the games, and the shows—but they are poorly described with very few details. The description of the rides is the only one the reader can picture. This paragraph probably kept the paper from receiving a lower score. Strong verbs, more details, sticking to the topic (the writer begins to talk about the prizes without describing anything else about the games), and good vocabulary would raise the score of this paper.

Focus	Organization	Support	Style, voice	Conventions
Medium	Medium	Low/medium	Medium	Medium

Example #9

This paper, obviously, should receive a **high** score, and it did—a **4**. While the introduction and conclusion might be better developed, the rest of the essay is excellent. The three focal points—the pool, the basketball courts, and the playground—are vividly described with nitty-gritty detail, strong verbs, good vocabulary, and great transitions. The writer uses transitional devices to walk you through the park which orients you to where you are. Details are so vivid ("blue sparkling pool that when you look at it, it makes your eyes water and invites you to dive in. It is three feet to fourteen feet deep.") that you feel as if you are there.

Focus	Organization	Support	Style, voice	Conventions
High	High	High	High	High

Example #10

This paper abandoned the descriptive genre and changed to an expository essay ("My first reason," "My second reason"). Despite this, however, it scored a **2** on the test. I would rate it a **low**. There are no strong verbs or really good vocabulary. While there are focal points mentioned in the introduction (the games, the music, the food, the clothing, and the rides), only one is developed. The others are mentioned without any detail or description. The description of the one ride, the "vortex," probably kept it from receiving a lower score.

Focus	Organization	Support	Style, voice	Conventions
Low	Medium/low	Low	Low-formulaic	Medium

Example #11

The three, fairly well-developed focal points (hanging out, shopping, food), obvious organization with a good introduction and conclusion, and clear picture of the mall itself earned this paper a **high** score of a **3.5**. The description flags a little when the writer talks about the good "cort" and gets off the topic, writing about getting the food rather than describing it. This, plus a lack of really good vocabulary, probably kept this essay from receiving a higher score.

Focus	Organization	Support	Style, voice	Conventions
High	High	High	High	High

32 Expository Examples

> **NOTE #1:** *Because there are so many types of expository essays, different states use different names (such as "expressive essays" or "evaluative essays" or "informational essays," etc.).*

> **NOTE #2:** *Because scoring differs from state to state, these samples are scored HIGH, MEDIUM, LOW, or ZERO for ease of translation.*

> **NOTE #3:** *The teacher of these students obviously has been working with her students to write with strong, active verbs (see **Step One**). It is amazing what fourth-graders can produce when they write in the active voice!*

Topic for Sample Set: "Everyone has a particular time of year that is their favorite. Before you begin writing, think about your favorite time of year. Now explain to the reader of your paper why this time of year is your favorite."

Example #1

Yea! Yea! My favorite time of year is December because Santa comes to my house's up the chincy hc gocs.

To begin with, Santa comes. One time I heard a lode boom on our roof top. I gazed a guy with a red cote and red pants with a long bired. Then I new how it was Santa Close. The he saw the cookeys my mom and I made for him and Hot cholect. He liked it very much. Christmas makes December a great month.

In addition we have two weeks off frome school. When I springed out of bed I was so happy that we hade two weeks off frome school. I'm excided that two weeks I got off school. Then my mom seaid "Good get your bathing sute because we are going to the beach." The waves were hi. My brother's ran to the water. It wasnt so cold and then i went in to. We hade so much fun there. it was cool going to the beach in december.

In conclusion. My favorite time of year is december. it is so cool. I love december for Santa and the two weeks off. That is why December is my favorite time of year.

Example #2

Wow! My favorite time of year? Not a problem. My favorite time of the year will come in June. Oh my gosh, that time of the year is good. My Birthday happens in June. They are always great fun. We take vacations in June. That's great too. I love the month of June.

To begin with, it's my birthday in June. "Today is my Birthday," I said to my mom and dad last June. They both gave me a present. It was a bakery set. I like those kinds of things. My brother was still sleeping so I jumped on him. He tolled on me. Then my parents went in one bathroom whitch had two sinks. They both brushed there teeth. Then in the living room were my fantastic friends and relitives. Then we all got into a car and went to Fun Time America. Everyone who came with me all talked with me. One hour later we were at Fun Time America! We all went inside. There were games, rides, and other cool stuff. First we went on the rolla-coaster that goes in circles. I got dizze. And we went on so many other rides. Then we all went to the games and got a lot of things. Then after one more hour we had to go. So we dropped everybody and went home and slept. Another time we had fun was my 7th birthday. We celibraded it outside our house. We called everybody to my party. First we all played bingo and limbo and other games too. Then we all drank soft drinks and ate. We also played musical chairs and I won. Then I cut my cake and my mom gave slices to everybody. Then we danced till 11:30 pm. But then they all had to leave. So I went inside my house and slept. Those were the great, marvelous birthdays I had.

In addition, I go on vacations in June with my family. Last year I went to India. I went with my mom and my brother. It was a long flight. Wnen we reached there we found my mom's dad and mom and went to their house. Then we were exausted and slept. Then the next day we went to meet my mom's relitives. And we had a sleepover. Then we went to parties together and shopping. We tried all kinds of foods and saw a lot of places and had so much fun. Every day was like a party over there. We didn't want to leave our Grandparents, but our vacation was over.

I can't forget that fun trip full of gifts, treatas, parties, lots of sleepovers, and especially spending time with my Grandparents. That was my favorite time and it happened in June. Another June I went to Washington DC. I went with my whole family. When we reached there, we saw my aunts, uncles, grandmas, grandpas, and my familys friends. We went to parties, places like malls and did shopping. Also my relitives had a baby that was adorable and I played with him. We all went to thier basement whitch had exircise eqipment, a tv, and games. Then it was 12:30 pm. So I had to sleep. So I did. Eight hours later I had to leave. So they dropped us off at the airport and we went home and relaxed. That was another fun time in June.

In conclusion, that's why June is the best time of the year. It is the best!

Example #3

Boom! go's the fireworks exsbloding in the night time sky. My favorit time of year is July as I say "wow" with the bright color's of the fireworks and the cool music of a band.

To begin with, it's the fourth of July month and my birthday month As I cry saying "god bless the U.S.A." Mom say's "this is the best day" as she sobs and dances with her sisters. My dad "yells me back" so I operate in a distance from my mom and Aunt's saying goodbye!!! In addition, it's my birthday. Jumping up and down shouting it in the house Its my birthday. After all that excitment, we went to King Richard's. When I turned nine I went on rides that I wanted to ride all these year's and finally I'm tall enough to ride the big scary one's like hunted house and other ride's/ After all those bumper car's we ate cake, pizza, and cookecacola. I was the king. I was so surprised a party for me! It was so awsome. I was so happy and yelled so much I lost my voice. I couldn't even speak. After all that I went to the games. It was fun playing with my brothers, anyways I got two thoused tickets. I won a huge price and gusse what! It's big, it's crazy, smells and look's like a hourse. Your right it was a donkey. Then I walked to my car out of the entrance saying wow!!!!! "I had a blast" I said to my mom and dad. And they said "you having fun" "Yes" I say and my dad said "I love you." Then I went to the house and thier was lot's of messesege's and calls.

In conclusion, July is my favorite time of year.

Example #4

I like July because of the fireworks. I also like Christmas. But my favorite time of year is January. Yes January is my favorite time of year. Where I live, January is when freinds come to visit because of the great weather. My birthday is in January too. THAT'S what makes it so fun.

This January I my freind Jessica came to my house. She is my Best freind. We played lots of games. The first thing we did was play Batleship. Batleship is a game where you have ships. And you have to say something like "A-5" and if you get it right four or five times, you sink a ship. Then that ship is out of the game. If you run out of ships, your out of the game too. Then I said, "You can't catch me," and then I dashed outside. Then we played tag. After that I said "Fetch me the cell phone." Then we played Space Impack. Its where you have to shoot things and at the end of the game you have to shoot a huge monster.

January is my favrite month of the year because it is my Birthday. Last year my Mom said, "You can have five girls sleep over." I chose Maria, Beatriz, Sabrina, Jakey, and Jessica. Jessica was the first one to arive. Then Jakey arived with Beatriz. Then Sabrina arived last. She said she had to find a way to get the huge present to my house. Then we played games and I ripped open my presents. The next day we screambled to my fort and then all my freind's parents came to pick them up.

My favrite time of the year is January because of my Birthday and the visiting of my freinds. January is my favrite month of the year.

Example #5

"Finally my very favorite time of year has arrived. The air is finally getting colder. The mosquitos are gone. We can spend time outside without getting eaten alive. People come from all over the world to visit our town. Christmas and my birthday are coming soon. There is excitement in the air at home. My favorite time of the year is winter!

Beginning with the best first, my birthday happens in winter. Last year when I turned nine I had my birthday at my house. After all my friends arrived, we started to have a great time by dashing out into my backyard, driving to Sue's Garden to order Shirly Temples, rice and noodles. After we all finished eating, my parents paid and we went back to my house. There we all had popcorn, Starbursts, and Skittles before my friends had to go home. Another time on my eighth birthday instead of my friends coming over, my cousins from England came to visit. Their names are Abigail and James, very English names. After we all played a fun game of tag we all decided to go to a restaurant. It was called the Snook Inn. We ordered our food and then my cousins and I all wanted to go to the dock so we could see the fish. We did, and we saw a couple of dolp;hins gliding and then jumping in and out of the water. My cousins were very excited. We had an awesome time together. I love wonderful winter!

Not only does my birthday happen in winter, but there is another great holiday—Christmas! Last year, we had my entire family over. After everyone arrived, we all revealed what we had gotten for Christmas. I told them I had gotten a big beautiful doll named Samantha. she had a checkered ribbon in her hair. I also got a walkman CD player which I loved, and I received a case for some of my CD's. After we exchanged presents and present info, my mom called out, "Dinner is ready." We rushed into the dining room, sat down at the table and ate a wonderful dinner of delishous mashed potatos, roast beef, and for dessert had ice cream.sundays which we all devoured very quickly.

There have been many other great birthdays and Christmases in my life. Those memories are what make winter so special. I just love winter, and it's not just for the wonderful cooler weather or no mosquitos. I love winter because it has a lot of special things that happen. You never know in my family!

Example #6

My favorite time of the year is May. I know that sounds wierd but I just love May. I wonder if my reader's favorite time of the year is May also. Two special things are in May, school gets out and I have my birthday! See why I like May?

To begin with, in May schools ring ring out and summers come in. With no more school I have time to play all my fun games. One time at the end of May I was playing Jack and Dexster 2 on Playstation and there was this giant lava monster I was resiling. I beat him up. I don't just play games in May. I get to play outside a lot. One time I I was outside skate-boarding. I went off a ramp, and I landed a pops-over-it. I thought I was gliding. Man that was s-w-e-e-t.

In addition, May is also my B-day. One time it was my birthday and I got a humongous presinte and I opend it and a gient dog came dashing out of the box! After thinking a bit and waiting a few days I named him Shoky becuse he was so fast. He chased me arond the house. I was winning but then he bete me by a mile. That dog was fast! And another time it was my birthday and I got a tiny presint. I riped it open and I found a small kitten inside. It was so cute. It was so small that I thote it was a rat at first. That's how small it was. Man it was c-u-t-e.

In conclusion, that's why May is my favorite time of the year. Getting to play games and getting neat prisents all in the same month is awesome. What is your favorite month?

Example #7

Boom! I wake up with the sound of fireworks. They only come one time in the year—July. I have so much fun in July that I just have to say it is my favorite month of the year. July is for trips, for adventure, and for fireworks! It is an awesome month.

To begin with, in July me and my family go to Ohio to visit our family. Last year we all went to Ohio and I flew all the way there on a huge white and red colored airplane. Our friends and family greeted us at the airport. That was nice but I got kissed by too many aunts. We slept at my Uncle John's house every night. My uncle likes to go hunting a lot, so he handed me a gun, and we scurryed out of the house to see what we could find. Once were where at his hunting spot he said, "We are going to shoot racoons." As we waited, I saw something come out of the bushes. I said to my uncle John, "What's that?" He shined his flash light near the bushes. It was a racoon. I cocked my gun and aimed at the creepy looking racoon and shot the gun. I fell backwards from the pressure of the gun.

He tiptoed over to see if I shot it, but I had missed. My uncle and I were tired and ambled home. Ohio is full of adventures like that. I can't wait until next July to go there again.

In addition, when I was younger me and my family drove to a enoroumous beach and watched fire works sparkle into the air on the fourth of July. We brang a blanket with us to sit on. As I glanced into the sky there were hundreds of lights and flashes and expolosions. The very last fire work was red, white, and blue. After the show, we drove back to our house and lit some small fire works of our own. My older brother tied a lizerd to a bottle rocket and lit the rocket. It shot off into the air and exploted. My other brother Bryce was playing with sparklers. He had two in each hand and was swinging them around saying, "I'm magic. Look what I can do." When we ran out of sparklers and could not find lizerds to shoot off we wobbled into the house and fell asleep.

In conclusion, July is my favorite time of year.

Example #8

My favorite time of the year is summer. Me and my dad play catch in summer time. Summer is the time to play all kinds of sports like football.

To begin with, I get to play takle football with my friends.

One time when I played takle football with my friends my friend Wesley threw a beautifull pass to me. I recived the ball and sprinted to the touchdown and made the touchdown and I did my Eagle move. Then we switched teams and I still kicked his butt. He understood how good I was at football. When I kicked his butt I chuckled. Last summer I played these guys that weren't good so wen my friend hiked the ball and I went for a short pass and recived the ball, I sauntered into the touchdown. Then we swiched teams again. I stated to them that they stunk and me and Wesley giggled for two hours after that. Then we stopped giggling and started playing hard again. Wesley threw a long pass and I caught it. The tried to tackle me, but they were to chubby and they tumbled over.

I will never forget that day because that was the best day of my life.

In addition, in the summer, me and my dad play catch with the football in the pool. One time when me and my dad played catch in the pool with my football I caught some marvolous passes. Some were in the pool and some were out of the pool. One time my dad throw me a beutiful pass in the pool. I leaped in the air and caught it and my dad sayed "Nice catch." I said, "Nice throw." He said "thanks." The next day me and my dad jumped into the pool to cool off then I got out and my dad throw the football again and I jumped in and caught the ball. Then we went home and played catch in the front yard.

In conclusion, I like summer. I love playing football with my friends and giggling and playing catch with my dad in the pool and in the yard. I like summer.

Scores and Analyses

Example #1

I score this essay as a **low-medium**, verging on a **low**. It is formulaic and, while it is on the topic and has an obvious organization, no voice is evident. The beginning and end, although clearly there, are not developed. The support is nothing outstanding, but it is there with some details (about the beach). There is no good vocabulary, and word use is limited. Though the student used quotation marks properly, the large number of convention errors (no commas, capitalization problems, usage mistakes, etc.) hurts the score. The repetition ("two weeks off school"), the formulaic layout, and the many spelling errors ("frome," "cholect," "sute," "cookeys," etc.) prevent this essay from earning a higher score.

Focus	Organization	Support	Style, voice	Conventions
High	Medium	Medium	Low	Low

Example #2

This essay is a good one despite the paragraphing problem. It would score a **high-medium**. The organization is obvious although the conclusion is skimpy and repetitive. Elaboration is excellent, but there are too many unnecessary details ("everybody went home and slept," "my parents went in one bathroom whitch had two sinks. They both brushed there teeth."). The writer used some very good vocabulary ("marvelous," "relitives," "exausted," "arrangements") but nothing outstanding. The voice, however, is very good. Obviously the writer was excited about going on those trips. In some states, this would score a low-high.

Focus	Organization	Support	Style, voice	Conventions
High	Medium	High	High	Medium

Example #3

This is another **low-medium** essay. Since most state writing tests consider the essays and narratives to be rough drafts, a lack of paragraphing does not lower the score very much if the organization is definitely there. This paper is definitely organized and begins well, but the conclusion is one sentence. The essay sticks to the topic. The writer has plural vs. possessive problems and makes way too many convention errors for a higher score. Vocabulary is ordinary. Sentences are not very varied. Spelling is poor but does not interfere with comprehension. There is adequate support, but it is poorly organized and unclear in places. The writer's voice is clear. The conventions, lack of an ending, and disorganized support are what keep the score to a low-medium.

Focus	Organization	Support	Style, voice	Conventions
High	Medium	Medium	High	Low

Example #4

This is another **low-medium** paper. It almost reads like a narrative. The focus is not quite clear. It is obvious that January is this student's "favrite" month, but he/she gets lost in his/her detail and ends up telling two stories. The beginning and end need work. Vocabulary is adequate ("dashed," "scrambled"), and the author uses some strong, active verbs, but there are quite a few convention problems although the author does know how to punctuate a quote correctly. There are quite a few spelling errors, but they do not interfere with comprehension. Voice is weak.

Focus	Organization	Support	Style, voice	Conventions
Medium	Medium	Medium	Medium	Medium

Example #5

I score this a **high**, but on the low end of high. The beginning is different and not formulaic. The organization is clear. Sentence structure varies. The author uses some good vocabulary ("devourer," "gliding") but could use better word choices in other places. The writer does, however, paint a few clear images (such as the dolphins and the dinner). There are plenty of details even if the essay verges on the narrative at times. For the most part, conventions are pretty good. The conclusion wraps it up without being formulaic. Voice is there but could be stronger. All in all, this is a very good essay.

Focus	Organization	Support	Style, voice	Conventions
Medium	High	High	Medium/High	Medium

Example #6

This is a good, solid **medium** paper. It remains on the topic, is organized, includes detail, and has a few good vocabulary words. The conventions are not great, and there are quite a few punctuation errors. Sentence structure is varied in places, but the writing is not outstanding. The writer's voice is there, but it needs development, and word pictures are not very vivid ("That dog was fast!"). The writer could use better vocabulary and more varied elaboration. Spelling errors abound, but they don't get in the way of comprehension.

Focus	Organization	Support	Style, voice	Conventions
Medium	Medium	Medium	Medium	Medium

Example #7

This is another **high-medium** essay. It sometimes reads like a narrative, but it addresses the topic. The organization is fine, but the end is one sentence. The author uses good vocabulary ("enoroumous," "scurryed," "creepy," "ambled," "wobbled") even if some are misspelled. The strong verbs are noticeable in this paper. While the shooting off of "lizerds" is repugnant, the essay is a fairly good one. The lack of an end brings the paper down to a medium.

Focus	Organization	Support	Style, voice	Conventions
Medium	Medium	High	Medium	Medium

Example #8

I would give this paper a **medium** as well. I am tempted to score it a medium-high, but there are too many subtle flaws. The focus is good, but, again, this paper verges on the narrative at times. The organization is OK, but the beginning and end are weak. The paragraphing is strange. The support is good, and the writer gives a vivid picture of playing football with his friends. Conventions are not perfect (such as indenting for a new speaker) but are adequate. What sets this paper apart from others is the use of strong, active verbs ("leaped," "played," "caught," "recived," "sprinted," "understand," "chuckled," "sauntered," "giggled," "tumbled," etc.). As you can see, the writer also has a good command of vocabulary. Spelling errors abound, but they do not get in the way of comprehension. The writer's voice is clear. With a little bit of work, this paper could receive a higher score.

Focus	Organization	Support	Style, voice	Conventions
Medium	Medium	Medium/High	High	Medium

Topic for Sample Set: "What book would you recommend that the whole class read? Give reasons why you recommend this book."

Example #1

"Book for Class to Read"

One book that I suggest the whole class to read is The Diary Of Anne Frank. This book narrates the many hardships that a thirteen year-old girl, Anne, had to endure during the World War II. The story began with Anne and her family hiding in an attic of a spice factory. Anne must spend most of her day in silences, and can not use the bathroom between seven o'clock in the morning till six o'clock at night. The author, Anne, in her writing conveys all the emotions she felt, and the settings are vividly describe. Although the story has a sad end, it is truly moving.

There is three main reasons why I choose this book. The first reason is that the students can easily relate to this book, and it can also teach the students about World War II. The last important reason why this is a good book for the class to read is because it is very moving.

This is a book that the student can relate to because it is about a girl our age. Anne had the same hopes and fears that we now experience. For this reason, the students can easily understand the feelings of the main character. For instance, Anne want to be a writer, and doesn't everyone have a dream?

Through discussion, the students can learn much about the World War II. The students learn first hand about the daily life of Jews. They also learn about Hitler and the Gustapo policemen. The students are also exposed to the concentration camps and much more. So by reading this book, the students can learn some history.

The last reason is that the book is very well-written. It is so well-written that the reader can feel what the character is feeling. It is almost as if you were Anne! For example, when the author describes a jubilant scene, you feel happy too. The book is also interesting and keep you hooked. Once you pick up the book you can't put it down until you finish it.

I believe the student will truly enjoy this book because of its cultural content. This book not only move the students emotionally, but also is educationally beneficial! All in all, this is a great book for the class to read.

Example #2

"The Book"

Yesterday my teacher chose me to pick a book that the class was to read. I told her that "The Incredible Journey" would be a good because of how the animal's pulled together to get to their master.

It will also show the students how to write well and how description can make a story good or bad.

Today she had "The Incredible Journey" and all the kids loved the beginning and my teacher was happy.

Example #3

"A Good Book"

The book I would choose I would probaly choose is Jurassic Park. Jurrusic Park is about a scientist who finds a huge mineral stone. When he was polishing it he finds a miscita in it. Since the rock was made millions of years before the mescita it had to be old.

The scientist takes the stone to another scientist were they find out the mosquito was over a million years old. Since the bug was in the ancient rock it had to be an ancient bug. Happened to contain DNA from dinasaurs. From their other scientist were able to reproduce the DNA and create real dinasaurs.

After hearing this a rich dinosaur searcher hired some private scientist and make his own dinosaurs. He soon makes over 250 dinasaurs. He has them all on a island that he will turn into a amusement park. The park was about to open when something went wrong.

The reason I would recomend this book is because it is very intrirty. When I first heard about it I thought it would be horribly. But after I read it I found out I was totally wrong. It was amazing in explain the detail even though it can be a little grousome it is a good book.

Example #4

"The Book to Read to All"

My teacher has asked me to write a paper explaining about a favorite book. It is The Once and Future King by J.H. White. This book shows the life of King Arthur to its fullest. In this story there is love, forbidden to those who want it. Also war, death at the hands of the mightest, and the dark secrets that creep between every crack in the wall like cockroaches.

The darkest secrets of this book effect love and war. Dark secrets and stories about people doing what shouldn't be told. For instance, when Guenevere and Lancelot fall in love, King Arthur lets them carry it on. Only if someone else were to reveal it, would he have to pontificate the matter in court.

Another good point about the book is the war involved. When Arthur started the Knights of the Round Table, his table given to him by Guenevere's father, all the knights desired to become part of it. He demanded that they all do good deeds. For only good deeds prevail at death.

Last of all, but already partially mentioned in this tragic tale when Lancelot beseached the Queen's love and she accepted. The funny thing is exactly what happened, one part of the book told them sneaking to each other's room. A good example would be the night when Arthur was away. Lancelot's friendly knight warned him he would be caught. But Lancelot went anyways for love.

Through hardships to the downfall of Arthur, love prevailed. This shows that war can be caused by love, but only good deeds can be caused within oneself. Dark secrets may lead the way to death when they are told, but whatever happens, people at least in this tale, follow their hearts' desire. Fearing the consequences, but still facing them head on.

Example #5

My english teacher asked me to recomend a book for our class to read. The book I would recommend is A Wrinkle In Time because it is an eighth grade reading level and a book of all kinds, mystery, drama, and all that stuff.

The reason this book is so great is you never know whats going to happen next. For instance Meg, the main character, has to figure out a way to destroy a big brain called It who has her brother under his control.

Another time in the drama part is when Meg finally sees her father again after 10 years.

I think anybody who knows how to read would enjoy this book more than any book in the whole world.

Example #6

"A Book for My Class"

I recomend the book A Spell for Chameleon by Piers Anthony. It is a great book to read. It has everything in it to make you want to read it. It has funny jokes, adventure, and magic. It is also good because it keeps you wanting to read it.

A Spell for Chameleon is about finding a special spell for someone. It has puns in it. And that makes it funny. When he goes looking for his spell he meets all kinds of intersting people like centaurs and a magican who lives in a castle. This keeps the book intersting.

This book keeps you wanting to read it. The hero goes hunting for his spell and gets into some scary scraps. There are fight places that also keep you wanting to read. You keep reading because you want to find out what happens.

A Spell for Cameleon is a good book. I recomend it to the class to read. Everyone, even the teacher will like it.

Example #7

"Animal Farm, a Book with a Message"

Recommend a book for the class to read? That is no problem! I recently read a book that every eighth grade student should read as soon as they can — Animal Farm by George Orwell. "Why read this book?" you ask. Besides being an intreguing tale of treachery and trickery that keeps even reluctant readers hooked, it is a story within a story that tells about the Russian Revolution in metaphor. George Orwell's book is also a message about the wrongs of totalitarianism. Even though you can read this book in only a few hours, it is one that no reader could ever forget.

In the first place, Animal Farm is the kind of book that appeals to eighth graders (after all, I am an eighth grader, and I loved it) because the action never stops. There is trickery as Napoleon manages to change the basic rules of the new farm and treachery as he gets rid of Snowball. The twists and turns of the plot twine around the reader's mind like a cudzu (sp. ?) vine, tugging and pulling the reader further and further into the plot and not letting go until the very end when the pigs are really humans in pork skin. This is a book you can't put down.

Animal Farm also grips the reader because of its hidden metaphor. It isn't really a book about pigs and farm animals. It tells the story of the Russian Revolution with the animals representing real people, like Napoleon being Stalin and Snowball being Trotsky. What a great way to study history painlessly! We eighth graders love hidden meanings and hunting for things. This book really lets us hunt and think and compare ideas about how bad totalitarianism is. Orwell even says in the introduction that his book is a protest against "all the horrors of totalitarianism." It's fun to learn things in this manner.

Finally, I recommend the book Animal Farm to be read by the class because it is one of those books that you read, like Charlotte's Web and Dr. Seuss's Green Eggs and Ham that you never ever forget. When my dad recommended this book to me, he told me that he had read it twenty years ago and he still remembered it today. Perhaps it is the fact that the story is a metaphor for a historical event or perhaps it is the unforgettable characters like Molly, Snowball, Napoleon, and the bleating sheep that make this book so unforgettable. In any case, this is one book that this eighth grader will not forget very soon.

In conclusion, I heartily recommend the book Animal Farm to be read by the class. It is a classic story that not only keeps the reader hooked, but it also has hidden meanings to hunt for. It is a book that my fellow eighth graders will not forget. Like the memory of a great football game where everything goes right, the book Animal Farm stays in your mind for a long time.

Scores and Analyses

Example #1

Despite its difficulties with verbs, this paper would score **high** even though it is a bit formulaic. There are not enough interesting transitions, but the organization is obvious. The vocabulary ("relate," "jubilant") is excellent. Sentence structure varies. There are some mechanical difficulties, but the overall essay sticks to the topic and explains the topic well with three distinct reasons why the author recommends this book. The introduction and conclusion also are well done except that the student, for greater clarity, could have restated the three reasons why he/she recommended the book.

Focus	Organization	Support	Style, voice	Conventions
High	High	High	Medium-formulaic	Medium

Example #2

This is obviously a **low**-scoring paper. On the test, the actual score probably would depend on the readers. The student does stick to the topic and does give two reasons for his/her choice of book. There is also some evidence of organization (note the three paragraphs). Aside from the other errors, there is no support for the topic, and this is what cinches the low score. With some support, vocabulary, and a conclusion, this could easily have scored in the medium range.

Focus	Organization	Support	Style, voice	Conventions
Medium	Low	Very low	Low	Low

Example #3

While, at first glance, this looks like a well-organized essay, it is not. While it does have a rudimentary introduction, the rest follows no pattern, and there is no conclusion. In addition, it wanders off the topic. The topic was to recommend a book and give the reasons why you recommend the book. This essay, however, is a synopsis of the plot of a book. For this reason, this paper would score a **low**. Not until the last paragraph does the student give any reasons why anyone should read the book. It is this paragraph which raises the score from unscorable to a **1**. There also are numerous mechanical errors. I think the writer has abandoned the use of commas! An attempt was made to include good vocabulary ("reproduce"), but one of the words he/she tried to use, "intrirty," is so misspelled that the reader cannot discern its origin.

Focus	Organization	Support	Style, voice	Conventions
Very low	Low	Medium, but off-topic	Medium	High

Example #4

This paper typifies what I call the "gifted hole" that bright children fall into when they write essays. Despite the misuse of "pontificate," the vocabulary is excellent ("breached," "prevail," "tragic," etc.), and the student even includes an appropriately used simile. Sentence structure is varied, and the piece is basically well-written. It is not, however, on the topic at all. This paper would receive a *very* **low** score because, no matter how well-written it may be, it does not address the topic. It tells the tale of the book and discusses it instead of giving reasons why it should be read. It would receive a very low score instead of being rated unscorable as the topic is stated in the first paragraph. Some states might ignore this and score on the quality of the writing, only taking off a little for getting off-topic.

This is the hardest kind of paper to score because the teacher in us wants to score it higher because of the writing. We cannot succumb! The scorers of the actual test can be ruthless in this respect. Papers must stick to the topic. This student even announces in the first sentence that he/she is writing a paper "explaining about a favorite book" rather than putting forth reasons why a teacher should require the entire class to read the book. There are few states, however, which take off some for being off-topic and mostly score for the quality of writing.

Focus	Organization	Support	Style, voice	Conventions
Extremely low	High	Medium but off-topic	Medium— formulaic	Medium

Example #5

This paper, despite its brevity, would receive a **low** score but not the lowest one. Vocabulary and sentence structure are adequate. There is some obvious organization in an introduction, a middle that gives examples, and a brief conclusion. The student would not earn a higher grade because of the paucity of support. He/she really only gives two reasons and supplies support for only one of them.

Focus	Organization	Support	Style, voice	Conventions
High	Low	Very low	Medium	Medium

Example #6

This is a **low-medium** paper. It is organized with a beginning, middle, and end, and it has some support, but the introduction and conclusion are not fully developed. There are no transitions. Vocabulary use is good but nothing out of the ordinary. Support is there, but it is not enough to earn the paper a higher grade. Sentence structure is mostly simple. And, while there are not too many mechanical errors, it is not a paper that stands out as did Example #1.

Focus	Organization	Support	Style, voice	Conventions
High	Medium	Medium/low	Medium	Medium

Example #7

There is no question about the score for this paper. It is a **high**. In fact, because it is so well-focused on the topic, is so well-organized, and uses sophisticated vocabulary ("intriguing," "treachery"), varied sentence structure, similes ("like a cudzu vine"), humor, flair, and even a quote from Orwell, it would probably receive the top score on any writing assessment test. This student shows knowledge of the book and history, revealing an insight beyond his/her years. (We studied the book in class, but the scorers do not know that, nor is that fact relevant to the essay.)

Focus	Organization	Support	Style, voice	Conventions
High	High	High	High	High

Topic for Sample Set: "If your principal asked you to head a committee to improve the lunchroom conditions, what would you suggest?"

Example #1

"Changing the Cafeteria"

If the principal appointed me to committee the lunchroom I would higher an exterminator to get rid of all the rats and roaches. Let the kids have a day when they get pizza delivered. Then I would higher new cooks to cook the food. The food would have to taste and look good.

If I did this the students would want to come to the lunchroom and would not talk about if parents would send their kids here just for the lunchroom.

If the kids are good I will make the servers be happy when they serve, and I will get 102 Jamz D.J. and put him on the stage so the students will be able to dance but only on the stage and if they be bad I will remove the D.J. and take away their pizza day.

If I did all this the lunchroom will be known nationwide and the kids will want to come even more.

The people with their own lunches will have to sit in one area and the people who eat the lunchroom sit anywhere except with the people with their own lunches. That would help the school out because people would want to buy lunches and it will bring more money.

The End

Example #2

"Lunch at Westwood"

Students aren't enjoying lunch time. There seems to be something wrong with the way they're handling it. I think I have some good ideas for a good way of change.

First, people come in, and try to pry themselves into the lunch line. On certain days you might have to wait in line for 20 minutes. By the time you sit down to eat, you only have about five minutes to eat. If we expand the time to 45 minutes — as much as a regular period — people will be much more pleased.

Second, people want to sit by their friends. The regulations we have now prevent us from sitting with anyone but whom is in your FAME class. There could be a sheet where you sign up to sit at certain tables for the whole year. That way there won't be as much "table-hopping." A happy student is a good student.

Another problem is the temperature. On some days, when it's cold outside, the Cafeteria may be down to 60. It is very uncomfortable. If the Cafeteria was set at a temperature that was comfortable, considering the outside climate, we could improve comfortness.

Another idea could be to paint the awfully dull walls blue. It has been proven that blue slows down the activity rate in your body. It would be hard to do, but maybe on a long holiday or even over the summer, it could be accomplished.

I hope you take some of my ideas to the fullest. I think this could be a good way to an enjoyable, instead of horrid, lunch period. From now on Westwood could have the best lunch time ever.

Example #3

"Lunchroom Improvements. We Need 'Em"

When I envision our school cafeteria, images of wretched food and unbelievable noise come to mind. It is an awful place, a place most students want to avoid. There is room for much improvement!

If I were to be appointed to a committee to improve the lunchroom, the first thing I would do would be to take some kind of input from the actual consumers, the students.
I would find out what kind of foods the majority of people would prefer. This menu wouldn't be all pepperoni pizza and coke, as some of you probably visioned. It would be a balanced, nutritious meal, complete with all four of the food groups.

As I complete my first changes, I would then deal with the Food Service Workers, better known as Cafeterians. I personally have no problem with them, yet my peers insist that they are rude, unsanitary, and cranky. Maybe a routine check of the sanitation devices, i.e. dishwashers, ovens, freezers, so on and so forth, would help.

From what I witness, most Cafeterians don't use plastic rubber gloves while handling unprepared food. This discusts me to no avail. I can not eat in a cafeteria knowing that the food I am about to digest has been handled by a pair of dirty, greasy, grimy hands.

More supervision is needed in our cafeteria. As I mentioned earlier, the decibel level in our lunchroom reaches unbearable heights. Granted, the noise is generated from talking, but if you've ever been in an enclosed room with three-hundred "talking" eighth graders, I need to explain no longer.

I feel that if there was more supervision, the pupils wouldn't be inclined to speak as loudly as they regularly would; which takes me directly into my next subject — punishment.

Punishment should be doled out upon serious infractions of THE RULES. The rules include not throwing food, no yelling, no fighting, and no breaking manditory school rules. Infractions of the policy will result in eating lunch on stage, in plain view of the entire student body, next to the principal of the school. Self-ridicule and just plain embarrassment will make this a dreaded punishment never voluntarily experienced again.

In conclusion, I feel that the lunchroom in our school is adequate, if not average, with a few glaring deficienceys. And, that's why I'm here.

Example #4

"The New Lunchroom"

The lunchroom was old. First the bricks lost their color of white. Second the tables bent in different directions. Third the food tasted hard and crusty. Fourth the floor was scattered with litter and food.

One day, the principal called me up and asked me to be the leader of the comitee to improve the lunchroom.

Expository Sample Set — "Lunchroom"

The first day we decided we would repaint the whole building. We sent the children outside to eat, and then we started painting. First we jet-sprayed the walls with water to get the extra paint off the walls. After that we power-sprayed the walls white. Third we took rollers and painted the places where we missed.

The second day we decided to switch the chairs and tables that were destroyed. First we moved the chairs and tables out, so they could be recycled. Second we went out and bought new chairs and tables that felt more comfortable. Third we moved them into different places, so the lunchroom would look a lot neater and better.

The third day we put trashcans by the tables, so people could throw away their trash. Second we called fast food restaurants to sell food at our lunchroom. Third we threw away the hard and crusty food (that tasted like astro turf) into the trashcan. Fourth, we got a new order of food that tasted a lot better, and a lot better looking.

On the fourth day we started to plant flowers around the lunchroom, so it would look nice and clean.

On the fifth day we decided to put a radio in. First we hooked up speakers around the lunchroom. After that we hooked up all the wires and see how the lunchroom would take it. The school shook like an earthquake.

When the lunchroom reopened, everyone went in to see what it would look like. It looked so nice that the principal awarded us with a trophy and some money. After the cleanup, no one ever trashed the lunchroom again.

Example #5

"Improve The Lunchroom!"

"Improve the Lunchroom!" our principal demanded. He said if the lunchroom wasn't fixed up in less than two weeks he would shut it down. "I'm tired of all the complaints I'm getting." he said.

We got down to buiseness right away. First we thought the kids should get to vote on what the school serves for each day. Then we thought up some stricter rules to keep everyone under controll. Third we tried to make up privaliges and fun games we could all play to award the students for good behavior. We are even trying to make lunch an hour instead of thirty minutes everyday.

Example #6

"Lunchroom Improvements"

The problem with the lunchroom today one is that it's not very clean. For instance right after the seventh grade eat the eighth grade comes in after them. Crumbs and spilt drinks that seventh graders left, fill the ground along with the tables and seats. I definitely would make sure that the janitors cleaned up the place after each grade ate. Second of all, the cafeteria smells as if a thousand animals were slaughtered there and eggs were cracked then left to rought. Finally, the lunchroom has no personality of it's own, and absolutly nothing to cheer it up a bit. It's just so plan!

The smell that's in the lunchroom I would put an end to by getting rid of any old food that might be left. Then after that was completed I would have people sterilize the lunchroom every week.

After that I would put in little airfresheners all over the room not enough to keck (gag) people, just enough to send a slight scent through the air. To make the lunchroom look a little bit better I'd add pictures and decorate the stage with more life, maybe put up some curtains nice curtains and keep them closed all the time.

My ideas would certainly brighten up the cafeteria, and give a little originality to our school's name.

Example #7

"Lunchroom Food"

Lunchroom food is horrible! Have you ever tasted the mystery meat hamburgers there? The chicken is so tough that you think it will turn to shoe leather in your mouth. And those casseroles!!! You could study them for hours and not discover what lurks in them for some poor student to eat. I recommend bringing your own lunch, packed by your loving mother with non-mysterious ingredients.

I usually bring my own lunch, being wise to the horribleness of cafeteria food, but one day last week, I was in a rush and left my lunch bag on the kitchen counter. After a quick look at the lunchroom menu, I decided to go without eating. A "kind" teacher, however, could not stand seeing a poor student go hungry and gave me money to buy a lunch. Naturally, being the considerate kid that I am, I had to get in line behind the other poor unfortunate eighth graders and get a lunch.

With the teacher looking down at me as I sat down at the lunch table with the cafeteria lunch in front of me, I had to eat it. My stomach growled in sympathy with my mouth. Somehow I had to eat that glop. It was a casserole of some sort, buried in a reddish sause and swimming in grease. Green specks of something that was once alive was in there. It looked repulsive. I smiled at the teacher and took a small bite.

It tasted worse than it looked! The grease rolled around on my tongue making the green stuff slide down my throat before I even swallowed. It reminded me of the time I ate dogfood — yuck! I wanted to rolf.

I resolved then and there, as I forced the rest of the mess into my unhappy stomach while smiling at the teacher, that I would never, ever leave my lunch at home again. I had learned my lesson!

Scores and Analyses

Example #1

This is a perfect **low-medium** paper. While it has some serious mechanical errors, such as a pointed lack of commas and repeated spelling problems, it is somewhat organized with a beginning and a middle. It lacks a conclusion which alone would prevent this essay from receiving a higher score. There are some specific suggestions that are somewhat developed. There is some extraneous information ("…if they be bad I will remove the D.J. and take away their pizza day"). The vocabulary is adequate. It needs much more elaboration and detail.

Focus	Organization	Support	Style, voice	Conventions
Medium	Medium	Medium/low	Medium	Medium/low

Example #2

This paper is a **medium/high**. On the actual test, it would score at the low end of high. The organization is excellent, even with the use of some boring transitions. Vocabulary also is good ("considering," "accomplished," "dull," "expand," etc.) but not outstanding. There are very few errors, and sentence structure is varied. The introduction and conclusion could be better developed, and the three ideas could be stated in each. This is a good paper with well-developed support and details.

Focus	Organization	Support	Style, voice	Conventions
High	Medium	High	Medium/high	High

Example #3

Like Example #2, this paper obviously deserves a **high** score. In fact, on the actual test, it probably would receive the highest score possible. It has humor, excellent vocabulary ("mandatory," "peers," "consumers," "granted," "envision," etc.), sophisticated sentence structure, and apart from some minor spelling errors, few mechanical errors. The organization also is excellent, though the introduction could be a bit better developed to disclose the three suggestions. Support is superior with many details provided. The humor certainly adds to the score. This is definitely a superior essay.

Focus	Organization	Support	Style, voice	Conventions
High	Medium/high	High	High	High

Example #4

This is a tricky one to score. It looks good at first glance, but the student really got off the topic by telling what he/she did to the lunchroom, rather than give suggestions as head of a committee, and turned it into a narrative. This immediately takes the score down by a few points. The introduction is clever, but the conclusion is weak and gets slightly off-topic, telling how happy the students were with the improvements. The overuse of transitions is confusing. There are frequent minor mechanical errors. Vocabulary, while adequate, is nothing to write home about. The student has used two similes which help, but the fact that the essay gets off the basic topic cannot be ignored. This essay probably would receive a **medium** score because it does not present suggestions as the

Expository Sample Set — "Lunchroom"

prompt demands. It instead states the changes as if they have already been made and describes their effects. It also verges on being a narrative.

Focus	Organization	Support	Style, voice	Conventions
Low	Medium/low	Medium but off-topic	Medium	Medium

Example #5

This essay would score a **very low** on the test since it is essentially a list with no support or detail and no conclusion. Vocabulary is adequate, but an essay that is a list with no support cannot score higher than a low since support and focus are the two main things the scorers are looking for in the essays. This essay even strays from the topic in that the student has made a narrative essay out of an expository topic. There is an introduction; the list follows. These keep the essay from being unscorable.

Focus	Organization	Support	Style, voice	Conventions
Extremely low	Low	Extremely low	Medium	Medium

Example #6

This essay is a **low-medium**. It has a short introduction and conclusion and has support for fixing the smell but only one sentence of support for cheering it up. There are English and spelling errors (misuse of "it's," for example). Vocabulary is good with use of words such as "slaughtered," "sterilize," and "keck." (The student got this last word from a Caught'ya and was told not to use it on the state assessment test as it is an archaic word, but at least he/she tried to use good vocabulary and similes.) Organization and support are the main downfalls of this essay.

Focus	Organization	Support	Style, voice	Conventions
High	Medium	Low	Medium/low	Medium

Example #7

This paper, in my opinion, is **unscorable** because it is a narrative, not an expository essay. It is the hardest type of paper to score since it is well-written and coherent (and funny), but if the student does not address the topic at all and turns it into a narrative, the paper cannot be scored. This example mentions food but has no suggestions to improve the lunchroom. Obviously the student is bright and writes well with a good command of vocabulary, but he/she committed the cardinal sin of not addressing the topic at hand: improvements to the lunchroom. I call this the "gifted hole" into which bright students sometimes tumble. Indeed, one wonders what went through this student's mind as he/she read the topic. Sometimes very bright students dislike the topic so much that they simply refuse to write about it, writing instead about something that pleases them. This writer chose to write a personal narrative. Obviously, he/she had a "beef" with the cafeteria food and wanted to write about it. No matter how well-written this paper is, it cannot receive higher than the lowest score on the writing test unless you live in one of the states that now gives points for good writing no matter how much a student gets off the topic.

Focus	Organization	Support	Style, voice	Conventions
Extremely low	Medium—end	Medium/high	High	High

> **NOTE:** To obtain these samples, I read more than 170 papers. In at least a third of these papers, the writer talked about a problem (or problems), elaborated on that problem, and did not propose any solutions. Other students listed several problems, discussed them in detail, and then gave only a one-sentence solution to each. As I noted in **Step Three**, getting students to read the prompt carefully and not seizing one word as the focus of the essay can be a real problem. Several suggested solutions (Ha!) can be found in **Step Three**, page 76.

Topic for Sample Set: "Every school has problems. Think of one problem your school has that bothers you. Now think of some solutions to that problem. Write an essay explaining those solutions to the problem at your school." (Problem/Solution Essay)

Example #1

Every school has problems or issues. One problem that my school has is with people skipping class and having unexcused absences! There are many ways that a school can overcome this problem. Some ways to prevent students from skipping would be to put up more camera's, graduation suspension if you have too many unexcused absents', and not being able to make up the work you missed.

One way to prevent students from skipping class or school could be to set more camera's up around the school. For example, the parking lot, because driving students have their own transportation to just leave. You could also place camera's in the hallways and other places to catch students who ditch class.

Another way to overcome students from skipping class or school, would be to suspend their graduation if they missed too much school. I think this is a good idea because it allows the student to realize how important it is to attend school. Students should never vandalize their future by not going to school for no apparent reason.

My last idea to help prevent students from missing school or class would be to not let the student make up work if they were not excused from being absent. It's not fair to the other students who were there and also for the teachers. I think not letting the students make up their work, would give the students a good reason to be at school.

Every school has problem or issues. Skipping class or school isnt just a big problem in my school, but in schools everywhere. Help the futures of young students, plan against skipping.

Example #2

A problem that my school has is it is easy to get away with skipping classes. One of my solutions to prevent this from happenning more often would be locking all the schools restrooms during class, Signning in school before it starts, And getting phone calls home to parents while you are cutting class.

My first reason to help prevent from happening was locking all schools restrooms during classtime. You will have a bathroom in each classroom in case of an emergency. The school's public restrooms will be only allowed to be used during break time's in between classes.

My second reason is signning in school before it starts. The students whould have Id card's that will be scanned in the morning before school.
That will then trigger into the schools computers and will tell if you have showed up at school. Then the teachers will know if you are skipping class when they call role.

My third reason would be when you cut class you will atomatically get a phone call to a parent or guardian. At the time that you are skipping that class. You then will be sent to the office and sent to ISS for the rest of the day.

Those are my solutions to my schools problem. One of the problems. Hopefully my ideas will give some thought and maybe one day be used in all of this county's schools.

Example #3

One of the biggest issues we have in our school, even in these modern days, is racism. Believe it or not, racism is a huge problem among students, peers, and even teachers. There are a few solutions that might make racism less of a appalling problem in school. I am certain that we could work together to become a better school community when it comes to non-racial acts. Why can't we stick up for a student who is being mistreated because of his/her culture or nationality? We could also start a program that would help us get along with each other and that would train us to treat each other with respect and as equals. I certainly do want to make racism a thing of the past, or at least a much smaller problem, in our school.

Now, our school is one of the most mixed school in our county, mixed by color, language, and nationality. As a school with such a varied mix of students, we need to learn how to get along. They say that school is practically our second home. But, home is a place where your welcomed. At our school, it's not like that. In order to make our school like our homes, we have to learn not to judge people by the color of their skin or the language they speak in the halls. I know if we wanted to, we could be together as a school. If each student made friends with someone from another nationality or race and spent some time with that person, it would go a long way to solving the problem. After all, we learn to get along with our brothers and sisters in our homes. Why not do the same in our second home.

In addition to the problem of racism created by the mix of students we have at our school, I have become conscious of the fact that alot of students are bullied and picked on by their peers. They are bullied because of the way they look, because of their nationality, and because of the language they speak (mostly Spanish and Creole). Most of the other students don't even bother to get involved in these conflicts and simply let the poor victim be picked on. They keep walking away while someone is being bullied, pretending that it isn't even happening. Maybe if a group of us stuck up for those victims, this would not happen as much. The racist people who picked on the kids they think are different from them might think twice. Why? Because they would know if they messed with one of us, they mess with a whole bunch of us. We can be like family.

To go even further to solve this shameful problem, our school could start a huge program against racism. If the teachers could help us with such a program in which we study how to get along, we might see each other as equals and more alike than different. Someone once said that "Differences are only skin deep." We are all the same age at the same school, rooting for the same football team. If our school could implement a program that could help us care about curing racism, and why it's important to stop it, people might just think before they are rude to someone or make fun of someone just because they look or talk different. Maybe we could even all study each other's languages to have a better understanding of each other and our different cultures. It's kind of like if they become one of "us" and we become one of "them," we can't be racist any more.

In the process of helping get out of a racist mode into a family mode, we students could help each other in the process. We could help keep anyone from being bothered and hurt because of racism. We as a school, with the help of our teachers, could make a program to educate us about racism (after all, this is a school). If we do these simple things, maybe someday soon at our school it will not matter what the color of our skin is. It will not matter what language we speak or whether we have an accent. It will not matter where our parents were born. What will matter is that we become equal and fair and kind to each other, just like a family.

Example #4

"Problems with School"

Have you ever had a problem that made you so made you just want to scream? Well thats how I fell about my schools lunch lines. They are so long I barley have time to eat.

The are ways to fix this we could make more lines so not so many people don't stack up in a line. We could have them premake meals so theres quicker distrubution.

I think if we had multi lunch periods we could really do it right. That way not so many kids are all trying to eat at once, and my be people might sit in the caferiria and eat instead of going alaround the school.

So see if we try to fix the lunch problem every one ight get to eat instead of half. Like I said earlier I barley have time to eat so why dont you help me and every one else set lunch the right way instead of none at all.

Example #5

My school has a lot of problems here. I had been here about 4 mos. already. The first problem is the line to get your lunch you may wait like 30 min in the line to get your lunch. others think its the schule, the other school haven't the same schule, I don't not why it is the same county.

The solution to the lunch is to have more than one lunch, at least two lik A + B. one can be at third block an the next can be at the time is right now. that all I know about problems here.

Example #6

No school is perfect. Every school has something wrong with it. Here at our school we also are not an educational utopia. I believe the main reason that I would like to point out is our FCAT scores.

The FCAT is not an easy test. It requires alot of preparation. We lack the nescessary preparation needed to be ready for the reading, math, writing, and science testing. We should be honing our skills in all of these subjects. "Practice makes perfect, we need to redeem our reputation.

To reitorate, I don't like our school's grade. To make this better we should practice our skills for the FCAT more often.

Example #7

Everyone knows that every school has problems. My school is no exception. Since I attend _____, as a student I know that this school has problems. Some problems are worse than others, but the main ones we have at my school are the food and the dress code. I think it is important to give you explanations of why these are such dreadful problems.

The food in the cafeteria is a major problem here at my school. Since there is a lot of obesity in the United States, they are taking it out on us. "How are they taking it out on us?" you may ask. They are taking away some of our regular food like fries for example, and are replacing it with nutritious food. I don't think that htis is fair because not everybody in this school is obesse, and to the ones who are annorexic, they don't give them more food. This is only one of the problems we face at this school.

Dress code is definitely one of the problems that most kids argue about. In this case the problem goes beyond a simple dress code. Some of my friends are being suspended from school for supposedly dressing like a gang member. I don't think that this is good because I don't think they should be suspended for this stupid reason. Most students have dressed this way since elementary school! They are only trying to be "cool." This is the reason why I think there is a problem with the dress code.

In conclusion I have told you just some of the problems at my school. From the food to the dress code, you might agree or disagree with my opinions, but believe me, they are big problems at my school. If you haven't thought about this situation, think about it now and I bet you'll come out with a lot of ideas. Think about it and express yourself freely because this school does have problems!

Example #8

Our school has problem but I believe there could be many solution to these problems. One major solution to these problem is students getting into too many fights. There is a solution to this.

The solution to problem of students fighting is to have cameras in all the hall ways. The school could also put cameras in parking lot. So then when someone gets in a fight the can go to the video to see what really happened.

So to solve the problem of fighting the school need to invest in some camera. Now they can determin what really happened.

Example #9

Not every school is perfect, and my school has its problems just like all the others. One of the main problems with our school is the requirement to wear a sort of uniform. The administration requires us to wear a collared shirt that is black, white, navy blue, or tan—boring. The required pants must be kaki—extra dull! While girls are allowed to wear kaki skirts instead of the pants, they must be knee length—give us a break! This isn't the eighties. The two reasons why having a uniform dress code is that it eliminates showing our individuality. The other reason is because it costs too much for the uniforms. There are solutions we could implement to end this problem. They are very simple— 1) put a stop to the uniforms and 2) create a strict dress code so that we don't offend any adults, and 3) enforce this dress code. Simple, huh?

To begin with, if our school administration voted to do away with the uniforms and create a strict dress code, it would be the first step to a complete solution to this problem. In the new dress code they could make strict rules against midriff showing and tank tops which so offend the teachers. For example, the school could state that no midriff should be showing when the student fully extends their arms upward. Another restriction the administration could create is to ban halter tops, spaghetti straps, tank tops, tube tops, and t-shirts that use swear words, hate phrases, or beer ads. The school could allow the straps on the shirts of both sexes to be at least three inches wide. This is a huge restriction that I believe myself and my fellow students would abide by just to express our personalities with splashes of color and varied outfits.

The next part of the total solution to this uniform problem is that the principal and dean could create strong concequences to anyone who violates the dress code. For example, the guilty student could get several days in ISS or OSs depending on the degree of the violation. For example, if a student violates the three inch strap rule by a half inch, they could be required to spend only one day in ISS with more days for worse infractions. Of course days of OSS would be the punishment for students that have violated the dress code several times.

To conclude, I speak for myself as well as my fellow students who also wish to express themselves in their choice of clothing when I say that the uniform dress code is a huge problem that can easily be solved by common sense. Students who attend my school would do ANYTHING to get rid of it. This is why I think that my solution would work. Having had uniforms and knowing what it is like, students would now be ready to accept a strict dress code with severe concequences for violations just to get rid of the hated uniform dress code in those dull colors.

Example #10

Every school has its problems. Big or small, they need solutions. This school has one big problem it has to solve. It affects the entire school and the attitudes of the students. The problem is the school's appearance. It is an old school, but that doesn't mean that it can't be clean and nice looking. Instead, there is trash, graffiti, and vandilizing..

For example, there is trash every where. It seems like the students don't care and leave their lunch garbage where it is after they eat it. Some even eat during class and don't even bother to put the trash in the garbage cans.

Some solutions for the trash could be to punish the kids who don't pick up their trash. Some kids do it more than once so just make the punishments harder. The school can also put more trash cans every other corner of the school, closer to all of the tables. The kids are just too lazy to get up and throw their trash in the trash can.

There are also some gangs who live near the school and graffiti it like it's their property. They have no respect whatsoever. Others just vandilize for the fun of it, like breaking the windows and doors. Or getting into lockers and throwing books on the floor.

A better way to make sure this doesn't happen is to tighten the security system. Make the fences taller so kids won't easily jump through after school. Also put alarms on every door. Chains are just not enough. Make the windows unbreakable. And no glass doors.

A school's appearance says a lot about the students and teachers. If it's beautiful then it's a good learning environment. The school just needs to be more serious about its appearance.

Scores and Analyses

Example #1

This essay proposes solutions and sticks to the topic. However, the author rambles and keeps repeating him/herself (the suggestion of cameras, for example). There are a few fragments, some confusion of apostrophes and plurals, and comma problems, but for the most part, the conventions are OK. This is a good example of a "rambling **medium**" essay. The organization is fine, but the essay is a bit formulaic. The voice is not clear. Vocabulary is adequate but certainly could be improved.

Focus	Organization	Support	Style, voice	Conventions
High	Medium	Medium	Low	Medium

Example #2

This essay is a **medium**. While it sticks to the topic, has no extraneous information, and is organized, it is so formulaic that the student's voice hardly is recognizable. In addition, there are numerous fragments ("One of the problems."), other convention problems such as confusing possessives and plurals, and a few spelling problems. Vocabulary is adequate but not outstanding. Words like "scanning," "emergency," "automatically," and guardian" indicate some sophistication, but are not above grade level. Support is consistent, but no examples or anecdotes are given, and the details are not carried out to the second level. The student also uses the word "reason" instead of "solution." The end is a bit skimpy.

Focus	Organization	Support	Style, voice	Conventions
High	High but formulaic	Medium	Low	Low-medium

Example #3

Not much needs to be said about this excellent essay. The student writes fluently with superlative vocabulary ("appalling," "bullied," "implement"). Although he/she does talk a lot about the problem, the author develops those solutions in detail, being specific about the problem as well. The writer's voice is clear and includes humor, asides, a quote, parentheses, and even a theme (family). The organization is clear. The support and elaboration are consistent and detailed. There are very few convention problems ("your" instead of "you're," for example). The student even put a comma after "but" when he/she began a sentence with that conjunction! This is a definite **high**.

Focus	Organization	Support	Style, voice	Conventions
High	High	Very high	Very high	High

Example #4

This paper is another **medium**, however, it is on the low end of the spectrum. The writer begins with a good question and follows it with an effective statement but doesn't develop the introduction much more than that. The paper is basically focused on the topic but at the end becomes persuasive ("so why dont you help me and every one else set lunch the right way instead of none at all"). Parts don't make sense or the meaning is obscured (as in the sentence above). It is organized correctly, but

Expository Sample Set — "Problem/Solution"

all parts are skimpy and lacking in development. Except for the word "distrubution," the vocabulary is simple. There are spelling errors, but none of them gets in the way of understanding the content except "alaround." The conventions are fairly poor. There are no commas or apostrophes, several run-on sentences, and numerous usage errors. But, the most glaring problem in this essay is the lack of detail and elaboration.

Focus	Organization	Support	Style, voice	Conventions
Medium	Medium	Low	Low	Low-medium

Example #5

This essay is a **low** one. It is on the topic and attempts an organization, but it doesn't get far ("that all I know about problems here") and lacks clarity. The word "schule" means "schedule." I only know that because I know the schools in this county. Thus, the spelling problems do get in the way of comprehension. Convention problems abound—punctuation, capitalization, usage problems, etc. There is no support at all for the solution.

Focus	Organization	Support	Style, voice	Conventions
Medium	Low	Extremely low	Low	Low

Example #6

This is a difficult (and a painful) essay to score. The vocabulary is outstanding! The student uses extremely sophisticated words like "utopia," "redeem," "reputation," "honing," and even "reitorate" (misspelled but recognizable). There is a beginning, a middle (albeit a very short one), and a two-sentence end. Support is bare minimum. Even in such a short piece, the voice is evident (if only in the vocabulary use). There is a quote correctly punctuated and used. The student keeps the focus and shows organization, but there is no real development. There are three spelling errors but few convention problems. Obviously, this student could have done better if he or she had put in a little more effort on the piece. It must be scored a **medium** due to the lack of support and elaboration of the main point.

Focus	Organization	Support	Style, voice	Conventions
High	Medium	Low	High	High

Example #7

This essay is one of those that just make you cringe because it cannot receive a score for good writing (although some states are not giving zeros for papers totally off the topic if they are well-written). This paper certainly is well-written with clear organization, many details, and few errors, but, and this is a big "but," it is so off-topic that, in some states, it might receive a **zero**. The voice also is clear ("How are they taking it out on us?" you may ask."). Vocabulary is nothing stupendous but adequate.

Focus	Organization	Support	Style, voice	Conventions
Extremely low	High	High for wrong topic	High except for vocabulary	High

Expository Sample Set — "Problem/Solution"

Example #8

This essay has major problems itself. The writer gets confused between "problem" and "solution." But, there is no extraneous information. The only support is the idea to have cameras. There is no vocabulary and the writer's voice never surfaces. This student, I suspect, is still in the process of learning English and thus mostly does not put an "s" on the end of plurals or third-person singular verbs and leaves out words. There is some minimal organization in that there is a definite beginning, middle, and end, but none are developed to any extent. Convention errors are numerous. There is not a single comma in sight. Vocabulary is simple only. This essay is a **low** one.

Focus	Organization	Support	Style, voice	Conventions
Medium	Medium	Very low	Low	Low

Example #9

This essay obviously deserves a **high** score. There is humor and a clear voice. The writer intersperses good vocabulary throughout ("administration," "restriction," "splashes," "infractions," "consequences," etc.). There is only one spelling error and very few mechanics or usage errors. The writer uses a lot of detail to flesh out his/her idea so that there is no doubt in the reader's mind how the solution would work. He/she even gives specific examples. Sentences are varied, and strong verbs are used in places. All in all, this is an excellent problem/solution essay with flair, humor, and pizzazz.

Focus	Organization	Support	Style, voice	Conventions
High	High	High	Extremely high	High

Example #10

This essay is a good, solid **medium** that, with a little bit of work, could be a high. It is on the topic, but the organization is confusing between the problem and the solutions. The author jumps around. Is there one problem or are there three? There are some fragments, but there are not too many errors. The author uses a few good words like "vandalize" and "environment," but the vocabulary is just adequate. There are just enough details to keep the reader going, but the writer does not go beneath the surface to fully elaborate his/her points and solutions. The voice is there, but it is not very strong or noticeable. There is little or no passion and pizzazz, but it is not formulaic.

Focus	Organization	Support	Style, voice	Conventions
High	Medium	Medium	Medium	Medium

24 Narrative Examples

NOTE #1: *Some states differentiate between personal and imaginative narratives, but a narrative is a narrative.*

NOTE #2: *Because scoring differs from state to state, these samples are scored HIGH, MEDIUM, LOW, or ZERO for ease of translation.*

Topic for Sample Set: "Every day you pass a door. It is always locked. One day, as you pass, you notice that the door is open. You step inside. Write a story about what was on the other side of the door."

Example #1

When I go to the garage to get my bike out or skates, I see a door. I always wonder what's inside, but for some mysterios reason it is always locked. One day when I went to get my bike I wanted to open the door and it opened. I was so impressed.

I then decided to check out what was in there. When I went in there I saw a bunch of spider webs on the ceiling. I didn't get to scared. After I passed the spider webs, I saw this beautiful garden. It was full of flowers like daisies.

I soon started to get tired, so I got out of the door. The next day I came and tried to open the door but it just would not open. I soon realized that it was my first and only chance to go in there. After that I never forgot about the garden.

Example #2

You go lock it. And go up staris. And come Back down. It is unlocked and open. Something is say get out the house. Get out the house NOW. You get out of the house. And go to a nobar house that you and your mom know. Call the poilce as soon as you get there. When you get on the Phone be com and make sure you tell every thing. And don't forget to tell your adsdres and Phone number to. When you see your mom or the poilce go outside and meet them.

Example #3

Every day I go past a certain door and every day it is locked. One day I walk past it and it is unlocked. I wondered what was inside so I decided to go in.

The very next day I went in. I opened the door as silently as I could. Then, out came a huge, "Creak!"

"Oh — no!!! Whoever lives here will catch me now," I thought as I ducked behind the bushes.

No one came out. I ran inside extremely fast huffing and puffing. You won't believe what happened next!

It was black, pitch plack. Then again I thought I could see large white blanket looking things above and around me. They swirled like ghosts in all directions. I tried to ignore them by walking into the next room. The swirling blankets wouldn't go away. To my horror a high pitched scream rang out of my throat.

The blankets swirled around me faster, faster. I wanted to run away from them but my feet wouldn't move.

"Honey are you okay?" my mother said in her soft, sweet voice that seemed to come from far away.

"Yes," I said that I just had a bad dream. "Yes," I said to myself this time

Example #4

I walk home from school pass a door that is always locked. One day after school while I was walking home the door was unlocked. Then, I slowly walked inside. Soon, I found a staircase next to it was a night in shining armour. Slowly something extraordanary happend. The night in shining armour became a six leged ten armed alien.

I turned away and ran up the crooked stairs, then, I triped. The one eyed six leged ten armed two body alien creature walked closer. I got up and ran to the window. The alien started shooting acid at me. Then, I jumped out the window. The alien turned to stone and I went home. What a day!

Example #5

When I had walk past the door and I had went back. I had open the door I was so scarred. I had look up. I was going around and around. It had feel like some one was turnig me around in a circle.

I saw this big fat thing in there on the cles. When I had look it was on the ground I had saw a sperier. Then the door had close. I was so scared. I did not no want to do when that door had clesed. I saw some cloes the had some back salf on it. I was looking at the balck caest. It got hot and hot in the clocet.

the end

Example #6

I walk to and from school every day exsept Saturday and senday of corse. I always pass a locked door but this time it is unlocked and I take a step closer and it open quit quickly. There is a glary light inside the creepy door. Inside the glary light there is a creepy I mean creepy figure. It looked lopsided. I was so puzzled?

I took a few more steps and ...SMACK...the door shut loder than an atomike bomb. Well, maybe not quit that loud. Then...B-O-O-O..., my own family every one scared me half to death. I was so terrifed.

Example #7

Every day on my way home from school, I walk past a door that is always locked. Today, it was opened. I decided to voyage inside and explore. I cautiously entered the open door and stepped inside. Then, I found out that there was no floor under me. "AAAAHHHHHHHHH!," I shrieked as loud as a siren. The sound echoed off the walls of what seemed to be an endless pit as I fell and tumbled down and down. However, I soon found out it was not endless as soon as I hit the ground with an extremely loud thud.

I found that I was on the ground surrounded by snakes. They all glared at me with eerie, beady red eyes, ready to strike if I moved a muscle. Horrified, I held myself more stiff than petrified wood. I then did the only thing I could do.

"HELP!" I yelled at the top of my lungs. My heart pounded as loud as thunder. Maybe even louder as it seemed to echo off the walls of the pit. The snakes slithered closer to me, their winding bodies looking like dark spaghetti twisted together and moving. Then, from somewhere in the dark, a door opened with a creak, shining a light on the snakes and me. I lept up and rushed through the door as fast as possible, trying to leap over the snakes in my best ballet jump.

"I need to get home," I said.

"I know how to get you home," said a little green man who had suddenly appeared on the other side of the door. "We can throw a rope ladder up to attatch it to the doorknob way up there. But, we will have an extraordinary chance of being eaten by snakes on the way. They are still on the other side of this door." "Anything is what I will do to get home," I said confidently. "We can do it."

So the little green man and I cauciously opened the door to the room with the snakes. We streaked through the room to the side where the doorknob was way above us. It seemed billions of miles away. I just stared up at the doorknob above us, wondering if it was possible for me to get home. The little green man took a rope from around his waste and threw it up high, so high it disappeared.

Then I saw the rope ladder was attached to the doorknob. I jumped for joy onto the bottom of the ladder. I climbed as fast as I could, higher and higher. I felt I climbed up miles. Then before I knew it, I was out of the pit and through the door to outside.

"Thanks," I called down to the little green man who was staring up at me from the bottom of the rope ladder and waving goodbye.

I think that was a very scary time. I hope I never get that scared again. I know I will never go through opened doors ever again without knowing what is on the other side.

Example #8

Every day, you walk past a door certain door and it always locked. One day however, you walk by and notice it is unlocked. When you pasted a door the door is unlocked and you go in the door to see what's in there. The room is dark and scary. You cut on the light to see in the room the room is imtea. The room had nothing in it. No bad no dresot no mirro it had no tv in t. "It was just imtea."

That is my sory.

Example #9

It was a beautifull Saturday morning in Gainesville, Florida. Mom and Dad had gone to a confrence and I got to stay home. I decided to go into my parents room. I looked up and down and back and forth like a spy. I was eying my parents closet that was always locked like a prison.

I built up the courage to walk over. Without having to touch the knob it opened. I slowly creped inside, and my eyes got used to the blinding light inside the closet. Surprisingly, there were no dirty socks hanging off the shelves. Instead, there were scattered pieces of moss hanging off tiny palm trees. Instead of shirts spraled across the floor there were ponds with huge orange swans. There were even stars in the sky when the sun was shining.

I stepped out for a second to make sure I wasn't dreaming when the door closed behind me. I tried franticly to get it opened but it was locked again! Now the door that was locked for years finally beheld it's magic, but now it is locked again forever.

Example #10

Maybe it is a man. A mean man. Maybe it was his secreat hideout. Or maybe is is a kid. A kid that goes at school. Maybe it is the kid workshop. When I went inside and what did I see. I saw a kid. I was right it was a kid. I guess a really good guess it was.

Example #11

One day, after Girl Scouts, I walked past a door that is usually locked. I found the door unlocked. Now this is strange. I decided to go inside. The walls were covered in greenish mold!

I walked farther down the hall. I then came to a room. The room was a bathroom. I peeked in. There was an old-fashioned bathtub in the corner.

I walked in to the bathroom. I found a trap door. Hesitently, I opened it. I found beautiful jewelry. The jewelry was gold, pearl, and silver.

I closed the trap door and went across the hall. I found a bedroom. There was curtains around a bed. I opened the curtains. The bed was dark purple.

I walked down the hall even farther and found a staircase. I went up the staircase and found another hall. I walked down this hall.

Unexpectedly, everything modernized! The walls became black. It was a strange black. Then, paintings appeared on the walls. Paintings of famous singers.

I was stunned! I ran all the way home. When I got home nobody believed my story.

I still can't figure out what happened behind that door!

The End

Example #12

I always walk by an old house that is locked. On a Sat. I found that the door was standing wide open. My mom had always taught me not to go in to other peoples houses. I stopped, and paused. I asked myself if I sould go in or not. Since the house was abanted why not go in and take a peek.

I walked up the stairs and peeked into the old house. All a sudden a bird flew out of the old house. A shiver ran down my spine and I started to shake. I had an urge to go inside so I walked inside and all a sudden the door slammed behind me and the room grew dark.

The next thing I knew the room turned into a magic world. Through a light mist I could see a magical city, lit up by lights that made it look like Cindarella's castle with waterfalls around it. There were beasts, wild animals, monsters who lumbered around on green medows, and a giant doll who started crying when she saw me. The magic world started to flood with the tears of the doll. All of a sudden this giant dargon comes out and trys to burn me but I smiled at him and he asked me, "Do you need a ride?"

I answered, "yes."

The dargon flew me to an edge of a forest. He said, "If you need me again shout "tree.""

I walked into the forest. Half way a tree grabed me and then all the trees grabed me. One of the trees made a fire out of its own branches and another made a pot out of bark and put water, spices, and fruits in it. As far as I could see they wanted to make a stew out of me! Then I rembered to yell, "tree." I shouted "TREE" at the top of my lungs and then the dargon appared out of nowhere roaring at the top of his lungs, and spiting out fire.

The fire burned the trees but it didn't burn me for some reason. I thougt it was the weirdest thing so I asked the firendly dargon and he told me that since I'm not a thing that lives here, in the old house, I can't get hurt.

I asked him how to get out of the old house and he said he would take me but it might take us a while and there were a lot of demons like the trees who made stew that would want to try to hurt me. After a while we came upon a ghost that looked like it was mist inside white sheets. The dargon knew how to get rid of him. All he had to do was sing a song but he didn't know any songs to sing so I started to sing "You Are My Sun Shine." The ghost started to disapare and we were on are way agian.

The next stop was to the exit. I fell asleep after a while right on the dargons back. When I woke up I was on the grass in my own back yard. I ran up to the door and my mom was waiting for me. She wasn't worried. I hadn't been gone very long. Maybe she knew about dargons and little girls...

Example #13

I always walk by this door the door is always locked, but one day it was open so I decided to go in. You will never ges what I found.

I went down a very dark tunel. It smelled like something died in here, finaly I got to the end of the tunel. And I found an old amusement park! I decided to take a look around it was etarordnary I had never seen anything like it.

While I was walking around I found a very big swich. I tried to pull it but it was hard so I pulled it down the power came on. I went to look for the the games but ensted I found the rides. Neat! This ride looked famtastick, it was called the swirley so I got in it made me extreamly disey I almost threw up but I held it in.

Then I found the video games! They had some very old games this one was put out of the market for being to vilent I found a quarter so I played a game that was my day.

That was a very fun and exsited so I liked It very much that was a fun day. And very nice day.

Example #14

One day after school my friend and I past a house. The house was big and black and white. When we past the house we notice that the door was open. Then we looked inside. The house was emty. Then we looked more.

First, we looked for foot prints. There where mud prints all on the carpet leding to all the rooms. Then we panitce. "There mustd have been robbed," said my friend. "Yes they musted haved been robbed," repild Sally. "I think we sould call my mom," said Sally.

Next, we called my mom but all she said was, "Quite goffing off." Then she said, "I got to go back to working. Then we called my dad. All he said is that "my mind was playing trick on me." I tryed to ixspain that they where robbed. All he said is, "go do your home work drauger.

Last we called Mrs. Stallbom. She said they where not robbed. That they where moving. I was so that they where not robbed but sad that they were moving. Now I was really sad thay my best friend was moving.

Scores and Analyses

Example #1

This example has a definite beginning, middle, and end, wrapping up the story quite nicely. It stays on the topic and even has some description in the middle paragraph (the garden). Mechanics are pretty good, and vocabulary is adequate. I score this paper a **low-medium** because it lacks detail in the middle, it has no attempt at a conversation, and the story needs to be expanded. It is a below-average paper with nothing special about it.

Focus	Organization	Support	Style, voice	Conventions
High	Medium	Low	Medium	High

Example #2

This example would have to be **unscorable**. First of all, it never addresses the topic of writing a story about what was on the other side of the door. In fact, it never mentions the word "door." It also immediately turns into a "how to" expository paper for a child who finds trouble: "Call the police as soon as you get there. When you get on the Phone be com and make sure you tell everything." There is no dialogue or good vocabulary. Almost every "sentence" is a fragment. In some states, this student would receive the lowest possible score just for writing something.

Focus	Organization	Support	Style, voice	Conventions
Extremely low	Extremely low	Low	Non-existent	Low

Example #3

This example, although fairly short, is a good, solid **medium** paper. It has a solid beginning in a paragraph all to itself. The middle is developed with descriptions ("large white blanket looking things"), similes ("like ghosts"), good vocabulary ("ignore," "swirled"), strong verbs ("swirled around me"), and varied sentence structure. The end has a dialogue that is, for the most part, correctly punctuated, and it wraps up the story. More detail and more story development would raise the score.

Focus	Organization	Support	Style, voice	Conventions
High	High	Medium	High	High

Example #4

This paper is a good example of a **low** score but not the lowest one. It does have a beginning, a middle, and an end and tells a story. Vocabulary is adequate ("extraordanary"). There is some description of the alien, but the story needs development, detail, and elaboration. The student never exits from the door. Almost all the sentences are simple.

Focus	Organization	Support	Style, voice	Conventions
Medium	Medium/low	Low	Low	Medium

Narrative Sample Set — "Door"

Example #5

This example has too many words that are indecipherable ("sperier" and "caest," for example) and, although some sort of story is evident and there is a semblance of chronological order, there isn't enough to score higher than a **low**. This is one of the few instances where the spelling is so poor that it interferes with comprehension (and therefore the score).

Focus	Organization	Support	Style, voice	Conventions
Medium	Low	Extremely low	Low	Low

Example #6

This paper has a definite beginning, middle, and end. There is even some descriptive detail in the middle ("creepy figure," "It looked lopsided"), but it is not enough to earn this paper a medium score. Chronological order is not really clear, organization is weak, and the ending doesn't wrap up the story. There is one good vocabulary word ("lopsided"). This would receive a **low** score but not the lowest.

Focus	Organization	Support	Style, voice	Conventions
Medium	Medium/low	Extremely low	Medium/low	Medium

Example #7

This paper is obviously a **high**. In fact, it would stand a good chance of receiving the highest score on the writing assessment test. The beginning is well laid out, clearly setting the scene. The middle is developed in clear chronological order with descriptions (of the snakes), similes ("as loud as thunder," "more stiff than petrified wood"), dialogue, and detail. There are not too many mechanical errors. Good vocabulary ("extremely," "beady") and strong verbs ("my heart pounded") abound. The story progresses slowly from scene to scene without jumping in action. The end wraps it up with a promise to himself/herself. This is an excellent story with verve, tension, and flair.

Focus	Organization	Support	Style, voice	Conventions
High	High	High	Extremely high	High

Example #8

While spelling is obviously a problem ("imtea"), it would not interfere with the score as the words are decipherable. The writer does have a brief beginning and has a little bit of detail in the middle, but there is not really a story here, and organization is poor. This paper would receive a **low** score.

Focus	Organization	Support	Style, voice	Conventions
Medium	Extremely low	Almost non-existent	Low	Low

Narrative Sample Set — "Door"

Example #9

This is a good story with a beginning, a fairly well-developed middle, and an end to wrap it up. There are attempts at good vocabulary ("spraled," "scattered") and even two similes ("like a spy" and "like a prison"). I would give this story a **medium**. This example would have scored higher with more narrative, a conversation, and a more developed end.

Focus	Organization	Support	Style, voice	Conventions
Medium	Medium	Medium/low	Medium	Medium

Example #10

This paper would be scored a **low** or **unscorable** depending on the state. It never really addresses the topic or mentions the door. The speculation about the "kid," however, could be interpreted as being on topic enough to give it a 1. This is not really a narrative but a questioning about what something is. It is too vague, lacking any organization. There is no dialogue or use of good vocabulary. This paper could have been assured of a 1 if the author had just once mentioned the locked door.

Focus	Organization	Support	Style, voice	Conventions
Non-existent	Non-existent	Non-existent	Low	Low

Example #11

This example is a well-written narrative. I would score this a **high-medium**. The author develops the beginning, fills the middle with description and detail about the contents of the rooms, and wraps it all up nicely at the end. Although there is no dialogue, the chronological order is clear, the vocabulary is good ("modernized," "stunned") and even spelled correctly in most cases. The writer even uses strong verbs ("Paintings appeared on the walls."). What keeps this example from earning the highest score is the use of only simple sentences, the lack of dialogue, and a lack of "pizzazz." The middle needs more detail. The repetitive "I walked" makes the paper dull.

Focus	Organization	Support	Style, voice	Conventions
High	High	Medium	Medium	Medium

Example #12

While this writer cannot spell very well, all of his/her words are decipherable ("dargon"). Chronologically, the story flows well from entry into the room to meeting the trees and the ghost and finally returning home. The writer even wraps it up, wondering if his/her mother knew about dragons. There is dialogue, and sentence structure varies despite the lack of commas. Strong verbs abound ("Shiver ran," "bird flew," "door slammed"). The vocabulary is excellent ("lumbered"). Since mechanics are the least important part of a score, and the story is well-written, this would score a **high**, probably even the highest possible score due to its content, originality, clear organization, details, and focus on the topic at hand.

Focus	Organization	Support	Style, voice	Conventions
High	High	Very high	High	Medium

Narrative Sample Set — "Door"

Example #13

This is a basic **medium** paper. It has a beginning, a middle with some detail, and a definite ending. It has some attempts at good vocabulary ("extarodnary," "fantastick") and paragraphing. The writer clearly follows a chronological order, going into the door, going down the tunnel, finding the park, trying the rides, and finally trying the video games. The run-on sentences, however, interfere with the understanding of the paper, and that keeps it from receiving a higher score.

Focus	Organization	Support	Style, voice	Conventions
High	Medium	Medium	Medium	Medium

Example #14

This student tried to write an expository essay, complete with transitions in the middle paragraphs, out of a narrative topic. While it has a definite beginning, middle, and end, and it does try to tell a story, the end is unclear. The author uses conversation (the phone calls), but parts are unexplained. (Who is Mrs. Stallbom, for example?) This paper would receive a **low to medium** score due to the lack of clarity and the obvious essay format in a narrative paper.

Focus	Organization	Support	Style, voice	Conventions
Low	Medium/low	Medium/low	Medium	High

Topic for Sample Set: "After the recent hurricane disaster, there were people who did some very heroic things to help those in need. First, think about what makes a hero. Then imagine yourself as a hero of the storm, and write a story about your heroism in the recent disaster."

Example #1

Hurricane Wilma was a disaster! Alot of people did heroic things to help. I was one of those people. It wasn't hard. Here is what I did.

Toward the end of October, a terrible disaster happened. Hurricane Wilma hit our town. While I sat in the house, listening to the wind howl and the rain pound hard on my roof, I waited. Finally, after about five hours of being in the middle of the hurricane and passing through the eye wall, Wilma passed. I jumped into my car and drove of to find people to help.

As I drove down the street, I saw many houses with trees on top of them. I saw trailers tipped to the side with roofs caved in on some houses. I ran up to peoples houses making sure they were ok and didn't need help but some did. I took them in my car and off we went.

After a restless drive home, I took every one inside and calmed them down. I fed them lots of food for they were very hungry. They managed to all gobble down the food. I fed them some steak, mashed potatoes and gravy, and some garlic bread that were in our freezer. I wanted to eat them up in case our electricity went out. They offered to pay for it but I insisted that they didn't.

They all also got hot showers. I had electricity back the day of the hurricane but others weren't so lucky. Some didn't have a water heater for weeks because of no electricity. So everyone was glad to be at my house to have that. Once again they offered to pay for everything they had gotten from me but I still refused.

Once people started getting electricity back, the started to leave for their own homes. From that day forward I considered myself a hurricane hero.

Example #2

It was a dark cool night, right after the disasterous Hurricane Wilma struck my town. Me, my sister (Sydney), Mom, and Dad were just getting ready to go over to our neighbor's driveway for a cookout when I heard a strange popping noise, just like what popcorn sounds like in the microwave when it is cooking. I looked around the room but couldn't see anything. I ran to my dad in the kitchen and told him about the strange popping noise.

My dad and I ran back to the living room to find smoke pooring from our T.V.! Dad immedately yelled, "Turn everything off including the generator!" Then he ran around the house unplugging everything.

As he did that, I realized that my sister was standing in front of the smoking TV paralyzed with fear! I grabbed her by her jacket, put my other hand on her back, and shoved her out the front door. Then I put my arm around her and walked her far enough away so she wouldn't be hurt. She was crying. A neighbor came to stay with her.

After my sister was safely at the end of the driveway, I ran back in the house, grabbed our cat carrier, quickly and silently dumped my cat in it before she knew what I was doing so she wouldn't scratch me, ran the cage outside to where my sister was still standing with our neighbor. My cat howled the entire time because she doesn't like being in her cage, but I knew that she would be safe..

Next, I raced back inside again, this time calling to our three large dogs as I ran. They came right to me and I quickly hooked them up to their leashes that were on the table by the door. Then I took the dogs outside and tied Niko, Maggie, and Toby's leashes to the tree in our front yard. They barked at me because they don't like being tied up like zoo animals, but I knew they were safe.

Knowing that my sister and our dogs and cat were safely outside, I dashed back inside where my father was still trying to get everything unplugged so that he could put out the fire in the T.V. I helped my dad carry the still smoking t.v. onto the side of the road. Shortly after that, my mom came running out of the house with our two birds. She had been in the bedroom and didn't realize what was happening until she heard my dad yelling.

About thirty seconds after we got the t.v. to the side of the road, my brain started functionning again and I grabbed the hose from our neighbors yard and sprayed water all over the t.v. to cool it off. All this had happened in only a few minutes!!

When those horrid few minutes were over, and everything was safe, we settled our animals into our house again. Then, exhausted and still shaking we headed over to our neighbor's for dinner. Before we reached the driveway, my mom and dad stopped me and told me how proud they were. They told me that I was their hero of the day. After that everything was just fine.

Example #3

The hurricane was really horrible, this time it knocked down alot of houses and food has been very hard to find. So this time I decided to help. I was going to donate something. Then I was gonna fly up there and help them rebuild their homes, and I will also give to them.

First I didn't just donate money I went to the next step and donated clothes, shoes, and I also donated money. That way they had more money to spend on food and shelter than clothes. And can have some extra money for themselves.

Second I also helped rebuild homes. I worked really hard as I put houses up and foofs on their head. Then we had to put all the furniniture in, but before that we layed out all of the fluffy white carpets. Everyone was very thankful.

Then I gave to people. I gave them food and water. And obviosly a Place to live. And I also gave them very special gifts. The gifts had to be very special because they loved and cherished them.

In conclusion I helped and became a huricane hero. By... Donating clothes, shoes, and money. Helping rebuild Homes, and giving to people. You should do it to. It feels good to help.

Example #4

This is the story of super I the greatest hero of all. Well superman beat me by a little but I can woop him. So any way you will hear about my action adventure and fighting.

Hello kids, I'm Super I, the great hero, I mean 2nd greatest super hero, one of the best next to superman, but anyway, I'm here to protect the city. The city of Lansing.

The city of Lansing is one of the best. It is also one of the most dangerous, good to live in, but dangerous. It is dangerous because of megaman, the worst villin of all.

One day as I was patroling the city, I spotted megaman at the city power plant. He was planning to suck the power clean so I flew into action, "Stop it you evil doer."

"You can't stop me, Super I. Not only will I suck the cities power but all the power in the world."

"What the world?" I asked.

"Yes the world. By hacking into all the computers in the power plant I wil control people's power and if they want power they have to pay me. Ha, Ha, Ha, snort, snort. Sorry I snort when I laugh."

"You'll never get away," I said. So we fought and you know I put one foot on his head and hit him hard. He had already sent the signal so I did the only thing I could think of.

So that's the story kids.

"But what did you do mister. Huh?"

"Oh well I flew in space, and I turned the satalite around so the signal missed and I saved the world."

Example #5

Over here! I found a person hurt really bad. After the Hurricane I let in some people who did not have a place to stay. I helped look for hurt people or stuck in their houses. It was a really bad hurricane. I was luckly that my house was still up. I saw this boy stuck in a tree with a broke leg and arm. I take him to a hospital. They take him in the back. I looked all around the neighborhood for hurt people. I find this man laying on the ground. I said "do you need a place to stay." Well he needed one becase his house was in pices. I give him clean cloths and food untill his house was build again. The kid that had a broken arm and leg stayed at my house to becase he did not know where his mom and dad was. I looked in all the shelters for his mom and dad, but did not find them. Then a day later I saw them outside looking for their son. I thought to myself I was a hero for what I was doing. The man had his house built and the boy was home safe. His parents said I was a hero for what I did. It is not bad to help out some. It feels good.

Example #6

The headlines screamed, "Catagory 3 Hurricane Destroys Southern Florida!" In an article under the headline, the newspaper reporter said that the day after Hurricane Wilma hit, south Florida desperately needed some real heroes. Our town had no power and a short water supply. My father's car was a total disaster. The streets were a mess, but I knew that I could at least go around the block and pick up the debree. The neighbors' yards and ours looked like a big dump on a construction site. "Maybe I should help the town clean up," I thought.

Hurricane Wilma had tossed a bunch of small trees and branches onto my father's car. That had to be my first priority. I grabbed two friends and we threw all the branches, roof parts, and screening off his new, black Jetta. When the debree was cleaned off, the top and hood of the dark colored car looked all scratched up as if a cougar had jumped on it and used its claws to killed something right on the car. Still, it looked better without the trees and branches on it. My dad was pleased with our work.

After cleaning the branches and stuff off daddy's car, Melanie, Nicole, and I took off around the block to see what we could do to help. We moved anything that was not supposed to be on the sidewalk to a place where people wouldn't be injured by it. There was a plethora of light gray and black roof tiles all over the streets and sidewalks. As we picked it up to move the pieces of roof, the rough, sharp edges of the tiles that had come from rusty roofs cut our hands and made us bleed. But as they all say, "everything was going to be okay."

We ran home to my mom and she cleaned and bandaged up our hands using water from the bathtub that we had filled before the hurricane. Then after my mom patched up our hands, we went outside again and stopped by a couple of houses that had been hit bad by the fierce winds of Wilma. The people in those houses needed help. The trees that had fallen over looked like a monster had come through the city and flipped the trees upside down like they were matchsticks. Wow! This hurricane had done some pretty bad damage! A huge banyon tree lay on its side like a whale in the front yard.

My friends and I couldn't help with the trees, but we did help people by babysitting their young kids while the parents cleaned up the mess in their yards and on their porches. We watched three little boys and played a game of hide and seek in the branches of a big banyon tree that had fallen down. The parents were very grateful for our free babysitting service.

I don't think we did very much, but my two friends and I stuck together and helped with the cleanup. Now our street and our houses don't look as bad as they did right after Hurricane Wilma hit. I guess we all were heroes because we pitched in and did what needed to be done. It felt good to be old enough to be able to help. My dad says that I was a real hurricane hero especially after my friends and I cleaned up his car!

Example #7

What would of done to help the victoms of Hurricane Wilma is...

Sense I'm safe up in NC what I could of done was that I would go down here in FL and help the victoms. I would do is with the money that I have in my bank account. What I would do with the money that I have is that I would use it to donate to the Red Cross. So if I were to put in half of my bank account they could be about $5000. I have that much because my parents put about $100 of they're pay check in my account. So what I would do is that I would give $1000 to each family.

Example #8

I, the Hurricane Hero did alot of things to help out our state from a disaster huricane.

I couldn't imagine what it would be like to have nothing, so I donated alot of things that the needy needed. I started fundraisers. I started fundraisers so we could raise money. That's when the donations came along. I gave toys from the fundraisers. Including usable clothing and blankets. But the most important thing I did was getting other people in the U.S. to show some charecter, so victims would learn that other people out of Florida care.

And that was my heroic "hurricane Hero" story. Are you a "hurricane Hero"?

Example #9

"Swish! Bang! Boom!" is what I heard when that evil hurricane named Wilma came surging through our town. After my family sat through 4 hours of that awful noise, not knowing what was going on outside, the storm was finally over, and we could go outside to survey the damage. My parents said that before we tackled anything at our house, we had to help my Aunt Ethel clean up.

We drove through the messy streets, avoiding the fallen tree branches and broken roof tiles. After we arrived at our destination, first my brother and I immediately tackled my aunt's yard. There were so many branches that it looked like someone had cut off every branch of a tree, threw them around, and didn't clean up! After we made a pile of branches by the road, we decided to fix the hedges. They were all laying down on the ground where the wind had pushed them. We had to pull them back and forth, back and forth to get them to stand back up. Then we cut off the worst parts where the harsh wind had burned them and turned them brown. When we had finished with the bushes, our pile by the road was as tall as me!

After we did the yard work, we decided to go inside my aunt's house. We helped Aunt Ethel take everything off the counters and put them back in place. Everything that had been moved upstairs to protect it from flooding had to get moved back down to its home downstairs. Since there wasn't any electricity, we couldn't use the elevator. So we had to go up and down, up and down the stairs until our legs ached. Ouch!

Then, after we had tacked down both of those chores, we had to make the touchdown. We had to go and haul over the generator outside and try to fix it so that my aunt could have some lights at night and keep her food in the fridge from spoiling. That thing was heavy!!! We tried to but couldn't fix it and finally we had to call an electrician on my mom's cell phone. He came over and got that generator working in no time. Then we went back into my aunt's house and opened the refrigerator that was now working and got a cold glass of homemade lemonaid.

Hauling all those heavy branches and trying to help move that big generator put my back out, but all the time I was happy because I was there helping my family. I didn't think I was a hero, but in Aunt Ethel's eyes, I was her "baby knight in bright armor."

Example #10

After the hurricane most of the people didn't have electricity and water. That's when I told my mom if we could go to places that help people and we'll help. I was outside helping people pack the supplies they needed for their houses. After a few hours I went inside, that was when they told me to go to another place to help other people, this time I had to help old people. Some busses came, they had old people in them. I was helping them get out of the bus and into the wheelchairs.

After I helped them get out the person who was the boss in that place told me to help some people that were in the kitchen preparing the food. After I helped them cook there was a guy who was carrying some trays and I asked him if he needed some help he said yes so I carried a couple of them into two seperate rooms. When I came back I had to wash dishes mop the floor and unpack some boxes of food into a storage room. When everything was done the boss of that place said thank you for your work we really needed someone like you. After a few hours he gave me some money but I told him I did this work for kindness not for people's money.

Scores and Analyses

Example #1

This example has a definite beginning, middle, and end. It stays on the topic and remains a narrative. There are a few usage problems, but for the most part, the mechanics are pretty good. The vocabulary needs to be improved, and there is no dialogue. There need to be more compound and complex sentences. (The majority are simple.) The story lacks a strong voice. And, the examples and details need to be used consistently throughout the story. There is some good description in the third paragraph, but it is brief. The author gives some detail—"I fed them some steak, mashed potatoes and gravy, and some garlic bread."—in paragraph four, but like the description, it is not consistent. This paper is a definite **high-medium**.

Focus	Organization	Support	Style, voice	Conventions
High	High	Medium	Medium/low	Medium

Example #2

This story undoubtedly should be scored a **high**. There are a few spelling problems like "disasterous," "immediately," etc. but nothing major. The beginning is strong, sets the scene, and builds the suspense. The middle is well developed in chronological order with plenty of details about the TV, the writer's sister, and the family pets. While there is no dialogue (only one quote from the father), there are plenty of good vocabulary words ("disastrous," "functioning," "exhausted," "generator"), a simile, and good strong verb use. The story progresses slowly enough from scene to scene without a break in the action and with each action completed. The end wraps up the story nicely and brings it around to the beginning where the family is heading to the cookout. The writer's voice is very clear.

Focus	Organization	Support	Style, voice	Conventions
High	High	High	High	Medium/high

Example #3

While this example has a beginning, a middle, and an end, it is written like an essay (and a formulaic one at that) and not a narrative. There is not really a chronological story progression, but the writer did do things in a kind of order—donated, rebuilt, gave things. There are seven spelling errors, many usage problems, fragments, and other problems with the conventions. The vocabulary is simple and so are all the sentences but one. Still, I would give this example a **low-medium** because, even though it is more of an essay than a narrative, it is on the topic, follows a logical progression from beginning to end, has some description (albeit minimal), and includes a few details ("clothing, shoes, and money").

Focus	Organization	Support	Style, voice	Conventions
Medium/low	Medium	Low	Low-formulaic	Low medium

Narrative Sample Set — "Hurricane Hero"

Example #4

This is one of those difficult and painful **unscorable** papers, although nowadays some states will score a paper mostly for the quality of writing and take off only a point for not being on topic. The story is a fairly well-written narrative with a few spelling errors but basically correct. Even the dialogue is correctly punctuated. But, the story really doesn't make much sense. Obviously the writer is relating a TV show or movie he or she has seen. If this narrative were on the topic, I would score it a **low-medium** because of the voice, the conventions, and the dialogue, despite the lack of detail.

Focus	Organization	Support	Style, voice	Conventions
Extremely low	Medium	Medium	Medium	High

Example #5

Although this narrative has no paragraphing, it is not a low paper. There is a definite beginning, middle, and end. The story progresses from a good, original start ("Over here") to a logical end. But, I score it a **low-medium** because of the lack of detail, the use of only simple sentences, the lack of any sophisticated vocabulary, and its punctuation and usage problems.

Focus	Organization	Support	Style, voice	Conventions
High	Medium	Low	Low	Medium

Example #6

This paper is definitely a **high** one. It begins with a bang ("The headlines screamed...") and continues the story using good descriptions (the car, the roof tiles), nice detail (the tiles cutting their hands), good vocabulary ("a plethora of," "desperately," "debris" spelled wrong, "construction"). The voice is clear, and the writer used some original similes ("like a big dump on a construction site," "like a whale in the front yard"). The fallen banyan tree in paragraph four is used again in paragraph five. All in all, this is an excellent narrative.

Focus	Organization	Support	Style, voice	Conventions
High	High	High	Very high	High

Example #7

There is no question that this paper deserves a **low** score. The story does not make much sense. There is no logical progression. Conventions are poor. There is no clear voice and no detail or description anywhere except about the amounts of money.

Focus	Organization	Support	Style, voice	Conventions
Low	Low	Extremely low	Low	Low

Narrative Sample Set — "Hurricane Hero"

Example #8

This paper is another **low** one even though there are a few details and the sentence structure is varied. The details, though, are minimal, and nothing is developed. There is one fragment and some spelling errors ("alot" "huricane," "charecter"), but the conventions are not bad. It is the minimal development of the story that keeps the score a low one.

Focus	Organization	Support	Style, voice	Conventions
Medium	Medium	Low	Low	Medium

Example #9

This paper is a **high**. It begins with the use of onomatopoeia and then briefly describes the hurricane and the scene at Aunt Ethel's yard. There are some usage problems (such as using "like" instead of "as" several times), but generally the conventions are good. There is only one spelling error ("lemonaid"), and the sentence structure is varied. Details abound (such as about the bushes and the generator). The voice is clear. This paper could be improved by the use of some superlative vocabulary, maybe some dialogue, and a tad more detail. The end is very nice and really wraps it all up.

Focus	Organization	Support	Style, voice	Conventions
High	High	High	Medium	High

Example #10

I would score this narrative a **low-medium**. There are some major convention problems (like the complete lack of commas except in incorrect places and numerous errors with verbs—"if we could go to places and we'll help"). There are a number of run-on sentences. The writer does tell a story with a chronological progression, but there are few nitty-gritty details and a lack of good vocabulary. There is a definite beginning, middle, and end, but all parts need more development. No great vocabulary is used. What keeps this story from earning a low score are the few details ("wash dishes mop the floor and unpack some boxes of food into a storage room") and the definite progression of the story from beginning to end.

Focus	Organization	Support	Style, voice	Conventions
High	Medium	Medium/low	Low	Low

23 Persuasive Examples

Topic for Sample Set: "Persuade a friend to move to your town."

Example #1

Hola, Miguel, you need to leave Mexico and come join me here in Naples, Florida! Think of the fun we could have if we were together in this exciting town. Don't you want to enjoy fabulous weather instead of hot, hot, hot? How would you like to celebrate more holidays and get more presents??? You must move to Naples. Besides, I miss you.

You have no idea how much fun we can have in Naples. What I mean by "fun" are the theme parks that are either in the city or nearby. One of them (my personal favorite) is King Richards. It is better than anything you have in Mexico. Let me tell you how amazing it is! It has a roller coster that makes you feel like you are flying. You can ride in bumper cars and hit other cars. When you hit the other cars in the back or front, it is like you crashed but did not get hurt. King Richards is so <u>cool</u>! The ferris wheel goes so high you almost can touch the clouds. It's kind of scary because it is so high, but that is what makes it so exciting! You just have to come and experience it for yourself. Besides, can't you picture us high up on that roller coster, letting go of the rail, putting our arms in the air, and screaming all the way down?

And there's more than the theme parks here! The weather is great! Naples is the best place to live because of the weather. You would love it. It has cooler weather than where you live in Mexico. Sometimes it is 85 degrees in the summer which is much better than Mexico where it's not 85 degrees, it's 95 or 100 degrees in May. To make it even better, there is always a gentle breeze that cools you down. Wouldn't you want to be in the cooler air where the humidity is less than in the hot, wet air of Mexico? If you move here, we could enjoy the wonderful weather and lay back and read a book and feel that breeze go right past your face like a feather. You know that's heaven.

Almost as good as the weather are the holidays here. Unlike in Mexico, we get to celebrate Christmas, Easter, and so much more. Do you know why Christmas is fun? You get nice presents. You get to see your family. Sometimes, because Christmas is special, you get to see family members that you never met before. This year I got to meet my cousin Juan. He is about our age. We played games for hours. Here you get to decorate your house and you get to see all the colored lights in your eyes. You also get to enjoy a wonderful Christmas tree that you and your family decorated. A few months after Christmas, you get to celebrate Easter. You make eggs, go on egg hunts at church, get more candy, get Easter baskets with all kinds of stuff in them. You would love all this! I know you like to get presents.

You just have to move here to Naples. You and I could fly at the theme park, lay in the sun with the breeze across our face to cool us down, and spend really cool holidays together. Why don't you talk to your parents? I bet your dad could find work here. Have I convinced you yet??

Example #2

My good friend of mine might come to Naples. I really want him to come to Naples so we can play like we did before. I have no brother's or sister's to play with so my good friend just has to move here. Please move.

First of all we have good weather. We have a sunny day allmost every day. Some days it rains so it son't get too hot. Also we don't get freezing weather like New York, Ohio, and Michigan where my friend lives.

Another reason to move here is that we have nice beaches. And you can swim if you don't have a pool. Also you can skim board, which is really fun. Theres surfing too. It is almost like skim boarding.

We even have fun activities here. We have baseball, you can play it all year round, because it dosn't snow here. Also we have hockey, you can play at German Areana. Finally we have basket ball teams.

Now I hope I persuaded you to move to Naples. First of all we have good weather. Second is that we have nice beach. Finally we have fun activities. I like living here.

Example #3

The reason why my friend should move to naples because there are many nice home's you can move in to. Also there Almost everyware in naples also Almost at every tern.

Another reason why I think my friend sould move to naples is because thare are very few hurricans in naples also very many hurricans are weak.

I Also think she should move to naples because there are many shopping centers mosly and ware you go at every end or stop you make.

Example #4

My good friend should move to Naples. If he would, I could do things with him, have fun, then hang out with him. Please move here Steven.

I would want to do things with you like play games such as monopoly or chess. We could also go many places on the Cat bus. Or we could just sit around all day watching TV shows like NFLNBA, NCAA basketball, Ncaa football.

We could also have loads of fun. We could play pranks on your mom. We could go outside and mess with each other. Or we could play sports like football, baseball, basketball, socker.

On the weekends we could take the Cat bus to the mall so we can chill and hang out with friends to. Then when we are board we can play around with each other. While we are at the mall we can by things too.

In conclusion, I wish my good friend would move to Naples. We could do all of these things together. Move here.

Example #5

Naples is a great place to live. Naples has everything you want and more. Naples has good weather, fun places to go to, and other great stuff.

First, Naples has great weather. You can enjoy a nice hot day at the beach and get a suntan. If you hate the snow Naples, Florida is the right place for you, no snow. The winter time in Naples is really nice, days are not too hot and not too cold.

Second, there are many fun things to do in Naples. You can cool down at the beach. You can see some cool animals at the Naples zoo. You might need to get some shopping done at the Coastland Mall, or you could just relax and breathe our fresh air.

Finally, Naples has many other qualities. There are many Gulf courses and resorts you can relax at. Naples has great restaurants to enjoy some great food at.

In conclusion, please move to Naples, it will be the best place you ever lived. Enjoy the weather, fun activities, and other great stuff because Naples has it all.

Example #6

Well, I here that you're moving, but you're not sure where. I can help you decide. What about Naples! It's beautiful, there's always nice weather, and the beaches are amazing! Yep, Naples is the perfect place to live!

OK, let me tell you about the beauty that lies in Naples. The skys are definitly the best part of Naples in my opinion. The skys are a brillient baby blue with puffy white clouds that look like cotten balls scattered about. Oh! Don't even get me started on the beauty of the wild life. The birds are amazing with their green, white, blue, and yellow feathers. Naples is a obiously beautiful.

Next, the weather is always nice. Normaly it is warm, but not hot with a nice cool breeze. Dispite all the hurracains, the weather is still nice. I also think that it's grait that it doesn't snow.

Furthermore, the beaches are amazingly beautiful. The sand is soft and almost white. And the water is also spectacular! When you look out into the ocean there is beautiful blue green water as far as you can see. also there are occashinally sailboats in the harizon.

In conclusion, dispite the hurracains Naples is a wonderful place that you my friend shuld definitly move to. There is beauty in every speck of Naples. The weather is always nice, and last but not least the beaches are amazing.

Example #7

Theres hotels great servirce cute girls great frends movie theaters comic book stores game stores movie store toys and a hole bunch of other stuff it's fun but you have to do good in school most of the time it's all fun and games but sometimes you have got to takes stuff seriously. then have people from other countrys to.

and you and you and me and my friends could hang out together and do a hole bunch of stuff and you could come to school whith us and do stuff like go the mall or playvideo games and... naples is a good place to live

p.s. I hape you move over here

Example #8

Wow! Naples is a great place to live! That's why I think you should move here. Naples has great weather, lots of activities, and a nice atmosphere. Let's move on.

If you love great weather than Naples is the place to be! Almost every day here it is sunny. When it's not sunny, it's raining and who doesn't love those rainy days where you can just sit back and relax? Let me tell you something, I sure do. Also for all you people who hate cold weather, there's none of that here!

Naples sure has lots of things to do! You can spend days on our beautiful beaches having fun in the sun! You can shop till you drop on 5th Avenue, a wonderful shopping district where you can very well spend that whole paycheck because of all those shops. Or, if you want, you can just enjoy the beautiful scenery walking downtown.

Last but certainly not the least, Naples has a wonderful atmosphere. It's very clean with little or no trash in the streets and no run down places. The people here are friendly and welcoming too. Naples is also newer than most places with it's beautiful homes and resorts.

All in all, Naples is the perfect place to live. It has great weather, lots of activities, and a nice atmosphere. What more could you want? That's why I think you should move to Naples today.

Example #9

Want to know a great place to live? Naples, Florida! It has gorgeous wheather and beautiful beaches. Naples also has wonderful landscaping. It's a good thing that I already live in Naples because I would nag my parents to move if I didn't. I wish you could live here as well.

The one thing I especialy enjoy about Naples is the gorgous wheather. It is almost always sunny here with a gentle breeze that keeps it fairly cool in the summer. The thing that is great about the sun is that, in Naples, you can go swimming in the winter! It never gets cold and snowy like up north where you live. In the summer, the water feels cool while you swim. Your parents would drool over the warm sun and the icy cool water on a hot summer day. They would love it here too. Why don't you move here?

One of my most favorite things about Naples is the beaches. If your a beach bum like me, you will love this awesome town. Most times in the year the water is clear. So if your mom is afraid of sharks or fish, she can see if anything dangerous surrounds her and know she is safe. Tons of soft sand wait for you on the beaches, so you can't hurt your feet on sharp shells or rough rocks. Best of all, the currents of the Gulf are calm, so your little brother won't get washed away by giant waves. (Even though sometimes you might want him to be.) These beaches are beautiful. People from all over the world come to Naples to enjoy the beaches! Why don't you move here?

A great site of Naples is the landscaping. Wonderful palm trees grow up from the ground like tall green or brown poles with dark and light green fronds. Green grass delicately blankets the ground. Trees and multicolored flowers decorate the sides of the roads. Flowers from the bushes grow brightly in small patches in almost every yard. Naples has the best landscaping. So why don't you move here? You love flowers.

So you see (I hope) that Naples is the place to live. There are gorgeous beaches, wonderful wheather, and beautiful landscaping to enjoy. Move to Naples. It's the right and the best place to live in the world! Besides, I'm here!

Scores and Analyses

Example #1

This essay is a definite **high**. It is well-written with plenty of nitty-gritty detail, such as "Besides, can't you picture us high up on that roller coster, letting go of the rail, putting our arms in the air, and screaming all the way down?" This excellent use of detail remains consistent throughout the paper. It is not formulaic. The voice is loud and clear, and the writer really sounds excited about living in Naples. He or she uses direct address, a definite must for a high score on a persuasive paper. Transitions are innovative: "And there's more than the theme parks here!" to begin another topic and "Almost as good as the weather are the holidays here" to move from the topic of weather to holidays. There are a few spelling errors ("ferris" and "coster"), but they do not detract from the essay. A few usage errors (using "like" instead of "as," for example) also do not detract from the content. A more mature command of vocabulary would help, although there is some good use of active verbs and words such as "decorate," "breeze," "personal favorite," etc.

Focus	Organization	Support	Style, voice	Conventions
High	High	High	High	High

Example #2

This paper definitely lacks detail. The writer is well organized but goes back and forth between explaining why he/she wants his/her friend to move to Naples and convincing him or her to do so. The beginning does not start out persuasive at all. There is no nitty-gritty detail for any of the writer's arguments, but there is some detail such as saying what can be done at the beach (skim boarding and surfing). Vocabulary is adequate but not spectacular. The paper is formulaic and does not really show much voice. It is a **medium**.

Focus	Organization	Support	Style, voice	Conventions
Medium	Medium	Medium/low	Low-formulaic	Medium

Example #3

The first problem with this paper is that it is not persuasive. The writer consistently uses the word "reason" instead of argument and never really addresses his/her friend. It also lacks elaboration, details, a conclusion, and vocabulary. There is an attempt at organization. Convention problems abound, specifically capitalization problems. The last sentence doesn't even make sense. Thus, this paper is an obvious **low**.

Focus	Organization	Support	Style, voice	Conventions
Extremely low	Medium low	Extremely low	Low	Low

Persuasive Sample Set — "Move"

Example #4

This **medium** paper is on the topic, is organized, and includes some detail ("Or we could just sit around all day watching TV shows like NFLNBA, NCAA basketball, Ncaa football."). The detail, however, is mostly lists without any real substance, ("football, baseball, basketball, socker"). To receive a higher score, this paper needs much more elaboration and some good vocabulary.

Focus	Organization	Support	Style, voice	Conventions
High	Medium	Medium/Low	Medium/Low	Medium

Example #5

This paper is another **medium**, but it is better than Example #4 in that there are a few real details ("You might need to get some shopping done at the Coastland Mall, or you could just relax and breathe our fresh air"), but they need to be pursued in much more depth. There are a few good words in it ("qualities," "resorts"), but there are also a few convention problems (although there are no spelling errors). Sentence structure is varied. The paper, however, is too formulaic. The writer needs to find some more interesting and varied transitions and make his/her voice stronger.

Focus	Organization	Support	Style, voice	Conventions
High	High	Low medium	Low-formulaic	Medium high

Example #6

This essay also is a medium, but it is a **high-medium**. There is excitement in the writer's voice. He/she includes some really nice description ("The birds are amazing with their green, white, blue, and yellow feathers."). There are a few good words such as "scattered" and "spectacular." The spelling is atrocious ("cotten," "thir," "dispite," "hurracains," and many more). However, the misspelled words do not interfere with the understanding of the essay. The paper still needs more elaboration and vocabulary if the writer wants a higher score.

Focus	Organization	Support	Style, voice	Conventions
High	High	Medium	Medium	Medium

Example #7

This paper is an obvious **low**. The convention problems make the paper difficult to read. There are very few capital letters! Spelling errors abound. There is no beginning or end, and the middle contains no detail. Even in such a short piece, there is extraneous information (about doing well in school). Vocabulary and elaboration are lacking. This paper, in fact, would score the lowest score above a zero on any state's writing test.

Focus	Organization	Support	Style, voice	Conventions
Medium	Low	Low	Low	Extremely low

Persuasive Sample Set — "Move"

Example #8
This author's voice is loud and clear. You almost can feel his/her excitement and passion for Naples. There are details ("When it's not sunny, it's raining and who doesn't love those rainy days where you can just sit back and relax."), but the paper could use more of that down-and-dirty, nitty-gritty detail. Vocabulary is adequate ("atmosphere," "resort"), but not outstanding. I rate this paper a *very* **high-medium**. Because of the voice, some states whose rubrics go to four might score it in the high range. The beginning and end need to be developed, though, and more support is needed in the middle. It is a very good essay but not an excellent one.

Focus	Organization	Support	Style, voice	Conventions
High	Medium	Medium	High	High

Example #9
This essay is an obvious **high**. It begins with a bang ("Want to know a great place to live? Naples, Florida!"). The support is excellent and consistent ("Tons of soft sand wait for you on the beaches, so you can't hurt your feet on sharp shells or rough rocks."). The writer uses humor: "Best of all, the currents of the Gulf are calm, so your little brother won't get washed away by giant waves." The student's arguments are well-developed, and he/she even weaves a theme throughout with "Why don't you move here?" which he/she repeats in almost every paragraph. Sentence structure is varied. He/she uses active verbs ("green grass delicately blankets the ground."), and vocabulary is more than adequate ("multicolored," "delicately," "landscaped," etc).

Focus	Organization	Support	Style, voice	Conventions
High	High	High	High	High

Topic for Sample Set: "Should Community Service be a requirement for high school graduation?"

Example #1

For many years it has been proposed that high school students be forced to do community service in order to graduate. This is outrageous! Why put kids in situations like that. It's forced labor. "Well, kids always are asking to be treated like adults," you might tell us, but let me tell you, the only adults who are forced into working without pay are convicts! Teens need time, time for things like homework, or activities to unwind after a hard day at school, plus it's just dumb for us to do what is essentially forced labor (no pay). Besides, what would happen if we got hurt on the job? I really doubt we would be compensated.

First of all, students like me have absolutely no time during the week or on the weekend for community service. Last year, I was in band which met every day after school untill November. Then, the day before band got out, I had soccer tryouts. I got on the team and practiced every day after school for the soccer season. Then, a week before soccer was done, I began basketball. In all, I only came home right after school about a total of three weeks (21 days)! When I wasn't at school, I was either studying or sleeping. I know for a fact that this is how some kids live their lives (yes, there are others besides me), and believe me, there is no time for community service in our busy schedules.

Second of all, its just stupid for us to be forced into doing something and not get a reward. To me it seems like we would be on the same level as a convict, only without the bright orange clothes! We would be working with no pay to get out of this hell hole, only to go to another one for even less of a reward (not even any learning).

Last of all, what would happen if we were to get hurt and couldn't go to school for a few weeks? Would we be compensated? I really don't think we would. How would we make up the school work AND the community service we missed? Could we? It would be physically impossible to do so.

In conclusion, its clear that we would have no time, no pay, and could really, if injured, lose out on a lot. I think community service is a dumb requirement for all these reasons (and many more as well), and should not be required for high school graduation.

Example #2

"Should be Requirement"

Community Service is a great requirement because you learn a lot of respect and responsability for your actions. Community Service makes you open your eyes to real life.

Requirement of community service I say "yes why not." Community service for a punichment is a great idea. It gives something that who or what did the crime a dose of reality of life. It also gives what they take or breake back by the time they finish.

Jobs. Jobs. Jobs. Community service is a job, not a paying job, but a job. You get experiens in what ever you are doing or selling for that matter you also get experiens in.

What ever you are doing or selling for that matter you also get perseverence is a big part in having a job or geting the job.

Persuasive Sample Set — "Community Service"

Community service is March of Dimes help make healther babys. With March of dimes you get payed not with money or prizes but you get payed by knowing you saved a life.

The Salvashon Army is another exampel of community service.

So in my conclushon I say "yes" to community services not for the fact that it is a good punichment or good job experiens or to have good refrens but for the fact of knowing that a life was saved or some one is not alone or even frezing. So yes community service should be a requirement so you get a dose of realyty of life.

Example #3

"Community Service Essay"

Now, first off, don't get me wrong. I'm not saying I hate community service completly. But, I think that doing it under different circumstances would be better for many a people if they weren't told "There it is. Go do it!"

Alright, we have schools saying that you won't be allowed to graduate unless you have so and so amount of hours of community service, but for some people that's really hard because they might already have a job that pays and you'll have to cut your hours down (a lot!). Then where is the money going to come from? Also, what if they tell you a certin day for community service but your already working and you miss work, gee! You can be fired!

Another reason would be that, what about all the jobless people who could use more work? Just out of curiosity!

I guess, some other reasons (got to think or Mr. Owens will say I can't correctly elaborate!) would be that, if you get injured you won't be insured by a business, can't get worker's comp. (If it's an expensive doctor's bill).

There's lots of things like this that would make people (and should) skeptical! (Just because you got to think with caution.) Like I said before though. I'm not saying it's a bad thing, but every option should be explored!

Example #4

"Community Service"

I think that if your doing community hours you should get paid because you'll probably be out there from sun till it's dawn and that's really some long hours without getting paid for it and that's hard work all the day long with no money. I don't think most people will fall for it because as you see there's no pay what so ever and that is probably about the thing and probably to lazy to work.

I think the judges probably be letting people off a little easy because instead of going to jail over little of nothing, but it probably need to be issued for students to graduate but like I said some people won't do it without pay and don't get me wrong some will do it to get there diploma, but I think if they give an order most of the students probably would do it if it is consider for graduation.

Example #5

"Community Service"

Should community service be required to graduate from high school? Community service is a good thing for those of us that can afford to do it, but many of us can't and it would only make graduating a harder task, as if it's not hard already.

First of all, many students don't have the time to volunteer their time. Going to school five days a week gives you a lot of homework and can drain you of your energy. With the free time I do have I'm either studying or trying to catch up on some of my sleep. I beleive if I lost the little free time I do have I would fall behind in school.

Second of all, many can't afford to work for free. Not everyone's parents can afford to send their child to college or buy them a car. Many high school students hold a job so they can have a car or save for college. Community service would take away from your job, which would take away money, which would not allow you to have the things or the savings you want.

Thirdly, many students have a hard time graduating as it is. By having to have so many hours of community service it would make graduating harder and the whole process longer. Many student's can just not do it. Not because they don't want to, but because they really can't.

In conclusion, I think it just would not be a good idea. Let people choose to do community service. More people would be willing to do good at what ever it was they were doing if they were able to choose. If you force someone to do something they are just going to push away and not do their best. Community service. I beleive it should be someone's choice.

Example #6

"Community Service"

I think that community service is great, but I don't think it should be a requirement to graduate from high school. I don't know about everybody else, but I don't have enough time as it is, much less having enough to perform community service. It also seems like a punishment. And, I think that we should be encouraged to do community service, but not forced.

To start of with, I don't have enough time now to get everything and do everything I need to. When I get home the first thing I do is get ready to go to work. And then when I get home around six o'clock, I do my homework. Then if I have time, I like to lift weights. And, that's not all the time-management problems! What about sports? I have a real hard time getting off work for important sports events much less community service. If I was forced to do community service, there is no way I'd have enough time to get everything done.

Secondly, whenever I think of community service it always reminds me of when my sister got three speeding tickets, and as a punishment they gave her community service. It's almost as if we are being treated like criminals. Why should the school board require of upstanding high school students what the penal system requires of those who break the law. What message is that giving us? Community service is great for volunteers and criminals who need to pay back society, but it should not be a requirement to graduate from high school.

Last of all, I think that to force a high school student who is struggling to maintain good grades to do anything non-educational is wrong. If I did have time, I would be more than glad to help the community in some way, but right now I have to concentrate on my future, and most importantly on my education. And, I don't see that doing community service would help me in any way at this point in my life. Now this may sound selfish, but when I'm done with college and have a good, steady job, then I'll do a lot if community service. I believe in giving to those who are less fortunate than I am.

In conclusion, I would like to restate something I said earlier in this paper. "Community service is a great thing, but it should be encouraged not forced or required." I say this because we students have a lack of time, look on forced work as punishment, and need to concentrate on our future. Community service? Not now, thanks.

Example #7

"Sure, No Problem"

Community service to me is a very good thing to me. This kind of work is the best kind, because 9 times out of 10 your doing it from the heart. Community service should not be something demanding or stressful, but something you realy care about.

First, it makes better people. An example of a person becoming better with themselfs. Say that a person has to team up with somebody different from his race, for community service, and as time goes on they become good friends.

Second, community service comes from the heart and is a good thing because of that. For example I like to work with little kids and it comes from my heart and I feel good about myself.

In conclushun, community service to me is a good thing to me. I like it. You will to.

Example #8

"No Community Service"

I think needing community service to graduat is quite wrong. What dose it show you did your parents haft to do it to graduat. Hear are my reasons I think us students shoud not haft to do it.

Time, why shoud we waste are time to do community service to graduat. My last year in high school I don't want to do community service, I whant to have fun. Students need to study, and be able to do there homework or project. Some students have job's and where can they find the time to fit this in to there schedel. Now this leads up to my next example.

Grads. All students that whant to go to college, haft to make the best grads they can, and shoud not haft to do the service to gratuat. You haft to do homework to pass any class, and doing this service takes time away from doing your homework.

But hear is the mane question in my mind, Why! Why shoud we haft to do this, you know your parents did not haft to do this, so why shoud we haft to do it to graduat. What do us students get out of it, so the city dose not haft to pay a person to do it, so a bissnes owner dose not haft to pay another persen to do work when you can get it for free.

Example #9

"Down with Community Service"

In my opinion requiring community service for graduation would just end up being a waste of time for everyone. For the students it would be a waste because they have busy schedules to complete that include work as well as school work. And for the manager it would be a waste because they'll have to take time out helping and showing students how things work. They'll waste even more time yelling at them to stay on task and do their job right. (You know teenagers. We need to be nagged or we get lazy!)

I personally think students have enough to worry about without community service. We need to keep our grades up. Senior years are usually pretty hectic with trying to find a good college to accept you and getting the grades to meet the requirements of the college. I know last year (9th grade) I started working towards a volleyball scholarship, but I could hardly stay on the team with a 1.9 grade point average. To get into most colleges you need at least a 3.0, so studying should be a top priority, and community service would definitely cut in on studying time.

A second reason community service should be forgotten about is the quality of work. If some is not going to get paid for their job, they're not going to work as hard, no matter what job it is. And if someone gets stuck doing something they really hate, they'll hardly put any effort into it. (If they're lucky, a friend will be there and they can both get screamed at together.) One of my friend's mom hates her job so much she sits at work thinking of ways to get fired. This doesn't help anyone much.

Working for free would not only waste the students time, but whoever they're working for as well. Someone's going to have to show the "fresh fish" how things work around there, and someone's going to have to help them when they screw up.

Transportation is another problem that could occur, and one day your worker just might not show up which would put you on the spot and possible waste more of your time looking for a replacement. If a student has another job already, working times may collide, and that's going to waste a lot of someone's time working that mess out (plus it might cause the student to get fired from their paying job.)

In conclusion I feel the community service requirement to graduate is selfishly organized and inappropriate. Students have too much other stuff to worry about like how to pay off their car. They need to concentrate on grades. And, the bosses will lose time as well. A community service requirement for graduation is a lose—lose proposition.

Example #10

"Community Service Should be a Part of Graduation Requirement"

I think Community Service should be a Graduation Requirement. It it was you would still be learning, but you would only be on the outside of the school. Thats were most students wish they was anyway.

The first reason would be to learn not to throw paper on the ground. If you or anyone else throw paper on the ground you don't want to pick it up. Do you think someone else wants to clean up behind you. You're not just doing something for yourself but for your community. You would also be proud that you made the community look better.

The second reason is you may found some interesting things. You may find a comic book that's worth some money. Someone might find a purse that needs returning to the owner. You may even find some money.

Last, but not lease. You may learn how to keep your home clean. Like if you was looking for a paper on your desk but you can't find it because your desk was to funky. One morning you was late for work and you was looking for something to wear so you put on the first suit you see but didn't know it wasn't clean. Then all day long you smelled like roadkill that's been dead for months. You could have visitors but you wont let them in because you haven't seen what your floor look like in 4 or 5 months. All of these things wouldn't have happened if you wouldn't have taken just one more class for graduation.

So see if you take this class it wouldn't hurt. You would learn things and keep your house up better. So say no to P.I.S. and yes to C.S.C.

Example #11

"Essay"

When I first thought about it. I said that there shouldn't have to have community service for graduation. Then I thought about it again. Then I said yes we should have it because we need to learn how to work. And start helping older people and sick people out. More then that will learn the value of money. And will also learn many trades. I will be more focus and responsabile toward life. Thats my argument.

Example #12

Community service should not be a requirement to graduate. People work to get enough credits to graduate and keep up their grades and they don't need to have another thing that they have to do. It is something that kids should want to do, not have to do. It is also criminal-like treatment and time consuming.

First of all, it is not going to help the community any if they are forcing people who don't want to help to help. There are plenty of people who love to volunteer and they should be the one's doing it. If you are forced to do anything, you are not going to want to do it. Kids who are pushed into it unwillingly are never going to be helping again because of the bad experience. Some people may like helping after having to, but they could have found that out willingly.

Secondly, isn't community service a punishemnt to criminals? We should be rewarded for going to school, not be forced to do something convicts do. You might have well have stole something and been sentenced to 20 hours of community service if it was required. The only thing missing is some jail time.

Finally it would take up a lot of time. It may sound selfish, but a lot of kids are balancing a hard schedule and it may be hard to fit that in. They could be making money to support themselves with that time. Kids nowadays have a lot of responsibilities, and it would be hard to do that.

In conclusion, it is always good to help out your community and it should be voluntary and not like it was a punishment. It should be something good and you wouldn't want people with bad attitudes doing it.

Example #13

"Essay"

I think community service shouldn't be a graduation requiremnt to get out of high school. The first reason I don't think it shouldn't be one is because you are going to help the city out and the city doesn't try to help you out with nothing but try to give the people in the city hard time. Then they ask them to do something for the city. But most of the time when the people of city go down town to city hall they try to be nasty to the people and give them a hard time.

For another reason I think it shouldn't be a requirement is because when you do it you don't get a grade for it or you don't get a credit for it and it doesn't teach nothing that is going to help you down the road of life.

For the last final reason I think it shouldn't be a requirement is because you are working without pay. That is not fair because the people that you are working or watching over you when you are working are getting paid but you are not that is not fair. You are doing it for free but if you call the city to do something they would like you to work for free.

Those are the reasons I think it shouldn't be a requirement for graduation.

Example #14

Community service should not be a graduation requirement. Students barely have enough time for homework now, let alone if we needed to go volunteer somewhere. Weekends should be reserved for fun or relaxation or catch up from the five day week, and time spent on sports and after school jobs make community service impossible to serve. Please, we high school students don't need another requirement for graduation. Enough!

When we get home from school, a majority of the students have at least two hours of homework to complete, sometimes more. After that, who would feel like doing community service? Besides that, our parents are usually working and unless you're within walking distance to somewhere to volunteer, you don't have any transportation. Also students need to study (above and beyond the homework) for upcoming tests and quizzes. Time, like a diamond, is precious.

The second reason we shouldn't have community service for a graduation requirement is because we would need to do it on the weekends as well as during the school week. Weekends, apart from catching up on any homework or studying for upcoming tests, are made for fun and relaxation from the rigors of the school week. This does not mean just hanging out with your friends (like most adults think), but also to catch up on sleep (definitely lacking during the school week) and to relax from the pressures of school. It is a catch up time for our bodies and our minds, not to mention for any homework hanging over our heads.

Thirdly, a lot of students have after school sports, which would leave no or little time for community service. Plus after you're done with your sports, you're too tired to go volunteer. And, even if you dragged yourself to volunteer after playing sports for two hours, then you would have no energy left to do your homework. You would just want to go home and sleep. Sports aren't the only problem with after school community service. Some students who, because their parents are not rich, have to work after school would never find the time to volunteer. It's not fair to penalize those students and keep them from graduating. Most students who work do so because they have to, not because they want to. They now don't have enough time for their paying jobs, let alone volunteer work. There just aren't enough hours in the day for high school students to fit in community service.

In conclusion, community service shouldn't be a graduation requirement. We have too much going on to worry about volunteering. We wouldn't have enough time to devote to homework, our weekends would be all work and no play, and after school sports or work may have to be cancelled totally to make the time to complete the community service requirement for graduation. I say, "No" to community service. Enough is enough!

Scores and Analyses

Example #1

I score this paper on the **low end of high**. It is fairly well-written, stays on the topic, gives examples (the writer's hectic life in soccer and basketball), and uses good vocabulary ("compensated," "proposed"). While there are no similes, sentence structure is varied. There is even a quote at the beginning. Mechanics and usage errors are few in number. On the writing assessment, this paper probably would not receive the top score. It could not earn a higher score. It is a really good paper, but it is not outstanding.

Focus	Organization	Support	Style, voice	Conventions
High	High	Medium high	Medium—a bit formulaic	High

Example #2

The problem with this example is that it is more expository than persuasive. The writer explains what community service is ("Community service is March of Dimes") instead of arguing for or against requiring community service for graduation. The writer goes on in this vein for four paragraphs. Mechanics, usage, and spelling errors sometimes interfere with the meaning of the paper (look at paragraphs #2 and #3). The writer makes one attempt at using good vocabulary ("perseverence"). Organization is haphazard, however. Because the writer does mention the topic in the first and last paragraphs and lists one or two arguments (with little support), the paper would score a **low** on the writing test.

Focus	Organization	Support	Style, voice	Conventions
Low	Medium	Medium/low off-topic	Medium	Low

Example #3

This paper does stay on the topic and, in all but the one place, he/she addresses his/her teacher, but support is poor. The conclusion is vague and doesn't really make sense in the context of the prompt ("every option should be explored"). The writer uses a few good vocabulary words ("elaborate," "skeptical") albeit incorrectly spelled. This is a good **low-medium** essay because of its lack of support and above-average number of errors ("your" instead of "you're" and the lack of commas, for example).

Focus	Organization	Support	Style, voice	Conventions
Medium	Medium	Low	Medium—formulaic	Medium

Persuasive Sample Set — "Community Service"

Example #4

This paper is expository, not persuasive. The student does not address the topic and instead talks about how important it is to get paid for community service. I don't quite understand the part about the judges. There is no apparent organization at all. The writer jumps from one topic to another. The only sentence that mentions community service as a requirement for graduation is the last one, and it does not make much sense. This paper also is replete with mechanical and spelling errors, but the lack of focus is what would give it a *very* **low** score.

Focus	Organization	Support	Style, voice	Conventions
Extremely low	Low	Unclear	Low	Low

Example #5

This is a perfect **medium** paper. The student stays on the topic, gives three arguments, has an adequate introduction and conclusion, uses adequate vocabulary, includes adequate support (although the argument in paragraph #4 falls apart), and writes fairly well. Spelling errors ("beleive") never get in the way of comprehension. Transitions begin each middle paragraph. All the elements are there, but it is in no way outstanding enough or well-written enough to earn a higher score.

Focus	Organization	Support	Style, voice	Conventions
High	High	Medium	Low medium	Medium

Example #6

This well-written paper deserves a **high** score. On the actual test, it probably would receive the highest or next-to-highest score, depending on the judges. The paper never strays from the topic. Its organization is clear. The arguments are well thought out. Transitions begin the middle paragraphs. Vocabulary is excellent ("penal," "upstanding"), and mechanical errors are few. The support is specific and thorough as when the author talks in paragraph #2 about his evening (homework, lifting weights). It is, on the whole, an excellent essay, written with flair and conviction.

Focus	Organization	Support	Style, voice	Conventions
High	High	High	Medium high— a bit formulaic	High

Example #7

This essay is *very* **low**. It is not a persuasive essay trying to give arguments as to why community service should or should not be a requirement for graduation. In fact, it never mentions graduation at all. This expository essay is an explanation of why community service "to me is a very good thing to me." Organization is also muddled although there is an introduction and conclusion of sorts. There are numerous mechanical and spelling errors but, as in Example #4, the bottom line is staying on the topic. This essay does not. It would receive a score (instead of "unscorable") because it does mention community service.

Focus	Organization	Support	Style, voice	Conventions
Extremely low	Low medium	Low	Low—formulaic	Medium

Persuasive Sample Set — "Community Service"

Example #8

Apart from the egregious and numerous spelling errors in every line (this student may be dyslexic in spelling) and numerous mechanical errors, this writer does, except in the last paragraph, stay on the topic. There is an introduction and conclusion, though only one transition is used, and there are two paragraphs with arguments against community service. There is extraneous information ("All students that whant to go to college, haft to make the best grads they can..."). There is very little development of the arguments, however, and there is no elaboration, just a list ("I whant to have fun. Students need to study, and be able to do there homework or project. Some students have job's and where can they find the time..."). For all these reasons, this essay would score a **low** on the writing test, but on the high end of low.

Focus	Organization	Support	Style, voice	Conventions
Medium	Low	Low and unclear	Low medium	Low

Example #9

This essay, obviously, deserves a **high** score but not the highest on a five- or six-point rubric. Except for the end of the third paragraph, the writer stays on the topic. The paper has humor ("You know teenagers..."), good vocabulary ("inappropriate," "proposition"), good support in the middle paragraphs, and clever use of transitions. It is clearly well organized and contains only a few errors. It would not receive the highest score because, while it is a very good paper, it is not outstanding, and support flags a little in paragraph three.

Focus	Organization	Support	Style, voice	Conventions
High	High	High	High	High

Example #10

The point of this essay is unclear. Is the student talking about keeping your community and house clean or about requiring community service for graduation? And at the end, what do "P.I.S." and "C.S.C." mean? The student talks about reasons ("The first reason") but then strays from the topic by going off on a tangent ("Do you think someone else wants to clean up behind you."). Spelling errors don't get in the way of comprehension, but sometimes punctuation errors do. While this is organized in the main topics, the sub-topics wander off. Because of all these problems, this paper would score **low-medium**. It is formulaic which also would bring down the score.

Focus	Organization	Support	Style, voice	Conventions
Medium/Low	Medium – beginning/end	Medium low	Medium low – formulaic	Medium

Persuasive Sample Set — "Community Service"

Example #11

This paper is clearly a *very* **low**. It could not earn higher than the lowest score on the actual test because of the lack of development. It does stay on the topic, but it is simply a list of reasons why community service should be required for graduation. There is no support at all, no introduction, no varied sentence structure, no good vocabulary usage, and only a one-sentence conclusion.

Focus	Organization	Support	Style, voice	Conventions
Medium low	Low	Extremely low	Low	Low

Example #12

This is a **medium** paper. It is a good paper that stays the topic, has an obvious organization with transitions, provides support for the three arguments, and does not have an excessive number of errors. All in all, it is a average paper. The support in the first paragraph is good, but the other two are a bit weaker. The conclusion is skimpy. Vocabulary is adequate. It is, in short, an OK but in no way outstanding essay, and it is a bit formulaic.

Focus	Organization	Support	Style, voice	Conventions
High	Medium (end)	Medium	Medium – formulaic	High

Example #13

This paper mentions the word "community service" in the first and last paragraphs and uses "it" everywhere else, so meaning is sometimes confused. The writer gets off the topic a few times, talking about the "nasty" people at city hall. The end of the fourth paragraph doesn't make sense, and all of the support for the arguments falls apart. There are only a one-sentence introduction and conclusion. Vocabulary is adequate. This is a **low-medium** essay because of the confusing sentences and lack of support.

Focus	Organization	Support	Style, voice	Conventions
Medium - unclear	Medium low – beginning/end	Medium/Low	Medium	Medium

Example #14

This essay is really good. It is clearly a **high** paper and probably would earn the top score on the actual test. It never strays from the topic. Organization is clear. Three arguments are well developed with lots of details and specific support. The writer even includes humor in the asides in the third paragraph. Vocabulary is excellent ("upcoming," "devote," "lacking"), and sentence structure is varied. There is a minimum of errors. There is even a simile (albeit a trite one). This is a good example of an outstanding persuasive essay.

Focus	Organization	Support	Style, voice	Conventions
High	High	High	High	High

Bibliography

References

Caplan, Rebekah and Keech, Catherine. *Showing Writing: A Training Program to Help Students Be Specific.* Berkeley, CA: University of California Press, 1980.

Culham, Ruth. *6 + 1 Traits of Writing.* New York, NY: Scholastic Professional Books, 2003.

Dean, Nancy. *Voice Lessons: Classroom Activities to Teach Diction, Detail, Imagery, Syntax, and Tone.* Gainesville, FL: Maupin House Publishing, 2000.

_____. *Discovering Voice: Voice Lessons for Middle and High School.* Gainesville, FL: Maupin House Publishing, 2006.

Florida Writes! Report on the 1994 (95, 96, 97, 98, 99, 2000, 01, 02, 03, 04) Assessment. Tallahassee, FL: Department of Education, 1994 to 2004, grades 4, 8, 10.

Forney, Melissa. *The Writing Menu: Ensuring Success for Every Student.* Gainesville, FL: Maupin House Publishing, 1999.

Freeman, Marcia. *Listen to This: Developing an Ear for Expository.* Gainesville, FL: Maupin House Publishing, 1997.

Kiester, Jane. *Blowing Away the State Writing Assessment Test, Second Edition.* Gainesville, FL: Maupin House Publishing, 2000.

_____. *Caught'ya! Grammar with a Giggle.* Gainesville, FL: Maupin House Publishing, 1990.

_____. *Caught'ya Again! More Grammar with a Giggle.* Gainesville, FL: Maupin House Publishing, 1992.

_____. *Eggbert, the Ball, Bounces by Himself: Caught'ya! Grammar with a Giggle for First Grade.* Gainesville, FL: Maupin House Publishing, 2006.

_____. *Juan and Marie Join the Class: Caught'ya! Grammar with a Giggle for Third Grade.* Gainesville, FL: Maupin House Publishing, 2006.

_____. *Putrescent Petra Finds Friends: Caught'ya! Grammar with a Giggle for Second Grade.* Gainesville, FL: Maupin House Publishing, 2006.

_____. *Giggles in the Middle: Caught'ya! Grammar with a Giggle for Middle School.* Gainesville, FL: Maupin House Publishing, 2006.

_____. *The Chortling Bard. Grammar with a Giggle for High School.* Gainesville, FL: Maupin House Publishing, 1997.

Books Used for Sample Passages to Identify Writing Types

Adams, Richard. *Watership Down.* New York, NY: HarperCollins Publishers, 1975.

Angelou, Maya. *I Know Why the Caged Bird Sings.* New York, NY: Bantam Books, 1971.

Milne, A. A. *Winnie the Pooh.* New York, NY: American Book-Stratford Press, Inc., 1954.

Rowling, J. K. *Harry Potter and the Sorcerer's Sto*ne. New York: Scholastic, Inc., 1998.

White, E. B. *Charlotte's Web.* New York, NY: HarperCollins, 1952.

About the Author

Jane Bell Kiester is the author of the popular Caught'ya books: *Caught'ya! Grammar with a Giggle*; *Caught'ya Again! More Grammar with a Giggle*; *The Chortling Bard! Grammar with a Giggle for High School*; *Eggbert, the Ball, Bounces by Himself: Caught'ya! Grammar with a Giggle for First Grade*; *Putrescent Petra Finds Friends: Caught'ya! Grammar with a Giggle for Second Grade*; *Juan and Marie Join the Class: Caught'ya! Grammar with a Giggle for Third Grade*; and *Giggles in the Middle! Grammar with a Giggle for Middle School*. Teachers all over the country also use earlier editions of this book to help improve their students' scores on state writing assessment tests. Jane continues to write new books.

In addition to writing books, Jane has given hundreds of workshops to fellow teachers around the country for the past sixteen years. Her subject? The same as in her classroom where she happily taught elementary and middle school for more than thirty years—teaching students to write well.

Throughout her more than three decades as a classroom teacher, Jane served many years as various department chairpersons and grade-level chairperson. She is also a past president of the Alachua County Teachers of English. Jane has been recognized five times by "Who's Who Among America's Teachers." In 2002 she won Teacher of the Year for her school and Middle School Teacher of the Year for her county. Now that she is retired from active teaching, Jane spends her time writing, consulting, volunteering in local schools, spending time with her family and friends, and enjoying living on the edge of the Florida Everglades.

On the CD

Step One Files

"Dead" and "Dying" Verbs to Avoid
Strong-Verb Practice Sentences
    Primary
    Basic
    Intermediate
    Advanced
Possible Answers for Practice Sentences
    Primary
    Basic
    Intermediate
    Advanced
Vivid-Verb Paragraphs
    Elementary Examples
    Middle-School Examples
    High-School Examples
    FYI—How Your Teacher Scores the SVVP
    Topic Sentence Suggestions
        Clusters
            Wild Cafeteria Cluster
            Clustering Blank
            Clustering Blank with Checklist

Step Two Files

Evaluating Anything Written
Basic Scoring Criteria
Six-Point Rubric
Practice Scoring Lesson Plans
Focused Analytical Score Sheet

Step Three Files

Sample Passages
Sample Passages—Key
Transitions
Grabbers and Zingers
Evaluating Writing
220 Practice Prompts
    40 Descriptive Prompts
    75 Expository Prompts
    45 Narrative Prompts
    60 Persuasive Prompts

Graphic Organizers
    Content Cluster
    The Hand
    Tried and True
    The Caterpillar
    Blank Flow Chart

Step Four Files

How a Writer Dazzles a Reader
90 Examples for Scoring Practice
    11 Descriptive Examples
        Place to Have Fun
        Analyses—Place to Have Fun
    32 Expository Examples
        Favorite Time of Year
        Analyses—Favorite Time of Year
        Book for Class to Read
        Analyses—Book for Class to Read
        Lunchroom
        Analyses—Lunchroom
        Problem/Solution
        Analyses—Problem/Solution
    24 Narrative Examples
        Door
        Analyses—Door
        Hurricane Hero
        Analyses—Hurricane Hero
    23 Persuasive Examples
        Move
        Analyses—Move
        Community Service
        Analyses—Community Service